CW01218247

SUNBEAM-TALBOT
& ALPINE
In Detail

SUNBEAM-TALBOT & ALPINE
In Detail

BY ANDERS DITLEV CLAUSAGER

Herridge & Sons
in association with the Michael Sedgwick Trust

Published in 2009 by
Herridge & Sons Ltd
Lower Forda, Shebbear,
Beaworthy, Devon EX21 5SY

© Copyright Anders Ditlev Clausager 2009

This work is published with the financial assistance of the Michael Sedgwick Memorial Trust. This Trust was founded in memory of the famous motoring researcher and author Michael Sedgwick, 1926-1983. The Trust is a registered charity (charity no. 290841) set up to encourage the publication of new motoring research and the recording of motoring history. Full details and contact address can be found on the Trust's website www.michaelsedgwicktrust.co.uk
The Trust welcomes suggestions for new projects, and financial donations to help with future work. Support by the Michael Sedgwick Memorial Trust does not infer any involvement in the editorial process, which remains the sole responsibility of the author, editor and publisher.

Designed by Ray Leaning
Special photography by Simon Clay

All rights reserved. No part of this publication may be reproduced in any form or by any means without the prior permission of the publisher.

ISBN 978-1-906133-13-9
Printed in China

Contents

Introduction	6
Chapter 1: **Rootes and Sunbeam-Talbot**	10
Chapter 2: **Britain's most exclusive light car: the Talbot Ten**	21
Chapter 3: **Building a range: 3-Litre, 4-Litre & 2-Litre**	49
Chapter 4: **Streamstyle and synchromatic: The 80 & 90**	69
Chapter 5: **Developing a winner: 90 MkII to MkIII**	88
Chapter 6: **"Bred in the Alps": the Alpine**	119
Chapter 7: **Excuses not needed: the competition story**	139
Chapter 8: **Sunbeam-Talbot rivals**	164
Chapter 9: **The legacy**	176
Chapter 10: **Ownership today** *by Paul Walby*	185
Appendices:	190

  1 Specifications, prices and colours
  2 Production and identification
  3 Competition entries, post-1945
  4 Bibliography & acknowledgments

Introduction

The low-mounted headlamps and additional fog and pass lamps immediately identify this as a 1948-50 "Mark I" model, in this case an 80 saloon, a rarer model than the 90.

On the 90 Mark II, here in convertible form, the headlamps were raised, there were separate side lamps and additional air intake grilles on either side of the radiator grille.

If the "man on the Clapham Omnibus" now remembers the name Talbot at all, it is likely that he thinks only of the short-lived attempt to re-badge the old Rootes, Simca and Chrysler products, following Peugeot's take-over of the European Chrysler companies in 1978. It would probably require some prompting to get him to recall *Sunbeam*-Talbot but he may remember the Talbot *Sunbeam*: "Oh yeah; didn't they use to go rallying, or something?"

Yes Sir, they certainly did. The Talbot Sunbeam Lotus was an extraordinarily purposeful rally car in its day, and won the World Championship for Manufacturers in 1981. But that was not quite what I had in mind, as I was looking back to an era some 25-30 years before that, when there was a car actually called the *Sunbeam-Talbot*, and which had no mean career in rallying either. At least the name of one of the team drivers still evokes instant recognition – Stirling Moss.

Rallying as a popular and widely-followed form of motor sport is now not what it was in the 1950s, or even as late as the 1980s; nowadays all we seem to get in the media is Formula One. In the 1950s, there was still a strong contingent of British amateurs or semi-professionals who took part in international (meaning European) rallying just for the fun of it, as they rarely had a chance of a good result; and yet, they could occasionally surprise us. The same was often true in other European countries. This none-too-serious approach led to wide grass-roots support for a sport which was much more accessible to amateurs than it later became, and its popularity in turn led to coverage in the media, mostly in those days the wireless and the daily newspapers, apart from motoring magazines.

At that time, a Sunbeam-Talbot was one of the cars to have, if you wanted to go rallying, or even if you just wanted to drive a distinctive car with a remarkable reputation. For sure, the Sunbeam-Talbots never quite enjoyed the status accorded to the Mini Coopers in the 1960s, or the Ford Escorts a little later, and unlike this illustrious pair, they are now largely forgotten, outside the coterie of devoted enthusiasts; but at the time they were Britain's most successful rally cars, and they deserve to be better remembered than they are.

It was not just the rallying story, either. The Talbot to Sunbeam-Talbot to Sunbeam story covers a period of just over twenty years, while the Sunbeam brand lived on for another twenty years. Some of these later cars, notably the Rapier, and the second car to bear the Alpine name, built an equally excellent reputation for themselves in their day, yet they too do not register highly on the radar screens, even of most classic car enthusiasts. One reason for this must be the tumultuous later existence of their erstwhile sponsor, the Rootes Group, which in turn became Chrysler, then Talbot, to finish up as simply the British branch of Peugeot, and even that is now no more. So, Sunbeam-Talbot is just another lost cause to add to the already depressingly long list of defunct British car companies.

Another reason may be that the Sunbeam-Talbot cars made and marketed by Rootes, even in their heyday were regularly the target of opprobrium and mostly irrelevant comparisons with the Sunbeam and Talbot cars that had been made before Rootes stepped in and took over, not to say rescued, the faltering companies. I absolutely agree that many of the original Sunbeam and Talbot cars were outstanding, but I do not see why enthusiasm for these should preclude an objective judgment of the Rootes-built Sunbeam-Talbot cars on their own merits – and many of them had great merit.

In any case, the Rootes Sunbeam-Talbots were cars of a very different type from the pre-Rootes cars, built for a different market, and in a different social and economic climate. Their appointed task was to act as premium products for Rootes, extending that company's penetra-

The Alpine roadster front view is similar to the 90. However, only the early 1953 Alpines had this style of front bumper and number plate; it was changed on the 1954 model.

As can be seen here, this 1954 90 Mark IIA features the new front bumper with the number plate fitted below it.

The Mark III is immediately recognisable by its larger side grilles, with side lamps incorporating flashing indicators.

The four-door sports saloon is the most common body style, here a Sunbeam Mark III of 1955 showing its classic proportions, and the characteristic side window shape. Originally there were trafficators in the centre pillars.

The convertible coupé, here in Mark II form complete with spats, has two much wider doors, and the trafficators are built in behind the doors. The hood folds down almost out of sight.

On the Alpine the doors are the same width as the convertible, but are of quite a different shape at the front, while the line to the top of the door is lower, and there are no external door handles.

tion upwards in the market place. If Rootes chose an established prestigious nameplate for this, much as Nuffield and later BMC did with Riley and Wolseley, or Standard with Triumph, it should not detract from the virtues of the cars themselves. If the established brand reputations contributed to the standing of the Rootes-built cars, so surely did the successes of these Sunbeam-Talbots add fresh lustre to the traditional brand values.

Badge engineering? Of course, to some extent, but it is curious that the most overtly badge-engineered cars described in the following were the early pre-war Rootes Talbots, while the post-war Sunbeam-Talbots were rather more different from other Rootes cars – that is until the Rapier which in 1955 turned the wheel full circle, having a similar relationship with a contemporary Hillman Minx as had the original Talbot Ten twenty years before. It was only in the late 1960s that all Sunbeam models became completely badge-engineered, with versions of the ubiquitous Imp and "Arrow" (i.e. Hillman Hunter) families. But at least from 1948 to 1956, Rootes appeared to strike the right balance between preserving the identity and individuality of the Sunbeam-Talbot marque, while at the same time maintaining a viable cost base by judicious use of components shared with their other brands (to quote Professor Garel Rhys who probably did not have Sunbeam-Talbot in mind when he formulated this).

So, to some extent, the story of the Sunbeam-Talbot – to continue to use the longest-lived of the three names bestowed on this family of cars – is the story of the Rootes Group from the 1930s to the 1950s. This was the period of expansion for Rootes, a company which had come from literally nowhere and which within an incredibly short period had achieved status as one of Britain's leading six motor manufacturers by 1939, in no small part thanks to the sheer dynamism and exuberance of its founders, especially "Billy" Rootes. The company held on to its position into the 1960s but was increasingly seen to be one of the weaker members of this elite, relying too heavily on the large-scale commercial success of just the Hillman Minx-based range. Their final effort to establish a second successful model with which to increase their market share in competition with BMC and Ford, the Imp of 1963, instead brought disaster.

In this epic drama, the Sunbeam marque (as it had by then become) was relegated to the sidelines.

Then there is an element in the unfolding story of making a silk purse out of the proverbial sow's ear. The early Rootes Talbots and Sunbeam-Talbots offered style at affordable prices but very little else. Their mechanical specification was always simple and conservative, but this at least usually had the concomitants of robustness and reliability; there is arguably a parallel with Volvo here. When the company's sales manager, the arch-enthusiast Norman Garrad, first began seriously to consider Sunbeam-Talbots as rally cars, he found the raw material woefully inadequate for his purpose.

Garrad was perhaps rather like the master potter whose skill is needed to turn a lump of unprepossessing clay into the finest ceramics. In this case, Garrad was fortunate to get a sympathetic hearing from his masters, the Rootes brothers, and their head of engineering Bernard Winter. Without deviating too far from the basic specification and inherent qualities of the cars, over the years Garrad's influence, aided by Winter on the engineering side, gradually turned a not very inspiring car into something far more worthwhile. A 1956 Sunbeam Mark III was a far better car than the first 90 of 1948. The reward came not only in the form of successes in the sport, but in much-improved sales.

There was one relative failure on the way: the Alpine did not catch on in the sports car market, which by now mainly meant the USA – but it still lived up to expectations of the brand by making its mark in rallying in no uncertain manner. Rootes had no previous experience of sports cars, and this first effort, intended to cash in on the burgeoning American demand for this type of vehicle, leaned too heavily on the saloon model on which it was based, steering-column gear change and all.

To some, the finest hour for the Sunbeam-Talbot, or now just Sunbeam, came late in life, with victory in the 1955 Monte Carlo Rally. The concept was otherwise now beginning to show its age, in styling as well as engineering, and a replacement was waiting in the wings in the shape of the Sunbeam Rapier. This in turn also took a lot of sorting out to get right, but at least it proved capable of a useful twelve-year production run, again with a number of worthwhile rally successes to its credit.

However, the bulk of the story that I intend to tell in this book effectively stops just as the Rapier enters the stage. It is the story of the various Talbot, Sunbeam-Talbot and Sunbeam models from the first Rootes-produced Talbot Ten of 1935 through to the final Sunbeam Mark III of 1956. I think it is a story worth telling, and unlike so many classic cars about which so much has been written, it is a story which has not actually been told before in detail. All too often, Sunbeam-Talbot aficionados have had to be satisfied with their cars being covered in brief introductory, not to say apologetic, chapters to the stories of later Sunbeams.

For me, to tackle a subject with which I could not previously claim more than a nodding acquaintance has been a challenge, but an enjoyable one: the historian likes nothing better than undertaking new research in a previously undocumented area. And there are interesting parallels or comparisons with other makes with which I could perhaps claim greater familiarity over a longer period – the BMC brands or Jaguar. As an example, I have been amused to see how many well-known Jaguar drivers of the period also turned up at the wheel of an altogether humbler Sunbeam-Talbot – Moss and Johnson, Adams and Hawthorn – and I conclude that these cars from the other side of Coventry must have had something going for them!

I would like to acknowledge the tremendous amount of help I have received in writing this book, especially from the Sunbeam Talbot Alpine Register (STAR) collectively, and in particular from Paul Walby, the editor of their magazine *Stardust*, who kindly agreed to write the chapter on ownership of these cars today. Also from Leon Gibbs who gave me free access to the 1948-56 sales ledgers, from the Coventry Transport Museum and their archivist Lizzie Hazlehurst who allowed me to raid her photographic collection, and from the Michael Sedgwick Memorial Trust who gave their financial support. A fuller list will be found at the end of the book. My sincere thanks to all of you.

Anders Ditlev Clausager
Coventry and Birmingham
April 2009

Chapter One

Rootes and Sunbeam-Talbot

The Rootes brothers, William (left) and Reginald, were among the movers and shakers in the British motor industry for more than 35 years. (Courtesy CTM)

The start of the Rootes Group was a cycle shop and engineering works at Hawkhurst in Kent, opened by William Rootes senior in the 1890s, and which soon became a car agency. The elder William fathered two sons in his first marriage: William Edward was born in 1894, and Reginald Claud in 1896. They were always known as "Billy" and "Reggie", and eventually became, respectively, the first Lord Rootes and Sir Reginald Rootes. Billy was apprenticed to Singer in Coventry in 1909 or 1910, and then set up a branch of his father's business at Maidstone in 1913. Reggie trained as an accountant and joined the civil service at the Admiralty. During the First World War, Billy joined the Naval Air Service and was commissioned as a Lieutenant in the RNVR.[1]

The two brothers spent most of their long working lives together, later assisted by Billy's two sons, Geoffrey born in 1917, and Brian born in 1919, as well as by Reggie's son Timothy born in 1925. Their company remained a family business into the 1960s. Billy once described himself as the engine in their joint enterprise, and Reggie as the steering and brakes. Billy was the salesman, dynamic and extrovert, sometimes even brash, with a rare flair for what the market wanted. Bespectacled Reggie kept more in the background, taking care of the company's finances and administration. Both exercised considerable influence over the design of their company's products. Their approach was reflected by the fact that Rootes cars were often styled according to the latest fashion, while remaining conservatively engineered.

The brothers set up their first joint venture, Rootes Limited, capitalised by their father, at Maidstone and began selling cars soon after the end of the First World War, including Martinis from Switzerland and General Motors products from the USA. They soon moved into London and for some time held the agency for Austin. They bought into other dealerships, such as Robins and Day in their native Kent, but also George Heath with branches in Birmingham and across the Midlands, Warwick Wright in London, and Tom Garner in Manchester. Rootes became the largest motor distributors in Britain and, it was claimed, in the world. They went in for the export business at an early stage, and established a special export depot at Chiswick. By 1931 they had appointed an agent in Japan.[2]

In 1925 Rootes bought the London coachbuilders Thrupp & Maberly. In the following year they opened a head office and showroom in the then-new Devonshire House in Piccadilly; for many years their next-door neighbour was Henlys, distributors for, among others, Alvis, Rover, Studebaker and famously, S.S. and Jaguar. Rootes had become the exclusive worldwide distributor for the Wolverhampton-built Clyno cars, and in 1927 offered to buy this company outright, but were turned down. Soon after, in 1929, Clyno went into liquidation.[3]

By then Rootes had taken over as distributors for Hillman instead, and the Rootes brothers fulfilled their ambition of becoming car manufacturers by buying into the two now merged Coventry car makers Hillman and Humber, together with their commercial vehicle subsidiary Commer. When manufacturing was added to selling, the Rootes Group became a rare example in the motor industry of a vertically integrated company. In the post-Second World War period, Rootes even established wholly-owned subsidiary companies to look after distribution and sales in the most important export markets, a pioneering effort for the British motor industry.

Both Humber and Hillman began as cycle makers. Thomas Humber had established his original workshop in Nottingham in the 1860s. He later expanded and set up plants at Beeston, in Wolverhampton, and finally in Coventry in 1889. Here Humber became involved with HJ Lawson's grandiose schemes for creating a monopoly in the motor industry, and made some Léon Bollée tricycles under licence, under the name Coventry Motette. The company also made motorcycles from 1900 to 1930. The first Humber car was made in 1899, and the company even showed an experimental *voiturette* with front-wheel drive.

A more conventional car was in production by 1901, the year when the French-born engineer Louis Coatalen joined Humber. The first Humberette light car appeared in 1903 and from then until 1908, cars were made both in Coventry and at Beeston, but afterwards production was concentrated in a large new factory at Stoke on the eastern side of Coventry. In 1926, Humber bought Commer, based at Luton in Bedfordshire. The staple late-vintage Humbers were fours of 9hp and 14hp (1056cc and 2050cc) together with a six of 3075cc and 20hp which was introduced in July 1926, followed by a 16hp six of 2110cc for 1929.[4]

In 1907, William Hillman, a millionaire Coventry cycle manufacturer, hired Coatalen away from Humber to design the first Hillman car. The company opened a factory at Stoke in 1910, in fact next door to Humber. By the 1920s, Hillman's most important model was a 14hp four, joined in 1928 by a medium-priced 20hp

The original Talbot factory in London, here on a wet day during the Second World War. It was built in 1903 and the office block at the front still exists. (Courtesy CTM)

Taken in the 1960s when Rootes still had a museum collection, here are, from left to right George Roesch, Bernard Winter and Norman Garrad admiring a 1924 Sunbeam GP car. (Courtesy CTM)

straight-eight. Neither Hillman nor Humber was doing terribly well, and in 1928 they merged, with Humber taking over Hillman. Around the same time, the Rootes brothers began to buy into the combined company, and by 1932 they had acquired complete control under the aegis of their holding company, Rootes Securities Limited, with financial backing from the Prudential Assurance Company. As will be discussed below, already then the Rootes brothers had effectively taken control of the Hillman-Humber production programme and had begun to put their ideas into practice.

Success To Disaster: The S.T.D. combine

Apart from in Coventry, the motor industry had taken root elsewhere in the Midlands, in Birmingham but also in Wolverhampton further west. Here Sunbeam, founded by John Marston, originally made "japanned" tin-ware. The trade mark of the rising sun is said to have been derived from this, and was first used when Marston founded the Sunbeamland Cycle Factory in 1887. The first Sunbeam production car was the unconventional Mabley of 1901 with wheels in a diamond pattern, but production was soon re-organised under the direction of Thomas Pullinger, and in 1903 Sunbeam adopted a Berliet-influenced design for a four-cylinder car. While Pullinger moved on to Humber, in 1909 Louis Coatalen joined Sunbeam from Hillman. One of his early designs for Sunbeam was a racing model which finished first to third in the 1912 *Coupe de l'Auto*, coming third to fifth in the concurrently-run French Grand Prix. This was the start of Sunbeam's long association with racing and record-breaking. In 1920, Sunbeam

The name is the same: Stirling Moss's Sunbeam Alpine rally car with Anthony Heal's Sunbeam 3-litre, 20 years its senior. (Courtesy CTM)

joined the Anglo-French Talbot-Darracq combine.[5]

The British partner of this was the Talbot company, set up in 1902 with a palatial factory in Barlby Road, North Kensington in London. The handsome administration block which formed the street frontage still exists, later renamed Ladbroke Hall, and is grade II listed. Modern street names on the redeveloped site behind now commemorate every imaginable Rootes brand *except* Talbot! Originally they made the French Clément (also known as Clément-Bayard) car under licence, with financial backing from the twentieth Earl of Shrewsbury and fifth Earl of Talbot (Charles Henry John Chetwynd-Talbot, 1860-1921) whose family name the British car adopted.

The badge of the Talbot car showed a beast surmounted by a coronet. the lion statant, tail extended, which is one of the crests of the family's coat of arms, rather than one of the Talbot hounds which support the arms. Quite appropriately in this context, the Talbot family is thought to have originated in France and to have come to Britain at the time of the Norman conquest; John Talbot was created the first Earl of Shrewsbury by Henry VI in 1442. For a long time the British company's official title was Clement-Talbot Ltd.

Talbot took less of an interest in racing than Sunbeam, but in 1912 Percy Lambert created a sensation at Brooklands when he ran a streamlined 25hp model and set class records at speeds up to 113.28mph (182.31km/h), and in February 1913 became the first driver to cover more than 100 miles in one hour, completing 103.84 miles (167.11km). In 1919, they were bought out by the Darracq company which had been founded by Alexandre Darracq in France in 1900. As part of a venture capital scheme, control of Darracq passed to a British consortium in 1903 although their factory remained at Suresnes on the western outskirts of Paris. By 1914 the company was one of France's largest car makers, number three after Peugeot and Renault.[6] When in 1920 Sunbeam joined as the third partner, the combined company became known as S.T.D. Motors Limited. For the next few years, there was some interesting crossbreeding of designs between England and France.[7]

Driven by the ambition of Louis Coatalen, who was now the chief engineer of S.T.D.,

Sunbeam spent too much money on racing cars, and in 1924 raised £500,000, through an issue of 8 per cent guaranteed notes, redeemable in 1934: an act which was to prove the undoing of the Anglo-French combine. If this were to finance their racing programme, it was pointless: Sunbeam's last major victories had been in the 1923 French and Spanish Grand Prix (drivers were Segrave and Divo respectively), with the "Fiats in green paint", and in the San Sebastian Grand Prix in 1924 (Segrave again). Grand Prix racing was abandoned after 1925, although Segrave set a new World Land Speed Record and was the first man to exceed 200mph (322km/h) in the "1000hp" Sunbeam in 1927. Sunbeam produced the outstanding 3-litre sports model with an advanced twin overhead camshaft engine which finished second at Le Mans in 1925. However, their touring cars declined in popularity, and their final model was the uninspired four-cylinder 13hp 1627cc Dawn of 1934, designed by HCM Stevens who later joined Rootes.

The French-made cars were renamed Talbot in 1920, but the Darracq name continued to be used when they were sold in Britain. Both Sunbeam and the French Talbot company introduced straight-eight engines for some of their touring models. During the later 1920s, of the three companies the British Talbot was the most prosperous, thanks to the excellent designs of the Swiss-born engineer Georges Roesch (1891-1969) whose advanced six-cylinder 14/45 model

The three 1932 Alpine Rally Talbots at Fox & Nicholl with their drivers, including a young Norman Garrad on the right. (Courtesy CTM)

The Humber Vogue was promoted on the strength of Molyneux's novel body design. (Courtesy CTM)

The original pre-war Hillman Minx, here a 1934 model, was the car that made Rootes's fortune.

was launched in 1926. Roesch developed a wide range of sports, racing and luxury models from this, culminating with the 105 and 110 (3½-litre) models of the 1930s.

These Talbot model numbers could originally have been supposed to indicate brake horsepower; if they were the expected top speeds, the higher figures were optimistic! The 90 and 105 models established Talbot in motor sport with a string of successes in 1930-32.[8] Bearing in mind the later successes of Sunbeam-Talbots in rallying, it is interesting that both Sunbeams and Talbots were rallied, and between 1929 and 1935 each marque had a total of three *Concours de Confort* awards in the Monte Carlo Rally to its credit. One of the crew who piloted the winning Sunbeam through from Umeå in 1932 was a certain young Norman Garrad...[9]

The success of Talbot, which was profitable, did not prevent the collapse of S.T.D. Motors in October 1934 when they could not pay the interest on, much less redeem, the ten-year old notes. The Rootes Group had already lent money to the company. In late 1934 Rootes bought the Sunbeam commercial vehicle business, which mainly made trolley buses, but it was re-sold to Brockhouse in 1946 and later to Guy Motors. In January 1935, Rootes bought Clement-Talbot Ltd. A receiver was appointed to manage the affairs of Sunbeam, and it took another few months for this company's fate to be settled. After an interlude when the machine tool maker Alfred Herbert of Coventry and William Lyons of S.S. Cars had been mentioned as suitors, Rootes clinched the purchase of Sunbeam in July 1935.

Only the French company remained independent. It was re-organised under the control of its managing director, the Italian-born entrepreneur Antonio (or Anthony, or Antoine) Lago who had previously been associated with Self-Changing Gears Ltd in Britain, makers of the Wilson preselector gearbox, and had been the British concessionaire for Isotta-Fraschini.[10] Lago continued to make Talbot cars, including the famous high-performance 4½-litre model which enjoyed success in racing and rallying. After the Second World War the cars were often known as Talbot-Lagos, but production slowly declined, in part because of the heavy post-war taxation of large-engined cars in France. The company was bought by Simca in 1957, and production ceased shortly afterwards.

Sorting out the Rootes range

After they first acquired an interest in the Hillman-Humber combine in 1928, it took some time for Rootes to develop a coherent strategy for the two makes; in fact for most of the 1930s there were some overlaps between the two ranges. One of Billy Rootes's ideas was to improve the export business, by offering the same chassis with two different engine sizes, the smaller for the home market, the larger for export. Thus for the 1930 season, the Humber Snipe had a 3½-litre six (80 by 116mm, 3499cc) in the same 10ft (3048mm) wheelbase chassis as the Humber 16/50 six (65 by 106mm, 2110cc), an engine size which had been introduced a year earlier. Both still had two traditional Humber characteristics, engines with valves of inlet-over-exhaust layout, and a right-hand gear change. With an extra 1ft (305mm) in the wheelbase, the Snipe became the Pullman limousine. Humber's 1932 models had centre gear changes, while the 1933 models had simpler side-valve engines of unchanged capacities, and the chassis acquired cruciform bracing.

On the Hillman front, the unloved straight-eight, latterly known as the Vortic, was soon ditched, and the old 14hp was replaced by the Hillman Wizard, launched with much ballyhoo at the Albert Hall in April 1931. This was a strictly conventional six, arguably modelled on American cars, again available with two alternative engines – the smaller was the 65mm by 106mm, 2110cc unit also found in the 1933 Humber 16/50, the larger had a 75mm bore for a capacity of 2810cc. Rootes tried hard with the Wizard and its Hillman-badged derivatives but they never quite caught on. However, the next new Rootes car hit the jackpot and was the cornerstone of their growth for the rest of the 1930s and beyond: the Hillman Minx which was introduced at the 1931 Motor Show.

Designed initially in 1929 by Humber's chief engineer Captain Irving and Alfred Wilde who had previously designed the Standard Nine, the Minx was as straightforward and conventional as the Wizard, but had a small four-cylinder engine (63mm by 95mm, 1185cc) rated at 10hp in a chassis with a wheelbase of 7ft 8in (2337mm). It was the first of the new breed of "Tens" which became the staple British family cars for the rest of the decade. Never quite the cheapest car in its class, nor be it said the most economical, the Minx was launched with prices starting at £159 and soon reached an annual output of more than 10,000 cars. Both the Wizard and the Minx used all-steel saloon bodies supplied by the Pressed Steel Company at Cowley, but both were offered with a wide choice of alternative body styles. There was also the semi-sporting Hillman Aero Minx of 1932 with a shorter chassis which was underslung at the rear; a model of particular significance to the unfolding Sunbeam-Talbot story.

After the Humber 16/50 and Snipe, the Wizard and the Minx, the fourth string to the Rootes bow was a medium-sized family car, the Humber Twelve launched in late 1932. The engine was a side-valve four (69.5mm by 110mm, 1669cc) and the specification held no surprises. Prices started at £265, the price also asked for an Austin "Heavy Twelve" saloon, and quite a bit above the 12hp class norm, a Morris Cowley saloon for instance cost only £180-185. Again, the standard saloon was by Pressed Steel, but there were several other styles, including the Vogue designed by the *couturier* Captain André Molyneux and launched in September 1933. This two-door saloon had no pillar between the door window and the rear quarter light, which had a reverse angle shape; this became somewhat of a Rootes styling characteristic.

For the 1935 season, when the first combined Rootes range had become well-established and had been shaken out, this is how the line-up looked:

The Hillman Aero Minx saloon soon adopted a similar pillarless solution for the rear quarter light. This car was clearly the forerunner of the Talbot Ten. (Courtesy CTM)

1934-35	Cyl.	Bore x stroke	Capacity	RAC hp	Wheelbase	Prices from
Hillman Minx	4	63x95mm	1185cc	9.8	7ft 8in (2337mm)	£159
Hillman Aero Minx	4	63x95mm	1185cc	9.8	7ft 4in (2235mm)	£225
Humber Twelve	4	69.5x110mm	1669cc	11.98	8ft 2.75in (2508mm)	£285
Hillman 16	6	65x106mm	2110cc	15.7	9ft 3in (2819mm)	£269
Humber 16/60	6	67.5x106mm	2276cc	16.95	10ft 4in (3150mm)	£435
Hillman 20/70	6	75x106mm	2810cc	20.92	9ft 3in (2819mm)	£269
Hillman 20/70 lwb	6	75x106mm	2810cc	20.92	10ft 3in (3124mm)	£340
Humber Snipe 80	6	80x116mm	3499cc	23.8	10ft 4in (3150mm)	£475
Humber Pullman	6	80x116mm	3499cc	23.8	11ft (3353mm)	£735

This elegant sports saloon was offered on the 1935 model Talbot 75 and 105 chassis.

The Wizard had now become the Hillman 16 and 20/70, with a long-wheelbase variant of the latter, and the Humber 16/50 had become the 16/60 with a marginally bored-out engine and a 17hp rating. The 1936 six-cylinder cars, Hillmans as well as Humbers, acquired the "Evenkeel" transverse-leaf independent front suspension, while the 1936 Minx was completely revamped as the "Minx Magnificent" which went on to double the production of the original. Standard saloon versions of the new Minx, and of the latest Humbers, had similar styling with swept rear ends and compound-curve front wings, with bodies from Pressed Steel.

By 1939, the six-cylinder Hillmans had been dropped in favour of an extended and rationalised Humber range, but a new big four of 1.9 litres and 14hp had been introduced, sharing a common chassis and body with most of the six-cylinder Humbers. The range now included three Sunbeam-Talbots which shared major mechanical components with Hillman or Humber models.

The 1940 range was much the same, except that the Humber Snipe Imperial was dropped and a Sunbeam-Talbot 2-litre was introduced, using the Hillman Fourteen engine in a lengthened Sunbeam-Talbot Ten chassis. The 1940 model Minx was Rootes's first model with unitary body construction, although it looked almost identical to the 1936-39 model. Post-war, the Hillman Fourteen became the Humber Hawk, the two biggest Sunbeam-Talbots were dropped, as was the Humber Sixteen, while the Snipe acquired a 2.7-litre 18hp engine of a size last seen in 1937, but there were still seven models in the Rootes range until 1948: the ubiquitous Minx, four Humbers and two Sunbeam-Talbots.

Decline of the Talbots

Then the Talbot brand was added to the Rootes mixture in 1935. As far as Sunbeam is concerned, all that Rootes initially did was to stop making the cars, and the Wolverhampton factory was eventually closed and disposed of. The final Sunbeam design, the Dawn, would only have offered unnecessary competition for the Humber Twelve, if barely that at £425, while the larger Sunbeams, sixes in the 20-25hp bracket, were getting old and were similarly expensive. By contrast, thanks to the genius of Georges Roesch, Talbot had a fine range of six-cylinder models which were selling in larger numbers, and which were capable of still further development. Roesch himself had ambitious plans for fitting his highly efficient six-cylinder engines in a new chassis with all-independent suspension, perhaps of the backbone type that he patented in the dying days of Clement-Talbot Ltd.

1938-39	Cyl.	Bore x stroke	Capacity	RAC hp	Wheelbase	Prices from
Hillman Minx	4	63x95mm	1185cc	9.8	7ft 8in (2337mm)	£163
Sunbeam-Talbot Ten	4	63x95mm	1185cc	9.8	7ft 9in (2362mm)	£265
Hillman Fourteen	4	75x110mm	1944cc	13.95	9ft 6in (2896mm)	£248
Humber Sixteen	6	67.5x120mm	2576cc	16.95	9ft 6in (2896mm)	£345
Humber Snipe	6	75x120mm	3181cc	20.92	9ft 6in (2896mm)	£355
Sunbeam-Talbot 3-litre	6	75x120mm	3181cc	20.92	9ft 10in (2997mm)	£415
Humber Super Snipe	6	85x120mm	4086cc	26.88	9ft 6in (2896mm)	£385
Sunbeam-Talbot 4-litre	6	85x120mm	4086cc	26.88	9ft 10in (2997mm)	£455
Humber Snipe Imperial	6	85x120mm	4086cc	26.88	10ft 4in (3150mm)	£515
Humber Pullman	6	85x120mm	4086cc	26.88	11ft (3353mm)	£750

The Sunbeam Thirty drew the admiring crowds at the 1936 Olympia Motor Show but never went on sale. Three years later, a similar Phaeton body appeared on the biggest Sunbeam-Talbot chassis.

However, Roesch was instead asked to take the Hillman Aero Minx and turn it into a small Talbot, launched shortly before the 1935 Motor Show and generally well received (see chapter 2). Meanwhile, the six-cylinder range was pruned and modified in many respects, not least with a view to reducing costs and thus retail prices. The following are comparisons between the final pre-Rootes range (1934-35) and what happened over the next two to three years:

In 1948, the new Minx adopted full-width bodywork in the American idiom.

1934-35	Bore x stroke	Capacity	RAC hp	Wheelbase	Gearbox	Prices from
65	61x95mm	1666cc	13.8	9ft 6in (2896mm)	Preselector	£460
75	69.5x100mm	2276cc	17.9	10ft 0.375in (3058mm)	Preselector	£565
95	75x112mm	2970cc	20.9	10ft 0.375in (3058mm)	Preselector	£650
105	75x112mm	2970cc	20.9	10ft 0.375in (3058mm)	Preselector	£750
110	80x112mm	3377cc	23.8	10ft 0.375in (3058mm)	Preselector	£850
95 limousine	75x112mm	2970cc	20.9	11ft 4in (3454mm)	Preselector	£850

The Rootes influence was felt by the discontinuation of the smallest 65 model, and the introduction of a synchromesh gearbox instead of Talbot's traditional preselector 'box on the 75, while this and the 105 were offered with a very Humber-like all-steel six-light saloon body. Talbot's expensive and heavy 24-volt system with a combined dynamo and starter motor was replaced by standard components. The bonus was that all models had an improved cruciform-braced, box-section chassis, and that most prices had come down.

1935-36	Bore x stroke	Capacity	RAC hp	Wheelbase	Gearbox	Prices from
75	69.5x100mm	2276cc	17.9	10ft 0.375in (3058mm)	Synchromesh	£485
105	75x112mm	2970cc	20.9	10ft 0.375in (3058mm)	Preselector	£585
105 Speed	75x112mm	2970cc	20.9	10ft 0.375in (3058mm)	Preselector	£625
3½-litre	80x112mm	3377cc	23.8	10ft 0.375in (3058mm)	Preselector	£825
24hp limousine	80x112mm	3377cc	23.8	11ft 4in (3454mm)	Preselector	£895

Also introduced in 1948, the Humber Hawk had styling similar to the Minx but retained a vertical grille.

1936-37	Bore x stroke	Capacity	RAC hp	Wheelbase	Gearbox	Prices from
75	69.5x100mm	2276cc	17.9	10ft 0.375in (3058mm)	Synchromesh	£425
105	75x112mm	2970cc	20.9	10ft 0.375in (3058mm)	Synchromesh	£495
105 Speed	75x112mm	2970cc	20.9	10ft 0.375in (3058mm)	Synchromesh	£595
3½litre	80x112mm	3377cc	23.8	10ft 0.375in (3058mm)	Synchromesh	£695
24hp limousine	80x112mm	3377cc	23.8	11ft 4in (3454mm)	Preselector	£795

For 1937, synchromesh spread to other models although the preselector box remained as a £25 option, and prices were further reduced.

Production petered out in the spring and summer of 1937, in advance of the introduction of the Rootes-designed 3-litre at £398 that October. Classic Talbot features such as torque tube drive and quarter-elliptic rear springs continued to the end. Production figures for the later models were quite low: between 1935 and 1937 there were some 500 75s, 297 105s, 89 3½-litres, 50 limousines – and perhaps still a few of those ambulances that Talbot once had a near-monopoly on supplying to the London County Council! Production of the 3½-litre 110 finished in April 1937, although such a car continued to be listed as a "1938 model", its basic specification and price unchanged from 1937; my conclusion is that any later deliveries were made from stock.[11]

Stillborn wonder: The Sunbeam Thirty

As explained above, it seems that initially the Rootes brothers had no plans for the Sunbeam name, but they quickly decided to revive it in a fashion that was both spectacular and unexpected, since they asked Georges Roesch to design a car which would be a fitting top-of-the-range model – allegedly with a view to soliciting the custom of HM King Edward VIII who as Prince of Wales had owned and used a variety of Humbers, and who had become a friend of Billy Rootes.[12]

Roesch came up with a magnificent 4.5-litre 150bhp straight-eight, following the design principles established with his Talbot engines; it was notably compact and weighed 6.5cwt (331kg) with gearbox.[13] The aim was a top speed of 100mph (161km/h), which was supposedly achieved in testing at Brooklands. The Sunbeam Thirty was launched at the 1936 Motor Show. The engine was an outstanding design, but was installed in the latest Humber chassis complete with "Evenkeel" suspension, with added radius arms, and a wheelbase of 10ft 4in (3150mm) – the same as the Snipe – in the short-chassis "Continental" version, with another 1ft (305mm) for the long version, topping even the Humber Pullman by 4in (102mm). Chassis were priced at £750 and £800, with complete cars from £1195 to £1475. The gearbox was a stock Rootes item, and the Bendix cable brakes were on this occasion – wisely – supplemented by a Dewandre servo. If the front view was suspiciously like a

Humber, the coachwork by Thrupp & Maberly was delightful. The car was introduced to the press at a luncheon party at Claridges, hosted by the Rootes brothers.[14]

From the 1936 Motor Show catalogue, the following cars were on display and were also described in the show issues of *The Autocar* and *The Motor*:

On the Sunbeam stand (128):
Thrupp & Maberly limousine on long chassis, finished in Black, trimmed in Black leather to front and Fawn cloth to rear (£1325)
Thrupp & Maberly Continental touring saloon on short chassis, finished in Jewelessence Ruby, trimmed in Beige leather (£1240)
Thrupp & Maberly Continental phaeton on short chassis, finished in Gun, trimmed in leather to match (£1295)
Together with a display engine.

On the Thrupp & Maberly stand (19):
Thrupp & Maberly Continental saloon on short chassis, finished in Elephant Grey, trimmed in Grey leather

On the HJ Mulliner stand (20):
HJ Mulliner sedanca de ville on long chassis, finished in Black, trimmed in West of England cloth

This suggests a production figure of at least five cars though the figure of eight has also been mentioned. However, some or all of the show cars may have been empty shells on mock-up stretched Humber chassis…

The oft-told story is that the Rootes brothers decided to take a prototype on a Continental run, and that the over-stressed chassis broke, curiously enough near Maidstone in Kent where they had started their business. If there was any serious structural deficiency in the longest chassis it would have taken a great deal of effort to overcome, and since the King for whom the car might have been intended abdicated before 1936 was out, this spelled *finis* for what could have been a remarkable motorcar. Whatever cars and parts were made were scrapped, and although the Australian enthusiast Archie Marshall in 2000 claimed to own a car which *might* have started out as a Sunbeam Thirty, since camouflaged as a Humber and of course *sans* straight-eight, this is best treated as "not proven". I am however told that according to the Thrupp & Maberly records, its *body* – of the phaeton style – came from one of the 1936 Sunbeam Thirty Motor Show cars, and other Sunbeam bodies were also recycled.[15]

After the Sunbeam Thirty was dropped, in 1939 Roesch left Rootes to take up the position of chief engineer to David Brown, who after having severed contact with Harry Ferguson wanted to develop his own tractor design. Working with the headstrong Brown was not a happy experience for Roesch either. During the Second World War he went on to join Frank Whittle's Power Jet company, and for the rest of his career worked on gas turbines. He died at the age of 78 in 1969.

The Rootes family and their company in later years

Billy had become Sir William Rootes in 1942 in recognition of his contribution to the war effort, and was ennobled in 1959 for the export achievements of his company. He died in December 1964, but Reggie, who had become Sir Reginald in 1945 and took over as chairman of the company on his brother's death, lived on until 1977. Their sons Geoffrey, Brian, and Timothy had all joined the family business. Geoffrey succeeded to his father's title, and after Reggie's retirement in 1967 became chairman of Rootes until 1973; he died in 1992, and his son Nicholas then became the third Lord Rootes.

The Rootes Group was already one of Britain's "big six" car manufacturers in the 1930s, together with Austin, Ford, Morris (Nuffield), Standard and Vauxhall. Their post-

Rootes last throw of the dice, the rear-engined Hillmand Imp of 1963, was not as successful as hoped.

war model range introduced in 1948 was, as always, led by a new Hillman Minx, which continued to be their most popular product, and which was equally successful in many export markets. The main factory after 1945 was the giant plant at Ryton-on-Dunsmore outside Coventry, built as part of the government-supported "shadow" factory scheme in 1939-40. The company expanded by further take-overs, in the 1930s of Karrier (the commercial vehicle maker originally based at Huddersfield) and British Light Steel Pressings (steel pressings and later complete bodies), after the war of Tilling-Stevens and Vulcan (commercial vehicles) and, in 1956, of Singer cars. However, in 1952 Austin and Nuffield combined to form BMC, while Ford grew rapidly, whereas Rootes, together with Standard and Vauxhall, stagnated. A plan hatched in 1955 to merge Rootes with their fellow Coventry car maker Standard-Triumph did not come to fruition.[16]

A long strike at the British Light Steel Pressings factory in London in 1962 severely damaged Rootes through loss of production and thus profit. The company planned to meet competition from BMC and Ford head-on by belatedly introducing a small car, the Imp launched in 1963, built in a new factory at Linwood in Scotland, with a body plant next door which Rootes bought from Pressed Steel; it had originally made railway wagons but also the bodies for the early Volvo P1800s. The Imp was quite advanced, fitted with a single overhead camshaft light-alloy engine based on a Coventry Climax design; unfortunately this was in the rear, at a time when other manufacturers were beginning to switch to front-wheel drive.

The cost of this project, coupled with the fact that the Imp was never as successful as expected, led Rootes to selling a stake in the business to the American Chrysler Corporation which at that time was expanding into Europe. Chrysler approached Rootes in 1963, and in June 1964 it was announced that they were taking 30 per cent of voting shares, and 50 per cent of non-voting shares, all for a now-risible £12.3 million. They had already bought the French Simca company, at first in 1958 taking over the shares that Ford had held in Simca since selling their French subsidiary to Simca in 1954, and completing the take-over in 1963. The existing British Chrysler operation, the Dodge truck company at Kew, was transferred to Rootes in 1965. In 1967, Chrysler completed the take-over of Rootes, and in 1970 Rootes became Chrysler United Kingdom Ltd, part of Chrysler Europe, which also had operations in France and Spain. The old brand names disappeared: Singer in 1970, Hillman, Humber and Sunbeam in 1976-77. From then on, all cars were branded as Chrysler, while the commercial vehicles became Dodges.

Then in 1978 Chrysler sold their European operations to Peugeot, and in 1979 both the French and the British products were renamed Talbot, since this name was part of the corporate inheritance on both sides of the Channel. The commercial vehicle business was sold to Renault, which continued to make trucks in Britain until 1993. The Linwood factory was closed in 1981, and car production was concentrated at Ryton. However, despite its rich heritage, the Talbot brand did not succeed in re-establishing itself in the market, and the name was dropped in 1986; a new large car, the Spanish-built Tagora of 1981-83, was an embarrassing flop. Afterwards, Ryton continued to make some models of Peugeot for the UK market, but even this came to an end in 2006 when the last British-built Peugeot came off the line and the factory was closed and sold for redevelopment. This event also marked the end of large-scale car production in Coventry, the city that had once been considered to be Britain's Detroit. By 2008, nothing remained of the Ryton factory.

---

1. Much information in this chapter builds on Bullock *Rootes Brothers* and Robson *Cars of the Rootes Group*
2. Information courtesy of Terry McGrath
3. Montagu with Sedgwick *Lost Causes of Motoring* (revised edition) pp.174-78
4. Demaus and Tarring *The Humber Story 1868-1932 passim*
5. Dowell *Sunbeam "The Supreme Car" 1899-1935 passim*
6. Laux *In First Gear* pp.212, 215-16
7. Nickols and Karslake *Motoring Entente passim*
8. Blight *Georges Roesch and the Invincible Talbot passim*
9. Symons *Monte Carlo Rally* pp.39-71
10. Montagu with Sedgwick *Lost Causes of Motoring, Europe vol.1* p.199
11. *Chassis Registers* in Coventry Transport Museum archive, cp. Blight pp.483-84
12. Frostick *The Cars that Got Away* pp.66-72
13. Roesch in The Institution of Automobile Engineers *Proceedings* vol. XXXVI 1941-42 p.327; he added "it was not my gear-box"!
14. *The Autocar* 16 Oct 1936 p.722
15. *The Daily Telegraph* 24 Oct 2000; information on Thrupp & Maberly records courtesy of Tim Sutton
16. Bullock pp.200-02

Chapter Two

Britain's most exclusive light car: the Talbot Ten

Anthony Blight in his monumental Talbot history did not mince his words. In his succinct opinion, what Rootes did to Talbot was nothing more or less than "Rape".[1] Within this frame of reference, it is likely that Mr Blight would have considered the Talbot Ten as the "bastard" offspring of such an ill-starred relationship.

The car that was launched at the 1935 Motor Show was neither the first, nor far from the last, example of what became known as "badge-engineering" from the British motor industry, but perhaps it broke new ground by being the most obvious case yet of a car, hitherto known under one name, assuming a new name and radiator in an effort to push it upmarket. By 1935, the British public had already been presented with a Bentley based on the Rolls-Royce, several MGs using Morris or Wolseley components, a rather incestuous family of Daimlers, Lanchesters and BSAs, and at the same show where the new Talbot made its debut, with a range of Wolseleys which bore more than a passing resemblance to equivalent Morrises.

As previously related, Rootes had only bought Clement-Talbot Ltd in January 1935. In order to introduce a revitalized Talbot range at the earliest opportunity, the Motor Show the following autumn, they had about ten months to come up with new or revamped designs. Apart from making changes to some of the older Talbots, the simplest way to have a new model at the show was to base this on an existing Rootes product. To avoid any overlap with the bigger Talbots, the logical answer was to design a new car based on the Hillman Minx, or to be more precise, the Aero Minx, a mildly-tuned sporting version which had been on the market since 1932 but which had sold in tiny numbers; production was only 649 cars.[2]

The most important difference between the Minx and the Aero Minx was the chassis, which on the Aero model had its wheelbase shortened from 7ft 8in (2337mm) to 7ft 4in (2235mm) and

This artist's impression featured on the front cover of the 1937 Talbot Ten brochure.

The dimensional sketch of the Talbot Ten shows that the car provided space for four, but it was a rather tight fit, especially in the rear seat.

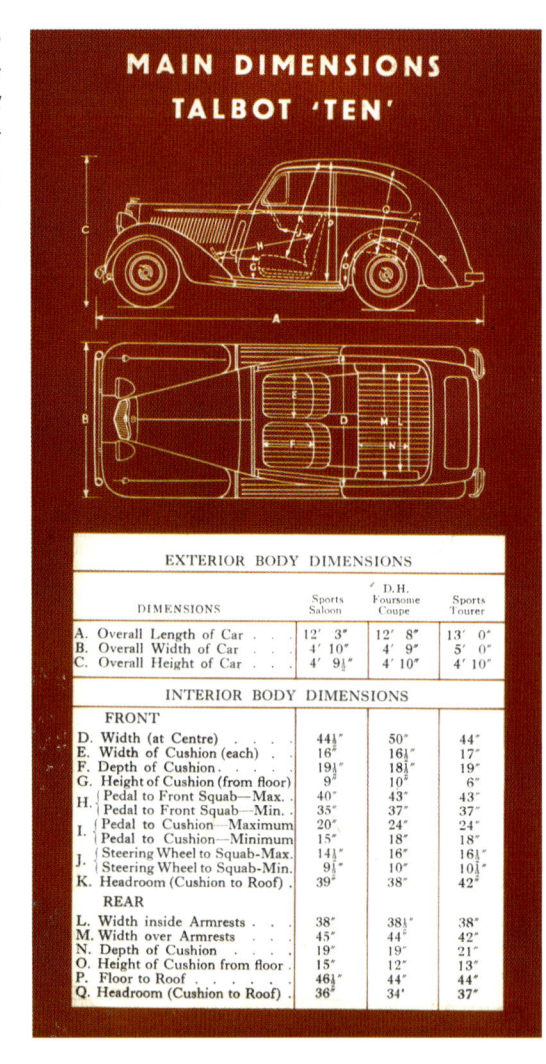

MAIN DIMENSIONS TALBOT 'TEN'

EXTERIOR BODY DIMENSIONS			
DIMENSIONS	Sports Saloon	D.H. Foursome Coupé	Sports Tourer
A. Overall Length of Car	12' 3"	12' 8"	13' 0"
B. Overall Width of Car	4' 10"	4' 9"	5' 0"
C. Overall Height of Car	4' 9½"	4' 10"	4' 10"

INTERIOR BODY DIMENSIONS			
FRONT			
D. Width (at Centre)	44½"	50"	44"
E. Width of Cushion (each)	16⅝"	16½"	17"
F. Depth of Cushion	19½"	18½"	19"
G. Height of Cushion (from floor)	9⅞"	10⅝"	6"
H. Pedal to Front Squab—Max.	40"	43"	43"
Pedal to Front Squab—Min.	35"	37"	37"
I. Pedal to Cushion—Maximum	20"	24"	24"
Pedal to Cushion—Minimum	15"	18"	18"
J. Steering Wheel to Squab-Max.	14½"	16"	16½"
Steering Wheel to Squab-Min.	9½"	10"	10½"
K. Headroom (Cushion to Roof)	39⅝"	38"	42⅝"
REAR			
L. Width inside Armrests	38"	38½"	38"
M. Width over Armrests	45"	44⅝"	42"
N. Depth of Cushion	19"	19"	21"
O. Height of Cushion from floor	15"	12"	13"
P. Floor to Roof	46½"	44"	44"
Q. Headroom (Cushion to Roof)	36⅝"	34'	37"

was carried below the rear axle, the "underslung" chassis design used by so many car makers of the 1930s in their efforts to build cars lower. The Aero Minx had been available with a variety of body styles, including a two-door saloon with a streamlined fastback shape, as well as open two- and four-seaters. An unusual feature of the saloon was that there was no centre pillar above the waistline, and the glass of the fixed rear quarter light overlapped with the glass in the door – a design feature originally introduced on the Humber Vogue in 1933. The mechanical specification was relatively little changed but included a special cylinder head with a higher compression ratio, which boosted the power of the side-valve 1185cc engine from 30 to 35bhp. The rest was standard Minx.

For the Talbot Ten, the underslung chassis was extended to a wheelbase of 7ft 9in (2362mm), presumably to add a bit more room in the rear seat, as the Aero Minx saloon had been somewhat deficient in this area. Tubular cross members were used but the chassis design was otherwise conventional. Suspension was by semi-elliptic springs front and rear, and there were transverse hydraulic lever-arm Luvax shock absorbers. As was appropriate for a car with a sporty image, Dunlop centre-lock wire wheels were fitted, with 5.25-16 tyres. Brakes were the Bendix cable-operated, self-servo type, with a pull-up handbrake with press-button release between the front seats; it operated on all four wheels. Steering was by Burman-Douglas worm and nut, with about two-and-a-half turns from lock to lock, and a four-spoke sprung steering wheel of 17in (432mm) diameter. That left-hand drive was available is confirmed by a preserved 1938 car in Denmark, chassis number 6451; this is also one of very few cars badged as "Sunbeam" for export, and was a chassis-only delivery, fitted with a special two-seater drophead body by an unknown coachbuilder.[3]

The engine was a simple and straightforward design, reflecting the conservative and careful approach of the Rootes engineers, and had proved itself since being first introduced in the Minx four years earlier. With four cylinders of 63mm by 95mm, capacity was 1185cc and the RAC rating was 9.8hp. The combined block and crankcase was cast iron, the crankshaft had three main bearings, and a short double roller chain drove the camshaft, which at first had two, later three, bearings, and operated the side valves on the left-hand side. On the Talbot, the cylinder head was aluminium and the compression ratio was quoted as 6.8 or even 7:1, high for a side-valve engine. A single Zenith downdraught carburettor was used, and the combined inlet and exhaust manifold provided a hot-spot. There was mechanical pump feed from a rear-mounted 8.5-gallon (38.6-litre) tank. Power output was claimed to be "over 40bhp at peak", which was 4200-4500rpm: an excellent figure for this type and size of engine at the time, when a Hillman Minx still had only around 30bhp. Cooling was by a simple thermosyphon system, assisted by a fan. The power unit was three-point mounted on rubber. Ignition was by coil and distributor, and the 12-volt electrics were fed by a dynamo with automatic voltage control.

There was slightly more interest in the transmission. Drive was transmitted through a single dry plate clutch to the Minx-type gearbox, which most unusually for the time had synchromesh on all four forward ratios. On the Talbot, change was by a short central remote-control gear lever, fitted in an extension to the gearbox. There was an open Hardy-Spicer prop shaft and a spiral bevel rear axle, with final drive ratios of 5.44:1 for the saloon and drophead coupé, 5.00:1 for the lighter tourer.

Of the three body styles available on this chassis, the two-door saloon was developed from the similar style found on the Aero Minx. The design is likely to have come from Ted White's body engineering department, and was made at the Talbot works in London, which meant in the old Darracq factory at Acton. The pillarless combination of door window and quarter light might in American parlance twenty years in the future have qualified it for the description "hardtop". Actually, together with the rounded outline it gave the car the look of a scaled-down S.S.I Airline, which in turn had been based on a Bentley designed by Geoffrey Smith, editor of The Autocar,[4] although the Talbot did not feature the then-fashionable falling waistline. The saloon cost £265, at a time when a "Minx Magnificent" was available at £159.

The other body styles were bought in. The body for the £260 open tourer came from Whittingham & Mitchel in London. The £295 drophead coupé had a body supplied by Abbott of Farnham, and featured a three-position hood with an intermediate "de-ville" position, where just the front part of the hood was folded. However after a few months a simpler two-posi-

The standard drophead coupé body was this "foursome" made by Abbott of Farnham. (Courtesy Ruud Lem)

Splendid artwork from the 1938 brochure showing all body types.

BRITAIN'S MOST EXCLUSIVE LIGHT CAR

THE NEW SEASON'S TALBOT "TEN"

(Above) The Talbot "Ten" Drophead Foursome Coupé in Ruby jewelessence finish (see ruby on cover).

(Top Right) The Talbot "Ten" Sports Tourer in Gun jewelessence finish (see silver grey on cover).

(Right) The Talbot "Ten" Sports Saloon in the New Lapis Blue jewelessence finish (see Blue on cover).

BRITAIN'S MOST EXCLUSIVE LIGHT CAR!

This 1938 model Talbot Ten tourer has the external-access boot with concealed spare wheel, new for this model year; earlier cars had the spare wheel outside, and boot access behind the rear seat. (Author)

The radiator ornament of the Talbot Ten has been called a "flying T". (Author)

As was traditional for the brand, the radiator badge featured the words "Talbot – London" on either side of the Talbot lion crest. (Author)

tion hood was introduced, presumably as a cost saving. A serious fire occurred at Abbott's factory in December 1935, and 22 Talbot Ten chassis, as well as others, were destroyed, but production was quickly back to normal.[5]

All three body styles were very smart and well-appointed as one would expect at the prices. The wings of compound-curve type were becoming a Rootes trademark at this time; they featured on some of the revised larger Talbots, as well as on the latest Humbers. A miniature version of the Talbot radiator had a grille with fixed slats and a stylized ornament (sometimes called a "flying T") rather than a filler cap which was under the bonnet. The headlamps were mounted on a bar passing behind the radiator grille. The bonnet and some body panels were made of aluminium. There was a full-width front bumper while at the rear, quarter bumpers flanked a built-in number plate. All models had built-in, self-cancelling trafficators and a reversing light. Dual electric wipers were fitted, with the motor mounted remotely under the bonnet.

The interior was nicely furnished; the seats featured Moseley "Float-on-Air" pneumatic cushions and leather upholstery, with tubular frames for the front seats. Foot wells gave extra legroom for rear seat passengers, and they also enjoyed a centre and side armrests. The saloon had a sliding roof, and swivelling front quarter lights operated by separate winders. Further ventilation was possible through vents on either side of the scuttle, adjustable by bevel gears. One demeaning feature of the original Talbot Ten was that it shared a nasty oval combination instrument with the Hillman Minx, with oil pressure gauge, fuel gauge and a clock built into the speedometer. Lighting from behind the translucent face was adjustable by a rheostat. The saloon had only a small boot, mostly taken up by spare wheel, so luggage had to be carried on the lowered boot lid. The drophead had a similar arrangement, whereas the tourer had an external spare wheel with a cover, and the luggage space was behind the rear seat backrest.

The Talbot Ten was also available in chassis form, there were 34 chassis deliveries over three seasons, including two or three for export, as well as nine others with non-standard bodywork, but it seems likely that most special bodies came from Abbott.[6] At the 1936 Motor Show, in addition to the normal foursome drophead, Abbott displayed a two-seater drophead coupé with a dickey seat that would accommodate another two passengers. The line of the tail was well rounded and the spare wheel was set almost vertically at the rear. The wings were not quite the standard type and interestingly the car had no running boards. To me, the *tout ensemble* had a somewhat Germanic, DKW-like look. Their 1937 show car had an auxiliary rear seat and the spare wheel concealed in the rear locker, while one of their 1938 show cars had a bench front seat. It is known that at least twelve were made, probably quite a few more, of which four are still known to the Sunbeam Talbot Alpine Register (see also appendix). In early 1937, there was an "experimental four-door pillarless saloon" probably by Thrupp & Maberly on chassis 2149, possibly a prototype for the style adopted for the 1939 model.[7]

Subsequently, Abbott developed a most unusual variant, a two-seater fixed-head coupé; *The Autocar* later illustrated one of these, which they described as a Sunbeam-Talbot although the wings and wheel discs indicate that it was a 1938 model Talbot. It has been suggested that the model was intended for the 1939 Motor Show. A survivor was reported in 1970. A similar body had already been built for the car registered ELK 7 that Norman Garrad entered in the 1938 Monte Carlo Rally. This must still have been a Talbot and had wire wheels, together with stubby and well cut-away helmet front wings.[8]

Georges Roesch, of course, was still the chief designer of Talbot, staying on until 1939. As the designer of some of the most efficient overhead-valve engines found anywhere at the time, reputedly he viewed the side-valve engine as a "primitive antiquity". However, he was widely credited in public with the design of the Ten, and was even mentioned by name when the Sunbeam-Talbot Ten appeared in 1938, although by then engineering responsibility had probably shifted to Coventry. It seems likely that he oversaw the modifications to the basic Hillman design, especially the engine improvements. Blight confirms this, and goes on to give a funny but rather sad description of Roesch introducing the 1936 Talbot range to the press: "Roesch passed to the next shed where the secret new Talbot Ten stood behind locked doors. He swung them open and stepped momentarily aside to reveal the car within. 'This', he announced, 'is the Talbot Ten.' No further word was spoken; the doors were closed once more, and Roesch's relief was barely concealed as the party moved on…"[9]

In fact the new model was subject to closer scrutiny by the press than this short glimpse into its garage, and was generally well received. *The*

The original 1936 and 1937 models used this not very sporting combination instrument also found on the contemporary Minx.

Motor referred to it as a "sports car" and "a small car de luxe …the workmanship, finish and equipment being all of the high order which is expected of Talbot productions." *The Autocar* described the Ten at the end of an article devoted to the larger Talbots and was perhaps a shade less enthusiastic: "this is a new conception of car to bear the Talbot name" and the

This car is one of the special Abbott drophead coupés, a two-seater with a dickey seat. (Author)

The dog lovers have rather got in the way but this was one of the 1936 season works rally tourers, CUC 10 driven by JE Scott on the Scottish Rally. (Courtesy Derek Cook)

engine was described as "a departure for a Talbot", but they conceded that it was "a very attractive little car."[10]

The Light Car by contrast headed their article "Talbots Return to the Light Car Field", referring to the 10-23hp and 8-18hp models of the early 1920s. They completely avoided mentioning Rootes and described the car as "an entirely new and very attractive Ten. The new car is neither freakish nor super modern. On the other hand, it is of thoroughly sound, up-to-date design... it is well capable of... speed with comfort." By the way, the words "super modern" were part of the British name for the first front-wheel drive Citroën, launched earlier in 1935. Similarly, the Rootes Group's own magazine *Modern Motoring* described the Talbot Ten as "the happy revival of an old and much-loved favourite in the Talbot range", waxing nostalgically that "The 10hp Talbot of early post-war days... was a superb little motor car... [and] reigned supreme among British light cars for many years." They went on to stress the "Talbot tradition and invincibility" of the newcomer – well they would, wouldn't they.[11]

The first road tests appeared in *The Autocar* and *The Light Car*. *The Autocar*'s test car was a drophead coupé registered CGP 120 which they described as "A Trim Little Car, Which Looks Well, Handles Well, and Has a Willing Four-cylinder Engine". While built on "established lines of small car design... its well-balanced appearance at once suggests that it is a younger member of the famous family..." The synchromesh merited praise, but "the gears were not entirely quiet... it is understood that later production cars are improved in this respect." The highest speedometer reading was 77mph (124km/h) but the best timed speed over a quarter-mile was 68.7mph (110.6km/h), and fuel consumption was in the order of 28-30mpg.

The Light Car and *The Motor* road tested the same saloon registered CGP 119 – they were after all sister journals published by Temple Press, and there were similarities in their test reports. *The Light Car* eulogized "...we feel that the Talbot is a car that will make a wide appeal; it has the appearance of a thoroughbred, and on the road it does not lack the essential characteristics that go to the making of the breed." Owing to "weather conditions and obstructions on the track" they recorded a mean top speed of only 64.29mph (103.5km/h) at Brooklands: "...we believe that under more normal conditions 70mph (113km/h) could be attained, if not exceeded." They quoted a 25.4sec time for the standing quarter-mile (400 metres). Amusingly they felt that the pillarless design "enables the back-seat passengers to enter or leave the car with greater convenience" which was accompanied by a rather unconvincing photograph. Their closing paragraph mentioned the Rootes Group and stated that the Talbot Ten "displays a number of features that have already been well proved by the companies concerned."

The Motor summed up the car as "An Attractive Car with a Lively Performance and an Extremely Comfortable Springing System", and although they, too, failed to record more than 64.3mph (103.5km/h) at Brooklands, "under more reasonable conditions it should be possible to achieve a timed speed of about 70mph (113km/h)..." Their standing quarter-mile time was also exactly the same as that measured by the sister journal. Fuel consumption was in the order of 27mpg, driven hard. They went on to say, rather candidly, "In mechanical design the makers have wisely made use of the special small-car experience possessed by the other manufacturing companies associated with Messrs. Rootes", but summed up the car as "a small sports car de luxe which should have a special appeal to those who appreciate refined performance and good workmanship."[12]

In *The Autocar*, there was further praise for the car from "The Scribe" in "Disconnected

Jottings". He had a saloon on loan for a weekend and could not "recall a more comfortable car; the seating comfort is a revelation." He was not tired after a 300-mile (480km) journey and found the car would cruise happily at 50mph (80km/h). "The running of the car is everything one expects from one of the Talbot breed, although its characteristics did not strike me as being related to the larger Talbots quite as one experiences throughout the ranges of other makes of car", which may have been damning by faint praise but he then put a gloss on it by adding "This Ten is entirely individual."[13]

Motor Sport road tested one of the 1936 season works rally tourers, CUC 11, which by this time had 20,000 miles on the clock. This lengthy report was apparently the very first road test by the new editor, a young man called William Boddy, and while it was as detailed as became that famous writer's custom, we may observe that he had not yet quite developed the skilful and ruthless analysis which became his trademark. However he stated openly that the engine "was developed from that used originally for the Aero model Hillman Minx." The steering and the synchromesh both impressed, and he found no fault with road holding and handling.

With the screen folded flat and the tonneau cover over all passenger seats, a lap of Brooklands was accomplished at 70.14mph (112.88km/h), and with one passenger on board a flying quarter-mile (400 metres) was covered at just under 72mph (116km/h). Boddy was quite happy in declaring this to be a 75mph (121km/h) car, a remarkable speed for a 10hp model at the time, which makes one wonder whether this works car had been specially tuned. Even allowing for the fact that the tourer was lighter and higher-geared, no other Talbot Ten ever approached 75mph (121km/h) on test. On the debit side, including the Brooklands test fuel consumption was 24mpg, which was fairly appalling![14]

The Talbot company had been quick to adopt the Ten for competition work. A team of three tourers, all in the same two-tone green colour scheme and fitted with wheel discs, was prepared for the 1936 season. They were registered CUC 10, CUC 11 and CUC 12 (issued in London in January 1936). The unofficial team leader was Norman Garrad, who had joined Talbot as a sales representative around 1931 and who had already competed with earlier models.

The two other drivers were JE ("Jack") Scott who, in the post-war period, became sales manager of Rolls-Royce, and Gunnar Poppe, one of three sons of the Norwegian co-founder of the White & Poppe engine firm, and later the manager of Thrupp & Maberly.

The first event for the team was the RAC Rally, which resulted in First Class Awards for Garrad and Scott, and a Second Class Award for Poppe. The three cars were then entered for the Land's End Trial, where Garrad took a Premier Award, Poppe and Scott Silver Awards. In the Scottish Rally, the cars were entered as part of the "Talbot Owners' Club Team" and the best result was a ninth in class for Poppe, while Ballantyne's privately-entered saloon managed fifth in class. Two of the works cars appeared again in the Welsh Rally, one of them driven by AG Douglas Clease of *The Autocar* magazine.

However the works effort then seemed to run out of steam. Their only major event in 1937 was the RAC Rally, where Garrad and Poppe ran two new cars, a tourer (DLT 2) and a saloon (DLT 1), coming second and eleventh in class. In 1938, there was just the one car, the fixed-head coupé ELK 7 (see above) which Garrad and none other than SCH Davis entered in the Monte Carlo Rally and finished fifth in the 1500cc class. Garrad could manage no better than sixteenth in class on the RAC Rally, and fourth in class on the Scottish Rally. ELK 7 was then sold to HJ Finden, who ran it in a couple of trials in 1939. Private owners fared little better, although Elliott was first in class on the 1937

In the 1937 RAC Rally, Elliott was second in class with his Talbot Ten saloon. (Courtesy Derek Cook)

In the 1937 RAC Rally, Garrad drove a new works tourer, DLT 2. That car was afterwards lent to Douglas Clease of The Autocar *who took this photo while on a trip to Cornwall. (Courtesy JDHT)*

Unmistakeably, S C H "Sammy" Davis. His and Garrad's 1938 Monte Carlo Rally car is in the background; was ELA 8 a practice car or a support vehicle? (Courtesy Guy Woodhams)

Scottish Rally and McDonald second in class on the same event in 1939. Most ambitious of the private efforts was that of Pilot Officer TGW Appleby, who took his tourer BCG 971 to a 64th place overall in the 1937 Monte Carlo rally. For fuller details, see the table at the end of this chapter. As a curiosity, in August 1938 a Rootes-sponsored race for Talbot Tens at Brooklands attracted ten entries, and was won by GA Wooding at 47.75mph (76.85km/h). He was protested for an alleged non-standard engine, and he had indeed run a supercharged Ten in the Sunbac trial of 1937.[15]

For its second season, the Ten continued virtually unchanged, but in September 1936, prices were reduced so that the saloon and tourer now both cost £248 and the drophead coupé £278. One of the show cars at Olympia in the following month was a saloon finished in "iridescent gunmetal". *The Motor* again tested a saloon, CYY 716, which was timed at 65.70mph (105.7km/h) and they were critical only of the lack of room for the driver's left foot: "it is necessary to rest the left foot on the clutch pedal all the time one is driving." Curiously, a year earlier *The Autocar* had specifically praised the fact that there was "a place for the left foot when off the clutch pedal..."

Ominously, *The Motor* withheld the "figure for petrol consumption... pending further tests" and later in the year they published an additional short test of a drophead coupé after "the makers [had] effected considerable research into the question of fuel consumption... it is now possible to get a petrol consumption on the favourable side of 30mpg." Indeed, when the 1938 model was launched *The Motor* headlined the fact that "Latest Developments in Ignition and Carburation Give High Performance with Low Fuel Consumption" and they were quick to road test another saloon, which now gave 32mpg with a best timed top speed of 68.2mph (109.8km/h). This they described as "High Performance With Exceptional Fuel Economy".[16]

Meanwhile, *The Autocar* had tested the same car, CYY 716, that *The Motor* had failed to get a reasonable consumption out of, but they made no similar comment and merely gave a figure of 27-30mpg overall. Compared to the drophead coupé that they had tested twelve months earlier, they found that the acceleration was slightly better but the best timed top speed was 66.18mph (106.51km/h). The gears were still not entirely quiet, but the synchromesh was good and the clutch light. Performance was better than "the normal type of lower-priced Ten", the steering was accurate and the brakes were deemed powerful but light to operate.[17]

The 1938 models were changed in a few respects. Pressed-steel disc wheels were adopted, but were covered by wheel discs. The cooling system was pressurised. The gearbox was still of the all-synchromesh type but had a normal gearlever. A great improvement was that the dashboard now had two Jaeger instrument dials, with the clock in the speedometer – which was marked in both mph and km/h – while a new combination dial included an ammeter. *The Motor* was happy to note that there was now room for the driver's left foot! The tourer fell into line with the other body styles by adopting an external-access boot which accommodated the spare wheel. Most paint finishes were now "jewelessence" (metallic) in Gun, Lapis Blue amd Ruby, while black was also available. The two door-saloon cost £255, the tourer remained at £248 and the drophead coupé cost £285. In August 1937 seven tourers were supplied to Maudes of Norwich with chassis numbers from 5090 to 5096; these are likely to be the Norfolk Police cars which were registered BVF 850 to BVF 856.[18]

The Autocar managed two road tests of the 1938 model, first of a saloon, EGF 855, and finally of a drophead coupé, EXF 856. In view of the praise bestowed in earlier tests and the modest changes made to the 1938 model, one is a trifle surprised to read in the saloon test that compared to earlier cars, "the general road behaviour is appreciably improved." Well, they high-lighted the quieter engine, but the lower gears were still not as quiet as they could be! The best timed top speed for the saloon was 68.18mph (109.73km/h) – the drophead was even a bit faster at 69.23mph (111.42km/h) – and petrol consumption was around 30-33mpg.[19]

The road tester of *Practical Motorist* was extremely brutal to the poor Ten saloon (EGF 855 again) that he had been let loose in, since he tested the synchromesh of the gearbox almost to destruction by changing down from top to third at 60mph (97km/h) and then down to second at 50mph (80km/h). This resulted only in "a certain whine as the drive was taken up again by the clutch" but would hardly be recommended practice when the highest speed on second was normally 32mph (51km/h). Still, it may have provided an alternative method of slowing the car down! – and it is a miracle that the engine did not over-rev.[20]

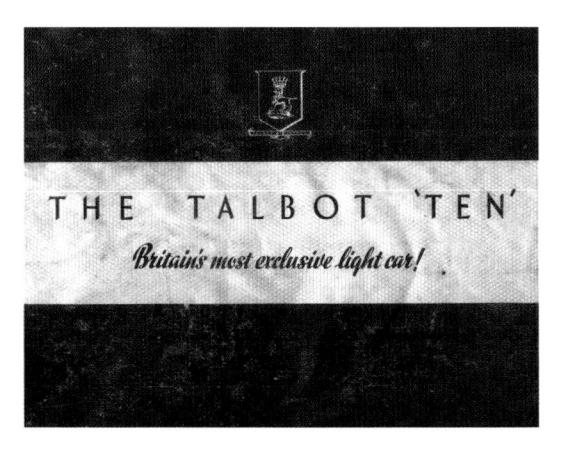

For a car of a fairly specialised type, the Talbot Ten was reasonably successful, with a production figure over three seasons of 3650 cars. If we disregard the contemporary "hype" which attempted to establish the model as a "sports car", we are left with the impression of an attractive, refined and well-equipped small car, with better than average performance for its size, of smart appearance and easy to handle, with commendable top gear flexibility for its size and able to cruise easily at around 50mph (80km/h). Equally important, it had a simple and straightforward mechanical specification – in short, all characteristics which would be handed down to its successors. Obviously there were still enough customers who were prepared to pay extra for the qualities of such a car, and for owning a car with a famous name and badge. One may also speculate that the Talbot was particularly popular with women car buyers.

Sunbeam-Talbot Ten

The Rootes publicists had two stories to tell in August 1938. Firstly, the Sunbeam and Talbot interests were now "fused"[21], the dual names adopted for the company as well as for the cars – initially without a hyphen but this was added within weeks. It is not clear why Rootes should have decided to adopt the dual moniker, but there may have been a genuine wish to keep the Sunbeam name alive and in front of the public, even after the fiasco of the Sunbeam Thirty two years before. It also cannot be denied that many prestige cars, then and later, had double-barrelled hyphenated names! On the new radiator badge, above the central Talbot shield was the word "Supreme" which harked back to the pre-Rootes Sunbeams. Later models remained "Supreme" until the end in 1956.

Secondly, there was a new Ten model, or rather, an all-new four-door saloon body on what was more or less the existing Talbot Ten chassis. The four-door body had been requested by the Rootes brothers, William and Reginald, who no doubt realised the limited appeal of a two-door in the market place. The engineering responsibility for the Sunbeam-Talbot range had now passed from Roesch in London to the ex-Sunbeam designer HCM Stevens, working in Coventry under Bernard Winter, who had become Rootes's director of engineering in 1935.

To give space for a four-door body, the

The frontal aspect of the Talbot Ten featured a radiator which was, more or less, a miniature version of the traditional Talbot radiator. The badge bar, fog lamp and indicators have been added on this car.

engine and radiator were moved forward by 3.5in (89mm). Although initial reports claimed that the gearbox was still of the all-synchromesh type, in fact synchromesh was no longer found on first gear; subsequently it was deleted from second gear as well. The new four-door body was acknowledged to be inspired by the sports saloon body on the Talbot 3-litre which had been introduced a year earlier. It was designed by Ted White, chief body engineer of Talbot, and his colleague Ted Green. It was of all-steel construction and was made by the British Light Steel Pressings company at Acton in London, which was next door to the old Darracq plant and had been acquired by Rootes in 1937. The front wings swept into the running boards while the rear wings kept the compound shape. All four doors were hinged at the rear, and the rear quarter light was still pillarless, with the reverse-angle shape recalling the Humber Vogue. Wheel discs contributed to a very pleasing overall appearance and the car was undoubtedly the most elegant small saloon of the period.

Fixtures and fittings were as nicely executed as ever. Rather than using wood, the dashboard and mouldings were in "Cellustra" (plastic) material in mottled brown or grey. Horizontal fluting ran round the cabin, from the dash along the top of the door trims and transversely across the backrest of the rear seat. To provide adequate rear legroom, the rear seat cushion was raised noticeably above the level of the front seats, but headroom in the rear was still reasonable, although to ensure this the sunroof slid back in full view inside, and the headlining was attached directly to the roof panel (which apparently gave trouble in hot climates).[22] The boot was appreciably larger than before, with the spare wheel flat in a separate compartment below it. The new saloon cost £265, while the tourer and drophead coupé models were still available at £250 and £285 respectively. Both of the latter had the new-style wings but were otherwise little changed

Performance was little changed from the previous model, with a top speed of around 68-70mph (109-113km/h) and fuel consumption of 30-34mpg. A 1939 tourer and a 1940 saloon tested by *The Autocar* both had a best timed speed of 70.87mph (114.05km/h). The saloon averaged 68.31mph (109.93km/h); the tourer was marginally faster at 68.44mph (110.14km/h) with the screen folded flat. Acceleration was not a priority at the time, but *The Motor* managed 0-50mph (0-80km/h) in 17.2sec and a standing quarter-mile (400 metres) in 23.4sec. More important for a 1930s motorist was the top-gear flexibility. Thus *The Autocar*: "Gear changing is not called for frequently... [it has] an exceptional capacity for a 10hp machine to hold a satisfactory rate up long main road slopes... Acceleration from low speeds on top is regular and fairly brisk". The car would accelerate evenly from 10mph (16km/h) in top gear, reaching 50mph (80km/h) in 30.8sec. The tourer tested by *The Autocar* stopped from 30mph (48km/h) in only 27ft (8.2m). As ever, the refinement was greatly appreciated: "the engine is smooth and pleasant at 50mph" (80km/h). The car was, according to *The Motor*, "an obvious choice for those who only want 10 horse-power but want the best."[23]

The Light Car was almost too enthusiastic, describing the Sunbeam-Talbot Ten as "possessing all the virtues of a luxury car [combined] with a real sports car performance..." and even the following paragraph of purple prose: "For many years the names Sunbeam and Talbot have been synonymous with all that is best in the production of quality motorcars. When the designers of both concerns collaborated in the production of the new Sunbeam-Talbot Ten it was evident... that the new production [was] one of the most handsome light cars ever built... it possessed that something known as refinement." Clearly Mr Blight whom I quoted at start of this chapter got it all wrong...[24]

The four-door body immediately broadened the car's appeal, and this was reflected in a much improved production figure for the 1938-39 season of 2752 cars, which still included 29 chassis, of which three were exported. There were also two "specials": chassis number 40002, effectively a prototype, had a Talbot Ten-type two-door saloon body, and chassis 42703 had a drophead body by Thrupp & Maberly. By now

After the finish of the 1938 Monte Carlo Rally, Davis and Garrad were photographed with their special-bodied Talbot Ten rally car registered ELK 7. (Courtesy CTM)

ELK 7 was soon sold to HJ Finden, who drove it in the 1939 Land's End Trial. (Courtesy Ruud Lem and Guy Woodhams)

The overall design of the Ten with the pillarless window is reminiscent of the S.S.I Airline, and the little Talbot is often known as the "Airline" as well, but does not have the falling waistline of the S.S.

Both front and rear wings are of the compound curve type, which is characteristic of Rootes styling of the period.

Appropriately for a car with a sporting image, centre-lock wire wheels are fitted.

BRITAIN'S MOST EXCLUSIVE LIGHT CAR

While attractive on the car, the two-tone colour scheme is unlikely to be original. The registration mark is a fairly recent "age-related" issue, since this car was re-imported from South Africa.

Headlamps and side lamps are stock Lucas items. The badge bar has been fixed to the headlamp bar proper.

A detail of the extra fog lamp.

The plain and simple rear view, with the reasonably large rear window. This car has a full-width rear bumper mounted higher than normal, and up-to-date rear lighting.

No, there is not a lot of room in the rear seat, but it is a cosy and comfortable space, with an excellent view out. There is also a folding centre arm rest, and we can just see one of the foot wells.

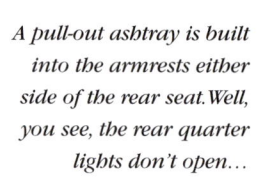

A pull-out ashtray is built into the armrests either side of the rear seat. Well, you see, the rear quarter lights don't open…

BRITAIN'S MOST EXCLUSIVE LIGHT CAR

There is nothing very fancy about the front compartment either, but the dashboard and cappings are at least in wood. On the steering wheel hub are the trafficator switch, horn push, and dip switch. We can just see the gaiter for the gear lever. The large knob to the right of the steering wheel is for the wipers.

The hand brake mounted between the seats (below left) and the ash tray for the front passenger (below right) – the driver did not get one!

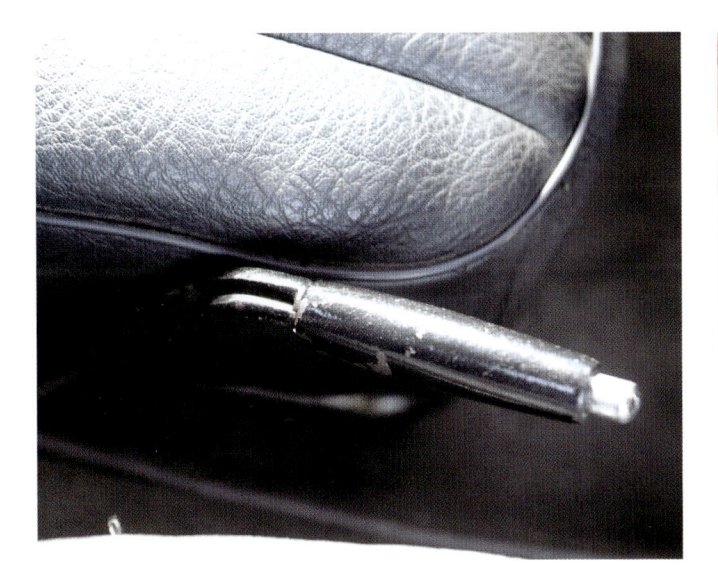

35

Under-bonnet accessibility is reasonably good, but the distributor is rather squeezed between the water outlet hose and the air filter. This car has been fitted with an electric SU fuel pump but the original mechanical pump is still "in situ". I am not sure that the engine should really be painted red.

The boot is almost completely taken up by the spare wheel. There is a bit of room behind this, otherwise luggage has to be carried on the fold-down boot lid.

This Talbot name plate is found on the boot lid.

BRITAIN'S MOST EXCLUSIVE LIGHT CAR

The useful ventilation flaps either side of the scuttle are operated by bevel gears, and open in either direction.

The right-hand side of the engine is rather cluttered, with the carburettor, manifolds and air cleaner, apart from the plugs, distributor (hidden) and coil. Somehow I think this car has been re-wired to cope with extra electrical equipment.

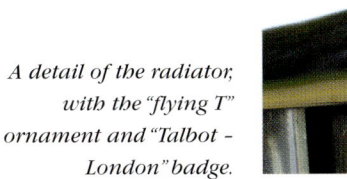

A detail of the radiator, with the "flying T" ornament and "Talbot – London" badge.

Here we see the gear lever properly, the rather scattered minor controls and the two small cubby holes. Below the mirror is the winder for opening the windscreen.

Although this instrument is marked "Talbot", a very similar combination dial was found on the contemporary Hillman Minx. The dual Imperial and Metric markings had yet to be introduced.

BRITAIN'S MOST EXCLUSIVE LIGHT CAR

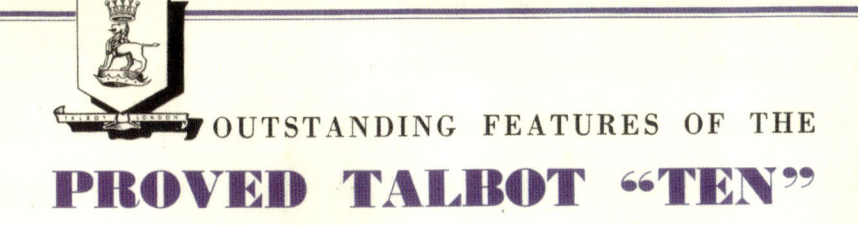

OUTSTANDING FEATURES OF THE
PROVED TALBOT "TEN"

NEW "INSTANT VISION" INSTRUMENT PANEL
With rheostat controlled pale green lighting. The instruments include a large speedometer marked in both kilometres and miles, with trip recorder, petrol gauge marked in litres and gallons, oil pressure gauge, ampere meter, eight-day clock and cigar lighter.

NEW TYPE OF GEAR LEVER
A rigid gear lever, specially designed for free unhampered entrance and exit, yet within instant reach of the hand for split-second gear changes.

IMPROVED PERFORMANCE
Performance is smoother, even more effortless now that the Talbot valve gear has been further improved. Yet petrol consumption is lower than ever.

A welcome change on the 1938 models was this more attractive set of instruments which for the first time had dual Imperial and Metric markings. Sadly the gear lever was now of the conventional type.

THE NEW SEASON'S TALBOT "TEN"

(Above) The Talbot "Ten" Drophead Four-some Coupé in Ruby jewelessence finish (see ruby on cover).

(Top Right) The Talbot "Ten" Sports Tourer in Gun jewelessence finish (see silver grey on cover).

(Right) The Talbot "Ten" Sports Saloon in the New Lapis Blue jewelessence finish (see Blue on cover).

BRITAIN'S MOST EXCLUSIVE LIGHT CAR!

The new "jewelessence" (metallic) paint finishes were made much of in the 1938 Talbot Ten brochure, which featured this lovely art deco style artwork.

39

1939-40 Sunbeam-Talbot Ten FLC 562 on road test, probably by The Light Car.

Taken at Brooklands in the summer of 1939, this Sunbeam-Talbot Ten saloon FXM 833 was road tested by The Motor.

owners' names were regularly recorded in the *Chassis Register,* and the Lancashire Constabulary had a batch of six tourers with chassis numbers from 40650 to 40655 in January 1939 as well as 42250, 42502 and possibly others; at least two still exist.[25] Very little was changed on the 1940 model announced in August 1939, but the handbrake was moved to the right of the driver in front of the door, there was an automatic choke controlled by a thermostat, and the wheel discs were of smaller diameter so that one did not have to remove them to get at the tyre valves! Modified Luvax piston-type shock absorbers were fitted, and the chassis frame was said to be "slightly wider". On the saloon the pneumatic seat cushions were replaced by spring cases with a sponge rubber overlay.

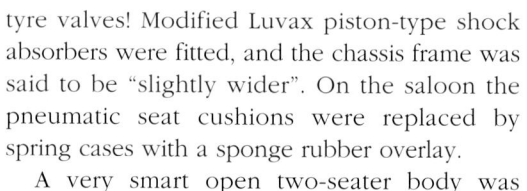

A very smart open two-seater body was added as a fourth body style, costing £248 as did now also the tourer; other prices were unchanged. Like the tourer, the two-seater was by Whittingham & Mitchel, it had cut-down doors and loose side screens. It offered plenty of luggage space in the tonneau area, and the long-tailed shape may well have been the inspiration for the Sunbeam Alpine fifteen years later. Before production was finally discontinued after the outbreak of war, another 852 cars were made, of which only eleven were two-seaters, and fifteen were chassis. During the period of the "phoney war" which lasted until April 1940, Sunbeam-Talbot like many other car makers maintained small-scale production, at least of the Ten, and made efforts to keep the export business going, to neutral markets such as the South American countries. Saloon production seems to have stopped in January 1940 so most of the later Tens had drophead or tourer bodies. Some 1939-40 Tens were supplied to the Police forces of Northumberland, Reading and Berkshire, and as late as March 1941 the Viscountess Astor took delivery of a Ten drophead coupé, which had been built nearly a year earlier.[26] She was of course the famous Nancy Astor, MP for Plymouth Sutton 1919-45 and the society hostess

BRITAIN'S MOST EXCLUSIVE LIGHT CAR

The drophead coupé was little changed from the Talbot Ten but, like the other Sunbeam-Talbot Tens, had the new swept front wings.

FOURSOME DROPHEAD COUPÉ

SUNBEAM-TALBOT 4 DOOR 'TEN'

1939 S-T Ten brochure

4 DOOR SPORTS SALOON

A slightly optimistic brochure shot – if all of this luggage had to be carried, the boot lid would have to stay down.

41

SUNBEAM-TALBOT & ALPINE IN DETAIL

These three side views show the 1940 model year Tens, with their smaller wheel discs. Note that only the tourer and two-seater had louvred bonnet sides. The short-lived two-seater was very pretty indeed. (Courtesy CTM)

of Cliveden (1879-1964).

During the war, Barlby Road became a repair depot for Rolls-Royce Merlin engines and also assembled Karrier Bantam light commercial vehicles. The factory was hit by bombs on 24 September and 15 November 1940 but was not badly damaged. The *Chassis Register* however shows that seven chassis were lost to "enemy action", probably when the Whittingham & Mitchel factory was bombed on 16 September 1940. Limited production of the Ten re-started in August 1945. The post-war models were described in *The Motor* on 8 August and *The Autocar* on 10 August, in the week before the Japanese surrender which marked the end of the Second World War. The Hillman Minx and the Humbers were re-introduced around the same time, so Rootes was one of the first manufacturers to complete its post-war range. Of the Sunbeam-Talbots, only the Ten and the 2-litre made it back, both in slightly modified form. The Ten had a wheelbase which was 1in (25mm) longer and the front end of the chassis had been partially redesigned with box-section cross members. It was claimed that the compression ratio had been raised, yet it was quoted as 6.8:1, the same as before the war, and that power output had been increased by 3bhp; it was now quoted as 41bhp. Figures later quoted by *The Autocar* were a 6.4:1 compression ratio and 39bhp![27]

The Zenith carburettor was replaced by a downdraught Stromberg, which supposedly improved fuel consumption by 2mpg. The crankshaft was now fully balanced with integral balance weights. Brake drums were cast iron rather than steel, and the Luvax shock absorbers were of an improved type. The final drive ratio was now 5.22:1 for all Tens, regardless of type of body. Among many other detail changes, *The Motor* noted that "the roof lining is attached by an improved method." The tourer and drophead coupé were still offered but the two-seater did not come back after the war. Prices of course had in round figures doubled, and were subject to Purchase Tax of one-third of the wholesale price, introduced in 1940. Prices in fact were only announced in November 1945, this being perhaps a more accurate indicator of when quantity production commenced. The price of the saloon was then £485 basic or £620 9s.6d in total. Basic prices for the tourer and the drophead coupé were £455 and £520 respectively, or to include the tax, £582 2s.10d and £665 3s.11d (for later increases, see appendix).

In the spring of 1946, assembly moved from the historic Barlby Road factory to the huge new Rootes factory at Ryton outside Coventry, which had originally been built to make aero engines as part of the government-sponsored shadow factory programme in 1939-40. The last cars came off the line at Barlby Road on 31 May 1946, and this factory now became Rootes's main London service depot. Sunbeam-Talbot saloon body production remained at the BLSP plant at Acton, while many other Rootes bodies, notably the Hillman Minx, came from the

42

Pressed Steel factory at Cowley. In 1946, the Rootes subsidiary Thrupp & Maberly took over building the Sunbeam-Talbot tourer bodies but it seems that drophead coupé bodies continued to come from Abbotts until 1948.

In September 1946, AG Douglas Clease of *The Autocar* and his wife gamely took a Ten Tourer (registered EWD 137) on a 2000-mile (3200km) tour of France, to the Riviera and back, with a party from the Junior Car Club, and wrote up the trip in his magazine: "The Sunbeam-Talbot Ten behaved splendidly, in spite of the low-octane French petrol. It sat down over rough patches in a way which elicited praise from the drivers of bigger cars, and it kept up its steady high cruising speed tirelessly." On good roads, the car cruised easily at 60mph (97km/h), while in the mountains "The little car's light steering and good lock made light work of the numerous hairpins" and there was no sign of overheating. In a separate article Douglas Clease praised "its capacity for conveying its occupants over long distances with a degree of comfort and an absence of fatigue more usually associated with much larger cars... Mileages of nearly 300 [480km] in the day left no feeling of fatigue, which was a tribute not only to the seating but also to the suspension." He reckoned that top speed by the speedometer was 70mph (113km/h) with fuel consumption of 30-35mpg.[28]

A Sunbeam-Talbot Ten was the fourth post-war car to be road tested by *The Motor*. For all the makers' claims to increased power output and improved fuel consumption, the results were actually quite poor, but the likely reason for this is that tests at the time were carried out using the low-octane Pool petrol. The table below, using figures from *The Motor*, compares the Sunbeam-Talbot Ten with some of its contemporaries of similar size:

One of the Ten tourers bought by the Berkshire Police, here performing escort duty for the Olympic torch in Eton High Street in 1948. (Courtesy Derek Cook)

Model, date of test	Engine size	Top speed	0-50mph (0-80km/h)	Standing 1/4-mile	Fuel cons.	Price in Feb 1948 incl. PT
Austin A40 3 Mar 1948	1200cc	67.1mph (108km/h)	20.5sec	24.4sec	32mpg	£429-442
Ford Prefect 4 Feb 1948	1172cc	59.7mph (96km/h)	26.9sec	25.9sec	33.8mpg	£390
Hillman Minx (1948) 10 Dec 1947	1185cc	62.5mph (101km/h)	25.7sec	25.6sec	31mpg	£493
Lanchester Ten 11 Sep 1946	1287cc	68mph (109km/h)	22sec	24.1sec	33.8mpg	£927
MG 1¼-litre 28 May 1947	1250cc	69mph (111km/h)	16.7sec	23.2sec	27mpg	£672
Morris Ten Series M 13 Nov 1946	1140cc	61.5mph (99km/h)	22.5sec	24.8sec	30.2mpg	£432-445
Peugeot 202 2 Jul 1947	1133cc	61.5mph (99km/h)	27.8sec	26.8sec	34mpg	n/a
Sunbeam-Talbot Ten 23 Oct 1946	1185cc	66.7mph (107km/h)	22.4sec	25.2sec	26.1mpg	£799
Volkswagen 7 May 1947	986cc	57.3mph (92km/h)	29.4sec	26sec	27mpg	n/a

Part of the war-time activities at Barlby Road, the body mounting shop for the Karrier Bantam. (Courtesy CTM)

The scene after the bombs fell on Whittingham and Mitchel on 16 September 1940, with two of the Sunbeam-Talbot chassis which were destroyed. (Courtesy CTM)

The first post-war Ten assembly line in the summer of 1945; it seems rather rudimentary but this was obviously a posed shot. (Courtesy CTM)

The Ten was just about able to hold its own on performance, although it lost out to the MG which had a much more modern engine, and its fuel consumption was noticeably high. In fairness, The Autocar quoted an "approximate fuel consumption" of 30mpg; on the other hand, Bill Boddy in Motor Sport quoted only 25mpg. It is by the way worth noting the similarly poor economy of the Volkswagen despite its smaller engine and streamlined shape, and the fact that the only all-new post-war design, the Austin Devon, did not offer that much of an improvement over the older types. Of other competitors, the Rover Ten (1389cc, £809), Singer Super Ten (1185cc, £608) and Wolseley Ten (1140cc, £537) were not tested by The Motor.[29]

The Motor Sport road test produced a best timed top speed of only 53.57mph (86.21km/h); at this time, Boddy's test results were so much poorer than those achieved by other contemporary journals that he actually shortly afterwards felt it necessary to describe in print the conditions under which he carried out performance tests, and then stopped quoting top speeds altogether! In fairness, on the open road he had momentarily attained a speedometer reading of 75mph (121km/h). The truth would be somewhere in between these two figures.

All the post-war road testers were very happy with the car. There was much praise for the quality and craftsmanship, for the refinement and lively performance, the smart and attractive appearance, and the passenger comfort that it offered. According to The Autocar it looked "very British, and yet decidedly dainty". The Motor discussed the lightness of steering, which

The Sports Saloon

This illustration was used in the post-war Ten brochure; it was in fact simply a coloured and mirrored version of a 1940 image.

The slightly generous brochure illustration of the saloon interior, a very neat design with many pleasing touches.

BRITAIN'S MOST EXCLUSIVE LIGHT CAR

The first post-war Ten in the yard at Barlby Road, HGF 444 (already with loads of club badges), soon followed by others. On the Commer truck are three of the Rolls-Royce Merlin engines which were refurbished in this factory. (Courtesy Guy Woodhams)

A Sunbeam-Talbot Ten tourer took part in the 1949 Monte Carlo Rally, here probably before embarking at Folkestone, amazingly with Bill Boddy and Dennis Jenkinson of Motor Sport *walking past in the background. (Courtesy CTM)*

they felt would "make an immediate appeal to women drivers." *Motor Sport* found a slight tendency to over-steer when cornering fast but "no more than the expected amount of roll", while the brakes were powerful, even fierce, but prone to lock during crash stops. The car tested by Boddy interestingly was fitted with a windscreen defroster.

The Ten carried on in production until the spring of 1948 when it was replaced by the new 80 model. Post-war production was in the order of 3718 cars, still including 21 chassis which were all for the home market, which averages out over two-and-a-half to three years of 1250-1500 cars per year; not in overall terms impressive but it compared well with 6158 MG Y-types over four years, 2715 Wolseley Tens from 1945 to 1948, 2640 Rover Tens over two years and around 2450 Lanchester Tens from 1946 to 1949. Some were exported, the best markets in 1947-48 being unsurprisingly traditional Empire markets such as Australia, and India until independence, but in Europe Portugal, Sweden and in particular Switzerland took quite a few. These three markets were deemed particularly important for British exports as their currencies were "hard", i.e. convertible to US Dollars.

In Switzerland and some other European markets, the brand was already then simply known as Sunbeam to avoid any confusion with the French Talbot cars; or perhaps this was "the Talbot so much feared abroad" that the name *had* to be changed.[30] This had been the case with a few cars even before the war. A French-language 1948 sales brochure referred to "Sunbeam" and featured a badge where the traditional crowned Talbot animal was coupled, rather perversely, with the words "Sunbeam – London".[31] Switzerland was considered important enough for Rootes to set up its own subsidiary importing company in 1951, replacing a hotchpotch of regional agents. In 1947, out of around 2300 Sunbeam-Talbots of both models, just over 900 were exported.

In those halcyon days of 1945-48, in the absence of German competition and with France and Italy concentrating on meeting home market demand, Britain could of course sell almost anything abroad, even if many cars were still only available with right-hand drive – which in many European markets was actually less of a handicap than might have been thought. However, the Ten was really a relic of the 1930s, designed with the home market in mind. Its *raison d'être* was the British horsepower tax, and when that was abolished by the Chancellor Hugh Dalton in 1947[32], demand for small-engined fairly expensive quality cars quickly evaporated. While the Ten outproduced the 2-litre, as we shall see, in the next generation the larger-engined 90 was more successful than the 80.

Selected competitive appearances of Talbot and Sunbeam-Talbot Ten, 1936-39:

Number	Entrant	Type	Reg. mark	Result	Notes
1936:					
RAC Rally, 24-28 March					
74/27	JE Scott	Tourer	CUC 10	1st class award	Works team
103/28	JE Scott, N Garrad	Tourer	CUC 11	1st class award	Works team
112/29	G Poppe	Tourer	CUC 12	3rd class award	Works team
Land's End Trial, 10-11 April					
306	WM Couper	Closed	DAR 963(?)	Silver award	
491	JE Scott	Tourer	CUC 10	Silver award	Works team
492	G Poppe	Tourer	CUC 11	Silver award	Works team
493	N Garrad	Tourer	CUC 12	Premier award	Works team
Scottish Rally, 1-5 June					
136	A Ballantyne	Saloon		5th of 12	Talbot club team
137	JE Scott	Tourer	CUC 10	14th of 32	Talbot club team
138	G Poppe	Tourer	CUC 11	9th of 32	Talbot club team
139	N Garrad	Tourer	CUC 12	11th of 32	Talbot club team
Welsh Rally, 14-18 July					
33/13	AG Douglas Clease (of *The Autocar*)	Tourer	CUC .. (?)	n/a	Works car
68	G Poppe	Tourer	CUC .. (?)	n/a	Works car
Alpine Trial, 20-26 August					
58	WEC Watkinson, Braithwaite	Open		Third prize	
1937:					
Exeter Trial, 1-2 January					
235	EJ Kehoe			Bronze award	
Monte Carlo Rally					
12	Pilot Officer TGW Appleby, McCarthy	Tourer	BCG 971	64th overall	
Sunbac Colmore Trial, 27 February					
44	GA Wooding			Retired?	Supercharged
RAC Rally, 9-13 March					
8	RM Proctor	DHC	BAK 888	17th of 20	
22	N Garrad	Tourer	DLT 2	2nd of 20	Works team
25	G Poppe	Saloon	DLT 1	11th of 21	Works team
26	CRY King	Saloon	CVO 888	13th of 21	
38	RL Thomson	Saloon		10th of 21	
47	WK Elliott	Saloon	DLU 10	2nd of 21	
Edinburgh Trial, 14-15 May					
73	JF Heaton			Premier award	
187	ER King			Silver award	
Scottish Rally, 17-21 May					
10	ER King	Closed		6th of 15	
65	DL Melvin	Closed		5th of 15	Talbot club team
116	Mrs Ian Fraser-Marshall	Open		Retired?	
122	WK Elliott	Closed	DXL 980	1st of 15	Talbot club team
155	J Martin Ritchie	Open		11th of 22	
Blackpool Rally, 4-6 June					
45	WK Elliott	Closed	DXL 980 (?)	n/a	
Welsh Rally, 30 June-3 July					
98	LJ Brown	Saloon	ASC 177	n/a	
116/18	RM Proctor	DHC	BAK 888	n/a	
MCC Torquay Rally, 16-17 July					
52	CRY King	Saloon	DNN 99	Bronze award	
97	AC Westwood	DHC	DXR 616	Silver award	
1938:					
Monte Carlo Rally					
75	N Garrad, SCH Davis (of *The Autocar*)	FHC	ELK 7	22nd o/a; 5th in 1500cc class	Works car
Land's End Trial, 15-16 April					
382	DH Perring	Open	DPJ 56 (?)	Silver award	Supercharged
402	LF Philipson	Closed	EXB 813	Bronze award	

RAC Rally, 26-30 April

7	Dr FW Schofield	Open		15th of 21	Works team
31	TC Wise	Saloon		22nd of 23	Works team
35	ER King	Saloon		11th of 23	
48	N Garrad	FHC (?)	ELK 7 (?)	16th of 23	Works team

Edinburgh Trial, 3-4 June

| 195 | D Perring | Open | DPJ 56 | Bronze award | |
| 212 | L Philipson | Closed | EXB 813 | Bronze award | |

Scottish Rally, 6-10 June

42	ER King	Saloon		7th of 16	
48	JH Brown	Tourer		13th of 27	
80	DL Melvin	Tourer		11th of 27	Talbot club team
81	WT Grose	Tourer	EXX 479	10th of 27	Talbot club team
82	N Garrad	FHC (?)	ELK 7 (?)	4th of 16	Talbot club team

MCC Torquay Rally, 15-16 July

| 82 | LF Philipson | Closed | EXB 813 | Silver award | |

1939:

Land's End Trial, 7-8 April

342	WR Cottee	Open	EXX 6	Bronze award	
347	HJ Finden	FHC	ELK 7	Bronze award	
446	R Truscott	Closed	DXE 891	No award	

RAC Rally, 25-29 April

| 18 | Miss SJL Baskin | Open | | 32nd of 39 | |
| 57 | AL Goodrich | 2-dr saloon | COV 73 | 13th of 31 | |

Edinburgh Trial, 26-27 May

| 125 | HJ Finden | FHC | ELK 7 (?) | Silver award | |

Scottish Rally, 29 May-2 June

21	DL Melvin	Tourer	FXF 359	15th of 21	S-T club team
22	WT Grose	DHC	FXF 213	4th of 17	S-T club team
74	T Leslie McDonald	Saloon	FLC 108	2nd of 17	

Blackpool Rally, 9-11 June

| 37 | G Eadie | Closed | | 2nd class award | |
| 39 | Miss H Berg | Closed | | n/a | |

Notes: Where a second rally number is quoted (e.g. 74/27), the second number applied to the coachwork competition.
All results are in class unless otherwise indicated.
This list is based on the late Donald Cowbourne's books *British Rally Drivers 1925-1939* and *British Trial Drivers 1929-1939*.

---

1. Blight *Georges Roesch and the Invincible Talbot* Part III, Chapter 5, p.429 et seq
2. Robson *Cars of the Rootes Group* pp.41-42
3. *Bilhistorisk Tidsskrift* no.51 1977
4. *The Autocar* 12 Jan 1934, 11 May 1934
5. Information courtesy of Nick Walker, citing Abbott records in Farnham Museum; *Chassis Register* in Coventry Transport Museum Archive
6. It has been suggested that there was a March(-bodied) version of the Talbot Ten but I think this is the result of confusion with the Hillman Aero Minx March Special
7. *The Autocar* 15 Oct 1937; *The Motor* 12 Oct 1938; *Chassis Register*, Lem *Rootes Talbot and Sunbeam Talbot Side-valve Register* 1936-1948 pp.111-13, 501
8. Abbott records; *The Autocar* 16 Aug 1940; Lem pp.115, 506-08, citing *Stardust* issues 160-164
9. Blight p.436-37
10. *The Autocar* 8 Oct 1935; *The Autocar* 11 Oct 1935
11. *The Light Car* 11 Oct 1935; *Modern Motoring* Oct 1935, see Lem pp.34-41
12. Early road tests in *The Autocar* and *The Light Car* both 7 Feb 1936; *The Motor* 11 Feb 1936
13. *The Autocar* 21 Aug 1936
14. *Motor Sport* Oct-Nov 1936
15. *The Motor* 2 Aug 1938; Boddy *The History of Brooklands Motor Course* p.326
16. Quotes from *The Motor* 16 Feb 1937, 1 Jun 1937, 10 Aug 1937, 31 Aug 1937
17. *The Autocar* 26 Feb 1937
18. *Thoroughbred & Classic Cars* Apr 1979 reproduced in Lem p.79; *Chassis Register*
19. *The Autocar* 17 Sep 1937, 8 Jul 1938
20. *Practical Motorist* 27 Nov 1937
21. *The Autocar* 19 Aug 1938
22. Bullock *Rootes Brothers* p.73
23. Quotes from *The Autocar* 16 Dec 1938, 16 Jun 1939, 4 Aug 1939; *The Motor* 20 Dec 1938, 1 Aug 1939
24. *The Light Car* 13 Jan 1939
25. *Chassis Register*; Lem pp.346, 357
26. *Ibid*; her car was chassis 932-010
27. Quotes from *The Motor* 8 Aug 1945; *The Autocar* 10 Aug 1945; *The Autocar* 7 Feb 1947
28. AG Douglas Clease "Road Impressions of 1946 Cars", *The Autocar* 25 Oct 1946; "France Lives Again" 20 and 27 Dec 1946
29. *The Motor* 23 Oct 1946; *The Autocar* 7 Feb 1947; *Motor Sport* Apr 1947
30. Shakespeare *Henry VI* act II, scene 3
31. Original in the collection of BMIHT, Gaydon
32. Announced in the House of Commons 17 Jun 1947, the flat-rate tax of £10 came into effect from 1 Jan 1948, originally on newly registered cars only

Chapter Three

Building a range: 3-litre, 4-litre and 2-litre

In the two years following the introduction of the Talbot Ten, as outlined in chapter 1 Rootes gradually scaled back and "Rootesified" the range of the original Roesch-designed Talbots. Once the badge-engineered little Talbot had established itself in the market, Rootes deemed the moment opportune for a big brother to be introduced, so at the 1937 Motor Show, the Talbot 3-litre made its bow: a car that bore a similar relationship to the big Humbers as the Ten did to the Hillman Minx.

According to *The Autocar*, the 3-litre was "a roomy family car at a very competitive price. Moreover, it is a car in which the Talbot traditions of high performance and quality are well maintained... In appearance, also, the new model is characteristically a Talbot" – which was a very diplomatic way of putting it. In their show report in the same issue the new model was described as an "innovation for Talbots... [It] is attracting considerable attention... and should make its mark."[1]

One detects a note of cautious exasperation in the show coverage of *The Motor*, where the 3-litre was described as "a complete departure from previous Talbot designs, having a six-cylinder side-valve engine, independent front wheel suspension, four-speed synchromesh gearbox and box-section frame." They were politer in the article in the same issue where the

The imposing front view of a 3-litre, in this case a 1939 Sunbeam-Talbot.

The style of the models' dresses and the design of the rug leave us in no doubt as to the period of this photo of a 3-litre six-light saloon.

The Talbot and Sunbeam-Talbot 3-litre brochures were illustrated with line drawings, including this of the "Evenkeel" independent front suspension.

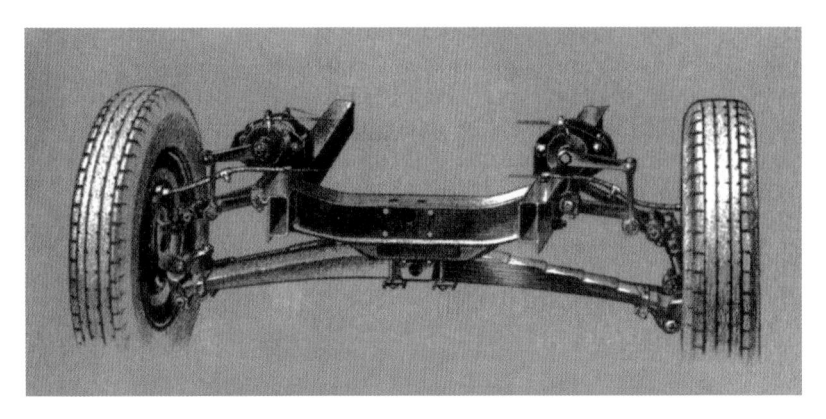

car was described in detail, as they credited the 3-litre "with the good performance and appearance that are traditionally coupled with Talbot… Although designed with a view to high performance and comfortable travel at high speed, the new three-litre Talbot represents in many ways modification of the Talbot tradition, inasmuch as it is designed with an appeal as a high grade family car. Thus the saloon model is notable for the interior passenger space available, quietness of running and the very moderate first price of £398."[2]

Since the standard Talbot 105, the earlier model which compared most closely with the 3-litre in size, had cost £585 in 1936 and £495 in 1937, never mind the even higher pre-Rootes prices, one wonders whether it was not the "very moderate price" which above all impressed contemporary observers. Like Amanda in Noel Coward's *Private Lives* (and she might well have driven a Talbot), the 3-litre held no mystery for anyone who had observed Rootes developments over the previous six years: all the basic building blocks were there.

Thus the six-cylinder side-valve engine of 75 by 120mm, 3181cc and 20.9 RAC hp was a direct descendant of the engine which had first appeared in the Hillman Wizard in 1931. The stroke had been increased from 106mm to 120mm in 1935 for the Hillman Hawk and its long-wheelbase derivative. Only two years later, the Hillman Hawk was discontinued although the Hillman lwb seven-seater model remained for another season. Instead of the £295 Hawk, alongside the Talbot 3-litre Rootes now introduced a new Humber Snipe with the same engine size, at £345. In the Talbot, the engine was fitted with an aluminium cylinder head and had a compression ratio of 6.4:1. A single Stromberg DBV36 carburettor with automatic choke was fitted. Power output was 78bhp at 3300rpm.

The transmission was in principle similar to the Talbot Ten, except that the four-speed gearbox had a normal central gear lever, and had synchromesh on only third and top. The characteristics of the car were such that for almost all types of ordinary motoring only these two ratios were required anyway. Otherwise, there was a single dry plate clutch, an open Hardy-Spicer prop shaft, and a semi-floating rear axle with spiral bevel final drive. The final drive ratio was 4.3:1. The pressed steel wheels carried 6.25-16 tyres and were fitted with full wheel discs, held in place by a large central nut.

The big Hillman, the Humbers and the new Talbot all used variations of the same basic box-section chassis, but with different wheelbases. On the Hillman Hawk, it had been 9ft 0.5in (2756mm); the Humber Snipe had a longer wheelbase of 9ft 6in (2896mm) which was also found on the new Hillman Fourteen and Humber Sixteen models, while the Talbot 3-litre had 9ft 10in (2997mm) between the axles. Even longer but different wheelbases were used on the Hillman seven-seater and the Humber Snipe Imperial, while on the Humber Pullman it stretched to no less than 11ft (3353mm).

All were however very similar, and all used the "Evenkeel" independent front suspension which had been introduced on the Humbers and big Hillmans in 1935. This system was inspired by the suspension designed by Barney Roos for the American Studebaker, although

The rare tourer was one of the alternative body styles for the 3-litre and was undoubtedly inspired by previous Talbot tourers. (Courtesy John Clark)

among those who worked on the Rootes version were future luminaries Alec Issigonis and Bill Heynes. It used a lower transverse leaf spring with single wishbones above, and was somewhat rudimentary in terms of wheel location. It was once described as "more independent than suspension", and it is alleged that Rootes adopted this form of suspension as they had a subsidiary company, possibly Jonas Woodhead, which made leaf springs but not coil springs. On the Talbot, the Luvax lever-arm type hydraulic shock absorbers were adjustable from a control on the dashboard. Brakes were of the Bendix cable-operated self-servo mechanical type, with a right-hand handbrake working on all four wheels. Steering was by worm and nut, with a four-spoke 18in (457mm) steering wheel on a telescopically adjustable column, and 2.75 to 3.5 turns from lock to lock (contemporary reports differ).

The standard four-door six-light saloon body of the 3-litre was made by Talbot at Acton, but probably used many panels from the Pressed Steel Company (PSC) at Cowley, since it was very similar to the bodywork on contemporary Humber saloons, or for that matter the Hillman Fourteen. The styling had first been seen on the big Humbers two years earlier, and also resembled the six-light saloons offered by Rootes on the Talbot 75 and 105 chassis. It was clearly inspired by contemporary American cars, but was quite restrained and rather handsome, especially on the new Talbot where it was combined with swept front wings and a Talbot radiator. Construction was effectively all-steel with very little wood, and none of it structural. A feature unique to the 3-litre was a small bustle for the boot lid, where the other similar Rootes cars still had flat backs.

Alongside the six-light saloon there were three alternative body styles, which were coach-built on ash frames in the traditional manner. Two of these were derived from bodies fitted to the earlier Talbots. These were a two-door four/five seater sports tourer by Whittingham & Mitchel priced at £435, and the most expensive of the range, a foursome drophead coupé by the Carlton Carriage Company at £525. A new note

Another body on the 3-litre chassis was the handsome sports saloon, on which the pillarless reverse-angle quarter light was introduced. This car is a 4-litre. (Courtesy Alan Glover)

Similarly inspired by earlier Talbot styles, the drophead coupé was made by the Carlton carriage company. This illustration actually comes from the 4-litre brochure.

The style of the interior trim of the sports saloon also set the pattern for many later Sunbeam-Talbots.

was struck by a very good-looking four-door sports saloon at £475, presumably designed by Ted White and Ted Green, with the pillarless reverse-angle rear quarter light inspired by the original Humber Vogue which was to become such a Sunbeam-Talbot hallmark. It was even found on the Roy Axe-designed fastback Rapier and Alpine models of 1967!

It was noted as unusual for the period that no woodwork was used for the interior trim, at least of the saloon, since on this model the facia and window surrounds were metal, painted to match the bodywork. Except for a rev counter, there was a full set of instruments in front of the driver, with adjustable lighting, and the speedometer and the fuel gauge both had Imperial as well as Metric markings, which became

another typical Sunbeam-Talbot feature. Equipment included self-cancelling built-in trafficators, two Mellotone wind-tone trumpet horns mounted externally, a single fog or pass lamp, and an automatic reversing lamp. Body finishes included a range of metallic "jewelessence" colours; Rootes was one of the pioneers in Britain in adopting metallic finishes. Broadly speaking, what the 3-litre customer got for an extra £53 compared to the Humber Snipe, was better finish and equipment, style, and slightly more performance.

Both the leading magazines tested the same 3-litre saloon (ELT 977) in early 1938. *The Motor* took the car on an extended Continental tour to Germany, coinciding with the Berlin Motor Show where Rootes was one of few British

The Sports Saloon

The Sports Saloon provides full accommodation for five persons. It has a flush lined sliding roof; draughtless window ventilators to front doors; wide-opening windscreen with centre control; adjustable-length steering column; two adjustable sun visors; arm-rests to both front doors and folding and side arm-rests to back seat. Rear blind is operated by the driver and control is concealed. Private locks are fitted to all doors and the luggage compartment, the lid of which opens for additional luggage. There is a wide parcel shelf behind the rear seat.

companies to exhibit. They spoke highly of the car's performance for long-distance touring and its comfort even over bad Belgian pavé roads, but noted that there was "some roll when the car is taken fully laden round sharp curves at about 70mph". *The Autocar* stated that "the springing seems soft for cornering purposes, allowing the car to heel over somewhat if fairly high speeds are held round bends" but they, too, praised the riding comfort. They noted the tendency for the brakes to fade, "after some severe high-speed work". Steering was found light but rather low geared. Performance was very good, with the best top speed timed by *The Autocar* of 84.91mph (136.65km/h) while *The Motor* measured the best acceleration through the gears of 11.6 seconds to 50mph (80km/h). Top gear performance was excellent, with only 8 seconds from 10 to 30mph (16 to 48km/h) in top, which fell to 5.4 seconds in third. Petrol consumption was 17-20mpg.[3]

The Motor later shed further light on the performance of the 3-litre. On that trip to Berlin in 1938, "During the course of the journey high speeds were maintained for some hundreds of miles on the autobahnen. Despite ice-covered roads on the outward journcy, 154 miles [248km] were covered in three hours, whilst on the return trip, when the roads were still frequently ice-covered but clear of thick snow, 198 miles [319km] were covered in three hours, making an overall average of approximately 66mph [106km/h]…"[4]

The Talbot 3-litre was an excellent performer in a straight line or on motorways, but does not appear to have had outstanding road holding or handling. At a very reasonable price, it offered good looks, generous equipment, space and comfort. It was competitive in its class, and offered a less staid alternative to the similarly-sized Humber. However, it was not a big seller, and the first season's production was only 639 cars. A VIP customer was the recently-resigned foreign secretary Anthony Eden, who took his sports saloon on holiday to Ireland in 1938. Four of the 21 tourers built were bought by the Edinburgh Police in 1938, and one of these, BWS 597, survives, formerly owned by *Stardust* editor Paul Walby. Another sports saloon FGY 861, by now badged Sunbeam-Talbot, was taken by Rootes publicist Dudley Noble on the Junior Car Club's "Cavalcade of British Cars" through the eastern USA in November-December 1938. This tour included a visit to the Chrysler factory in Detroit.[5]

The change from Talbot to Sunbeam-Talbot occurred soon after it had happened to the Ten and was publicized in the magazines in September 1938, but in case of the 3-litre there were two important improvements, also shared with the updated Humbers: Lockheed hydraulic

A 4-litre touring limousine was displayed on the Thrupp & Maberly stand at the 1938 Motor Show. (Courtesy CTM)

This famous photo was originally published in The Autocar *in 1939. A rather apprehensive-looking "Billy" Rootes stands by at the Berlin motor show while Hitler inspects a big Sunbeam-Talbot. Goebbels is on the extreme left, and Goering half-hidden to the right of "Billy". Soon the Rootes factories would be doing their bit to bring down the German dictatorship. (Courtesy CTM)*

SUNBEAM-TALBOT & ALPINE IN DETAIL

Despite the elegant swept front wings, there is no getting away from the fact that the six-light saloon body is very similar to the big Humbers, except for the added boot bustle.

The wheels discs feature the Talbot lion badge, encircled by the dual brand name.

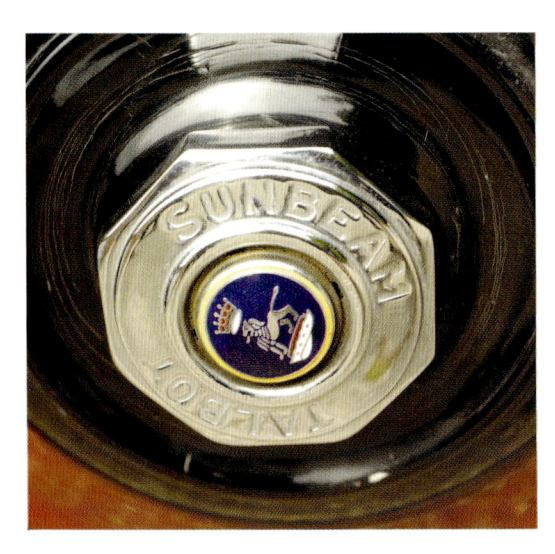

The waist line is accented by chrome trim, on which the door handles sit.

BUILDING A RANGE

The rear number plate is fitted below the spare wheel compartment lid, and is flanked by two D-lamps and quarter bumpers.

The central dividing pillar of the rear window is continued by a chrome trim strip on the boot lid.

The fog lamp and trumpet horns were standard equipment.

55

SUNBEAM-TALBOT & ALPINE IN DETAIL

A study in brown: rear seat accommodation is in marked contrast to the Ten seen in the previous chapter…

…and there is also loads more leg room, even without foot wells.

This Sunbeam-Talbot badge is found on the glove box lid.

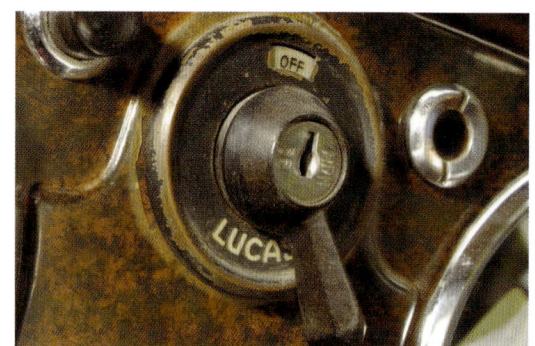

56

Instruction dials got very "busy" with the dual markings. Note the mottled paint finish of the dashboard panel.

Horizontal flutes across the seat backs and on door panels are typical of Sunbeam-Talbots. The hand brake can just be seen bottom right.

The ignition lock and lighting switch is awkward to reach, behind the steering wheel.

The fuel and oil gauges also have dual markings, but not the temperature gauge.

SUNBEAM-TALBOT & ALPINE IN DETAIL

On the big six-cylinder side-valve Rootes engines, the valves, manifolds and carburettor are all on the left-hand side. Note the water pump at the front of the cylinder head and the prominent oil filter.

All the electrical ancillaries are grouped on the right-hand side, with the distributor low down on the cylinder block.

brakes, with the handbrake now working only on the rear wheels, and cruciform bracing of the chassis frame which made it much more rigid, although according to the parts list this was only introduced from chassis number 8739 in early 1939, and even then not on all cars. As the cross-braced frame was common to the 4-litre, I *think* this was also the point when a torsion-bar stabilizer was added to the rear of the chassis, although it was not mentioned in the journals or the sales brochure and the only reference I have found to this is in the road test of a 4-litre in *The Motor* in April 1939. On 1939 models the compression ratio was increased to 6.5:1, and power output went up to 82bhp at 3800rpm. A six-light saloon now cost £415, the tourer £445 and the sports saloon £485, while the drophead coupé was unchanged in price.

The Motor road tested the revised model but despite the extra brake horsepower and unchanged weight they measured top speed and acceleration figures which were markedly worse than the original Talbot 3-litre. It is equally puzzling that the hydraulic brakes required *higher* pedal pressures to stop the car. 120lb (54.5kg) was now needed to stop the car from 30mph (48km/h) in 35ft (10.7m), whereas the mechanically-braked car stopped in 37.5ft (11.4m) with 110lb (50kg) pedal pressure; at least "a former tendency to fade when driving really fast is entirely eliminated." It seems that handling had been improved: "Cornering is good, reasonable freedom from rolling being attained by making full use of the hand-controlled shock absorbers... The difference that this makes to the suspension characteristics must be experienced to be believed... [on the hardest setting it becomes] a relatively stiff, firm car that imbues one with confidence in cornering." Hence my suspicion that this car, like the 4-litre, had the rear anti-roll bar referred to above.[6]

Then as a last-minute surprise before the Motor Show in October 1938, the 4-litre Sunbeam-Talbot was introduced. This was simply a 3-litre fitted with the 4086cc 26.9 RAC hp engine from the Humber Snipe Imperial, Super Snipe and Pullman models, developing 100bhp at 3400rpm, and with a higher final drive ratio of 4.09:1. Basically this was a big-bore version of the 3-litre engine, 85mm instead of 75mm; the 120mm stroke was the same. It is worth noting that this was the biggest engine offered in Britain at the time outside the luxury class; other top-of-the-range saloons from the mass-producers were of 3.2 to 3.6 litres.

In terms of power output, of its peers this Rootes engine was however bettered by the Wolseley 25 (108bhp from 3485cc) and the SS Jaguar 3½-litre (125bhp from the same size), both of which had overhead valves. Nor of course was the 4-litre anywhere near as powerful as the last of the Roesch Talbot 3½-litre models which had 123bhp from 3377cc (all bhp figures as claimed by the makers). It may be argued that Sunbeam-Talbot and Humber were by now at a disadvantage in the prestige class by having side-valve engines, which among

These four cars were the Sunbeam-Talbot Owners' Club entry in the 1939 Scottish Rally, here outside the RSAC club house in Glasgow's Blythswood Square. Apart from the two Tens, there are two 3-litre (or 4-litre?) saloons. Garrad is in the centre in a dark shirt, with his hand on the door handle, and Douglas Clease of The Autocar *is flanked by the two ladies on the right. (Courtesy JDHT)*

similarly-sized engines were otherwise used only by Austin and Ford.

Model for model the 4-litre cost £40 more than the 3-litre, but there were two additional body styles not at first available on the smaller-engined car, a touring saloon at £598 and a touring limousine at £630. These shared a Thrupp & Maberly body of the fashionable semi-razoredge design, which like the sports saloon had a pillarless rear quarter light. The only difference between them was that the limousine version had a division and a bench-type front seat.

The new model was once again well received. *The Motor* described it as "a fine car offering a combination of attractive qualities rather rare among the products of the British industry", combining a fine performance and good acceleration "with a remarkable degree of smoothness, quietness and general refinement… and the car contrives to be one of the most stylish on the road without offering affront to conservative English ideas on appearance." Road holding, handling, accommodation and comfort were all praised, and the price of £455 was found "distinctly moderate". The adjustable shock absorbers and the torsion-bar stabilizer at the rear of the chassis combined to reduce both pitch and sway. Top speed was quoted as a very respectable 85mph (136.8km/h), and acceleration from 0-50mph (80km/h) was accomplished in 11.2 seconds. Fuel consumption was 14-17mpg.[7]

Similarly, *The Autocar* found it "an outstanding example of a powerful but docile British car at a reasonable price". They described the standard six-light saloon as spacious and comfortable, and eulogized the top gear performance. Compared to their figure for the 3-litre, weight was up by about three-quarters of a hundredweight (say 35kg), and the 4-litre offered a higher top speed but not by much: *The Autocar* measured a one-way best top speed of 87.38mph (140.63km/h), but their average was surprisingly low at 81.82mph (131.68km/h) or only 0.4mph (0.6km/h) better than their 3-litre figure. Their 0-50mph (80km/h) time was 12.2 seconds, and they quoted fuel consumption as 17-19mpg.[8]

Based on the road test results from both magazines, the conclusion is that the 4-litre had better performance than the 3-litre but by a narrower margin than could have been expected with an extra 18bhp for only a slight weight increase. The conclusion is that even this extra power struggled against the weight and the aerodynamic properties of these cars. One might wickedly suggest that the subsequent road test of a 3-litre in *The Motor* which gave so much poorer performance figures was deliberately arranged by the Rootes PR people to portray the 4-litre in a more flattering light!

Unusually, the two big cars were very little used in contemporary rallies, although with their good-looking and luxurious coachwork at moderate prices they ought to have made an impact in the concours-mad 1930s. The matter is further complicated by the fact that a few earlier Talbots were still being rallied, so the entry of a "21hp Talbot" may be either a pre-Rootes 95/105, or a 3-litre! Honourable mention must

This recent photo does not really do justice to the special-bodied 4-litre drophead by Cox, but at least we see the v-shaped windscreen. (Courtesy Ruud Lem)

Summary of 3 and 4-litre performance:

		Top speed	0-50mph (0-80km/h)	10-30mph on third	20-40mph on top	Standing ¼ mile	Fuel cons.
3-litre	*The Motor* 22 Mar 1938	82.2mph (132km/h)	11.6sec	5.4sec	8.0sec	20.6sec	18mpg
3-litre	*The Autocar* 1 Apr 1938	84.91mph (137km/h)	13.7sec	6.1sec	9.3sec	n/q	17-20 mpg
3-litre	*The Motor* 30 May 1939	77mph (124km/h)	13.4sec	6.4sec	10.3sec	21.7sec	18mpg
4-litre	*The Motor* 11 Apr 1939	85mph (137km/h)	11.2sec	4.6sec	7.8sec	20sec	14-17 mpg
4-litre	*The Autocar* 21 Apr 1939	87.38mph (141km/h)	12.2sec	5.2sec	7.7sec	n/q	17-19 mpg

go to T Abel Smith who took a 3-litre saloon (registered ENK 345) through the 1939 Monte Carlo Rally starting from John O'Groats to finish 64th overall, four places ahead of Miss S Rowan Hamilton's Talbot 95 (or 105); Humbers in fact did rather better, with the Super Snipes of Lord Waleran and Norman Garrad in twelfth and fourteenth places, and Graham's Snipe sixteenth. Garrad entered a 3-litre saloon (FUV 6) on the Scottish Rally and on the Welsh Rally. On the former occasion he was kept company by AG Douglas Clease of *The Autocar* in a similar car (FUW 860), and they finished fifth and twelfth in class. Wilkins's 4-litre was the only big Sunbeam-Talbot on the 1939 RAC Rally.

With the wide selection of catalogued bodies, there were very few of the big Sunbeam-Talbots delivered in chassis form for special coachwork; there were only a baker's dozen of chassis, eight 3-litres and five 4-litres, and some of these were exported (see appendix). A few special-bodied survivors are known to the Sunbeam Talbot Alpine Register and are documented in Ruud Lem's *Register*.[9] These include an example of Maltby's Redfern saloon tourer and an Offord fixed-head coupé, both on the 3-litre chassis. On the 4-litre chassis there is a two-seater drophead with a dickey seat specially commissioned by the first owner, Captain Schreiber RN, from Cox of Watford, an otherwise little known coachbuilder. The Maltby Redfern body was also seen on other chassis of the period ranging from Morris to Rolls-Royce; it was a four-door drophead coupé, with no centre pillar above the waistline, and these bodies often had a hydraulic hood.

For the 1940 season, the 3- and 4-litre models were improved in detail, and the touring saloon and touring limousine bodies were now offered on the 3-litre chassis as well, although just one 3-litre was made with a touring limousine body. In addition there was an all-new body style which harked back to the abortive Sunbeam Thirty, in the highly unusual form of an open four-door phaeton with a bench-type front seat. This was the most expensive version at £645 for a 3-litre, £685 with the bigger engine, but sadly this handsome style got no further than the catalogue and none were built. *The Autocar* published no illustration of the phaeton while *The Motor* printed a rather obviously doctored photograph. However, one wonders how much this body style was related to that of the famous war-time Humber staff car.[10]

The engines were modified with a new casting for the cylinder block and crankcase, the water pump was moved to the front of the cylinder head and the circulation improved, while engine ancillaries in general were re-located and tidied up. The saloon interior was now fitted with a walnut facia, garnish rails and window fillets, and the two instrument dials were arranged symmetrically in the centre of the facia. On the drophead, the spare wheel was moved from the boot to a recess in the boot lid, as already seen on the other body styles except the standard saloon. Smaller diameter spring-loaded wheel discs were fitted.

Like the 3-litre, the 4-litre did not really catch on, with a total production of 229 cars over its brief lifespan of little more than a year, while only 430 of the 1939 Sunbeam-Talbot 3-litres were made, and some 197 of the short-lived 1940 model, giving a total of 1266 3-litres (see appendix). They were always outsold by the equivalent Humbers: there were for instance an estimated 1500 Humber Super Snipes in the 1938-40 period, and 2706 Snipes from 1937 to 1940. Other comparisons are the 1309 SS Jaguar 3½-litre cars built from 1937 to 1940, and possibly around 2000 of the biggest Wolseleys, the 21 and 25hp Super Sixes over the same period.

It seems that Rootes had slightly misjudged the market, and did not really need a second brand of large, prestige saloons in addition to Humber. In Britain this market sector was always limited by the horsepower taxation rating of such cars; the annual tax of £15.15s and £20.5s for a 3-litre and 4-litre respectively went up to £26.5s and £33.15s in the 1939 budget, and remained at these figures after the war.

Production of the two big cars stopped in November 1939, with some deliveries only being made in 1940. It is no great surprise that the 3-litre and 4-litre models were not re-introduced after the war, although it would have been possible to do so, as they shared their fundamental mechanicals with the Humbers. Rootes instead took Sunbeam-Talbot in a new slightly different direction, on to a path that would eventually bring them a great deal more success in every sense of the word, yet they almost faltered at the first step, taken with the new 2-litre which was launched on the very eve of war.

Although this illustration of the sports two-seater is taken from the 1939 2-litre brochure, the car photographed is probably a Ten, as there is no rear bonnet catch visible.

Sunbeam-Talbot 2-litre

The Autocar, in fact, described the 2-litre in their issue published on Friday 1 September 1939, at the start of the weekend when Britain found itself at war with Germany. They called the car "intriguing" and stated that it is "A Car Which Has an Excellent Performance". It "greatly broadened the appeal of the Sunbeam-Talbot range" and "bridges the gap which formerly existed between the famous Ten and the larger 3- and 4-litre cars." They were at pains to state that it was "not merely a Ten with a larger engine... but has been carefully designed from stem to stern, the aim being to produce a small car of quality with a sparkling performance."[11]

The Motor followed on Tuesday 5 September. According to their writer, "The new two-litre has... been introduced to meet the needs of those people who desire a really quick car... coupled with endurance, reliability and moderate overall dimensions." They described the coachwork as "generally similar" to that of the Ten – for which read "the same" – and praised the bodies as being "amongst the best now on the British market" whereas "The chassis, engine and axles are... specialized".[12]

Yet one has a feeling that this first 2-litre was more or less a Ten with a larger engine, and I may add that according to the *Chassis Register*, the first two prototypes in March 1939 were based on Ten chassis (numbered 42001 and 42002).[13] There is indeed little point in describing the model in detail, since it was so similar to the smaller car, other than those areas where there was any difference. Thus the wheelbase was 3.5in (89mm) longer than the Ten, but the track was the same.

The extra wheelbase length served to accommodate the bigger engine under a longer and more impressive bonnet with two catches either side, and the four body styles did indeed look exactly the same as those of the Ten. There were very few differences in the chassis, but the 2-litre used Lockheed hydraulic brakes, and had a "sway eliminator" – or anti-roll bar – for the front suspension. The final drive ratio was 4.44:1. At a glance it was difficult to tell the Ten and the 2-litre apart, except that the 2-litre had twin external wind-tone horns and a central fog or pass lamp, similar to the bigger cars.

The side-valve four-cylinder engine was a typically simple Rootes design. It ancestry could be traced back to the first Humber Twelve of 69.5mm by 110mm and 1669cc in 1932. However, when the engine was fitted to the new Hillman Fourteen in 1937, the bore was increased to 75mm, for a capacity of 1944cc and 13.95 RAC hp. In the Sunbeam-Talbot 2-litre it had an aluminium cylinder head, a compression ratio of 6.5:1 and a single Stromberg carburettor. Unlike the Ten engine, the 2-litre engine had pump cooling. Power output was 52bhp at 3800rpm, not a great improvement over the Hillman Fourteen which gave 51bhp!

Prices were very keen, with the saloon at £315, the sports two-seater and tourer both £298 and the drophead coupé at £335, exactly £50 more than the equivalent versions of the Ten. On paper, the 2-litre was an attractive proposition, with around 25 per cent more power yet only around 1cwt (51kg) heavier than the Ten. Its excellent power-to-weight ratio allowed comparatively high gearing, and the promise of good performance with reasonable economy.

Indeed, when *The Autocar* road tested a tourer – admittedly one of the lighter body styles at 20cwt 13lb (1023kg) – at the launch of the new model, they measured a mean top speed of 76.44mph (123.02km/h), and a best-timed speed of 80.36mph (129.33km/h) with the windscreen folded flat. Acceleration from 0-

If the registration mark on this saloon in the pre-war 2-litre brochure is real, the car dates to June 1939. The new model was claimed to be "In the First Flight for Performance" but rather than taking a photo with aircraft, they chose horses.

50mph (0-80km/h) through the gears was accomplished in 14.3 seconds, and in-gear acceleration was similarly improved over the Ten, while fuel consumption was in the order of 28-31mpg, at the worst only 10 per cent more than the smaller-engined car.[14] In the Hillman Fourteen, the same engine had to haul some 27.5cwt (1400kg) of saloon body around so the top speed of that car was 69-72.5mph (111-117km/h). *The Motor* does not appear to have road tested a 2-litre at this time.

It seems likely that the Achilles heel of the original 2-litre was the chassis, which was fine for the Ten, but not quite up to the additional power of the 2-litre engine. The suspension was rather soft and set up for comfort rather than handling. However, as was the case for the bigger Sunbeam-Talbots, performance was good for the size, and the car was just as handsome as the Ten. If considered simply as an upmarket saloon without any sporting pretensions, it was perfectly fine, and had war not intervened, it would no doubt have established itself as a useful addition to the Rootes range. As it was, only 181 cars were built before production was abandoned in October 1939; rarest was the two-seater of which just three were made.

The theory that the original chassis design was inadequate is probably borne out by the fact that the post-war model had an entirely redesigned frame, with side members as well as cross members forming a "structure [which] is commendably rigid. So marked is its effect on the road behaviour of the car that its designers have dismissed the anti-roll bar previously fitted to the Two-litre in its earlier form".[15] The concomitant was that weight for a saloon model was now 22.25cwt (1131kg). While it was claimed that the compression ratio had been increased, it was quoted as a *lower* 6.4:1! Similarly it was claimed that the final drive had been raised from 4.6:1 to 4.44:1, but this was the same figure which had been quoted in 1939. The power output was now claimed to be 56bhp. Post-war production of the 2-litre started in February 1946, six months later than the Ten, and very few cars were built before production moved from London to Coventry.

It is an interesting speculation that Donald Healey, who spent most of the war working for the Humber company, might have influenced

This 2-litre saloon is believed to be from 1939. Even in the side view it is difficult to spot the slightly longer wheelbase compared with the Ten, but the bonnet catch at the rear confirms the model. (Courtesy CTM)

It is only really the 1947 Warwickshire registration which tells us that this is a post-war version of the 2-litre. (Courtesy CTM)

the redesign of the 2-litre frame. It was at Humber that he met up with Ben Bowden and "Sammy" Sampietro, who both later joined him in the Healey car venture. One experiment by Healey – and, presumably, Sampietro – was fitting a Sunbeam-Talbot with independent front suspension cannibalised from a Volkswagen. Healey tells us that "it was not a great success, as I had overlooked the fact that a whippy chassis-frame could never allow the i.f.s. to do its job properly".[16] It was the only example of the smaller Sunbeam-Talbots to be fitted with i.f.s. before 1950, and while Rootes then adopted a more conventional independent suspension with transverse wishbones, Healey used a Volkswagen-like trailing link set-up on his own cars from 1946.

As for the Ten, in the post-war 2-litre range the two-seater body was dropped, and prices were sharply increased so that the saloon price, which was quoted only from May 1946, was £575 or £735 9s.5d including Purchase Tax. It took another two months for the tourer and the drophead coupé to appear in the price lists, at £595/£761 0s.7d and £660/£844 1s.8d respectively. There were subsequent increases so that by October 1947 a saloon cost £725/£927 2s.9d (see appendix). This was getting on for being expensive for what the car offered, especially as the 2-litre faced a much wider range of competitors in its size bracket, ranging from inexpensive family cars to a selection of sports or prestige saloons. The data below have been taken from road tests carried out by *The Motor*:

Model	Date of test	Engine size	Top speed	0-50mph (0-80km/h)	Standing ¼-mile	Fuel. cons	Price in Feb 1948 incl PT
Austin Sixteen	9 Jul 1947	2199cc	74.7mph (120km/h)	15.5sec	22.9sec	21mpg	£709
Citroën Light Fifteen	5 May 1948	1911cc	73.3mph (118km/h)	14.5sec	22.8sec	22.9mpg	£646-£735
Humber Hawk (1948)	24 Sep 1947	1944cc	64.1mph (103km/h)	22.6sec	25.6sec	20mpg	£889
Jowett Javelin	21 May 1947	1486cc	76.3mph (123km/h)	13.4sec	21.9sec	33mpg	£819
Riley 1½-litre	22 Oct 1947	1496cc	78mph (126km/h)	16.5sec	23sec	26-28mpg	£863
Standard Fourteen	2 Oct 1946	1776cc	68.5mph (110km/h)	18.9sec	24.5sec	24.7mpg	£672
Sunbeam-Talbot 2-litre	26 Nov 1947	1944cc	69.5mph (112km/h)	19sec	23.9sec	24.8mpg	£927
Vauxhall Fourteen	25 Feb 1948	1781cc	67mph (108km/h)	21.8sec	24.9sec	26.4mpg	£589

As was the case for the other body styles, the 2-litre drophead coupé used the body from the equivalent Ten. (Courtesy CTM)

Of other cars of similar size and price, the Jaguar 1½-litre (1778cc, £865-£921), the Rover 14 and 16 (1901 and 2147cc, £921-£964), the Triumph 1800 saloon (1778cc, £991) and the Wolseley 14/60 and 18/85 (1818 and 2322cc, £684-£755) were not tested by *The Motor*, nor did this magazine test the AC 2-litre, the Alvis TA14, the Armstrong Siddeley Sixteen Lancaster, or the Lea-Francis 12 or 14, which all by this time cost £1272-£1277. The Sunbeam-Talbot 2-litre does not come off too well in this company, which includes the two outstanding new post-war 1½-litre models from Jowett and Riley, but the Citroën of 1934 vintage also had the 2-litre licked. Compared with Sunbeam-Talbot's own Ten, the 2-litre scored better, with improved acceleration and top speed at not that much greater overall fuel consumption. However, the advantage of the bigger car was perhaps not as great as could have been expected with 56bhp against 39-41bhp. The weight of the 2-litre was now around 2.5 to 3cwt (125-150kg) more than the smaller model, a greater differential than had been quoted in 1939. The following are the direct comparisons between the two models, using data from both the leading magazines.

It should be remembered that apart from the poor quality low-octane Pool petrol which was then the only fuel available, the worse performance figures obtained after the war were possibly also due to the fact that Brooklands was no longer available for measuring top speeds. Another significant statistic is that while, according to *The Motor*, both cars would stop in 33.5ft (10.2m) from 30mph (48km/h), on the Ten with mechanical brakes this required a

Believed to have been taken by The Motor *for their 1947 road test of a 2-litre saloon, this shot shows the style of interior trim, common to the Ten.*

Model, date of test	Weight	Top speed	0-50mph (0-80km/h)	10-30mph on third	20-40mph on top	Standing ¼-mile	Fuel cons.
Ten, *The Autocar* 7 Feb 1947	20cwt 21lb (1026kg)	n/q	23.4sec	9.8sec	14sec	n/q	30mpg
Ten, *The Motor* 23 Oct 1946	20¾cwt (1055kg)	66.7mph (107km/h)	22.4sec	9.5sec	16.4sec	25.2sec	26.1mpg
2-litre, *The Autocar* 17 Jan 1947	23cwt 7lb (1173kg)	n/q	18.8sec	6.8sec	10sec	n/q	27mpg
2-litre, *The Motor* 26 Nov 1947	23¼cwt (1182kg)	69.5mph (112km/h)	19sec	7.6sec	11.8sec	23.9sec	24.8mpg

On 22 May 1948, HRH Princess Elizabeth visited Coventry to open the new Civic Centre, and also toured a special display in the city's Memorial Park of the products of the local industry. Here she is with the Lord Mayor of Coventry, inspecting a Sunbeam-Talbot 2-litre, perhaps rather wistfully since this car was for export to Hong Kong. A 2-litre tourer is visible behind. (Courtesy Leon Gibbs)

FAC 963 was the 2-litre tourer which caused Garrad so much grief on the 1947 Alpine Rally, here on the quayside prior to loading on to the cross-Channel ferry. (Courtesy CTM)

pedal pressure of 100lb (45kg), while on the 2-litre with hydraulic brakes only 50lb (23kg) of pressure was necessary. The smaller amount of pedal pressure on the Ten resulted in a stopping distance of no less than 89ft (27.1m)...

Some interesting comments on the 2-litre were made in the road test in *The Motor*. They found the car to have lower fuel consumption at constant speeds between 30 and 60mph (48 and 97km/h) than they had measured for the Ten. They were openly critical of the gear change, which was unusually heavy, and it was difficult to engage gear at rest. They glossed it over by adding that gear changing was rarely necessary, as the flexible engine made it essentially a top gear car, but it was at odds with a car which was otherwise so easy to handle that, according to *The Autocar*, "it presents no difficulty to the... woman driver." It was generally accepted that the car was strictly a four-seater, "with no pretence at accommodating more." However the body was adjudged "very comfortable" although "the upright seating position does not allow of tall rear passengers wearing a hat"; this was the 1940s, after all. The 2-litre was summed up as "a driver's car" which should induce "understandable pride of ownership" and was "most appealing to the man who likes something distinctive and out of the common run".[17]

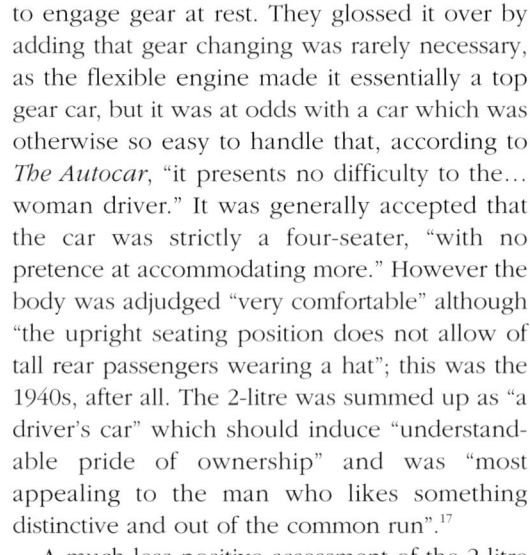

A much less positive assessment of the 2-litre came from inside the Rootes Group. Sales manager Norman Garrad used a 2-litre to cover the 1947 Alpine Rally, which he wrote up for the Rootes magazine *Modern Motoring and Travel*, and submitted a withering report to engineering director Bernard Winter. "He found the 2-litre... exceedingly dangerous to drive fast down the mountain passes, because of serious brake-fade. The shock-absorbers lasted only about 2½ hours, fuel vaporised in the pipe-lines, the gear-ratios proved unsuitable for Alpine work, third gear in particular being too low, the steering swivel-pins tightened up alarmingly, tyres gave trouble and power fell off badly at high altitude".

A very summery-looking Mrs Douglas Clease photographed by her husband with their 2-litre tourer during the 1947 Alpine Rally. (Courtesy CTM)

Furthermore, "after three or four hairpins the steering became so stiff that it required all the force he could muster to turn the steering wheel at all!"[18]

In complete contrast, when in 1982 Garrad remembered his drive with Douglas Horton (service manager for Rootes) in this car, a tourer chassis 389-200 registered FAC 963, he claimed that "it was a most interesting little car, never gave any trouble at all... your car did very well; it was quite comfortable and [had] quite a good performance", even if this rose-tinted reminiscence was tempered by Garrad's recollection that "later in life, we had an awful lot of problems to cover before we could go back properly into the Alps and do our stuff". Yet another conflicting statement comes from Garrad with a vivid description of having to slow the car going downhill from Mont Ventoux using only the gearbox, as the brakes had completely gone. "We completed the rally, which in effect told us how bad the car was."[19]

Garrad's candid report is credited with having convinced Winter to make those improvements which would make subsequent Sunbeam-Talbots so much better cars, with an enviable competition record to their credit. However, on the same rally AG Douglas Clease of *The Autocar* actually took part in another 2-litre tourer, EWD 222 chassis 388-200, and finished sixth in the 2-litre class, the most important but not the only use of this model in competition, and a very modest first effort in an event which later became a Sunbeam-Talbot benefit. In complete contrast to Garrad's experience, Douglas Clease later wrote that during the rally his car "never needed a tool applied to it, not even for brake adjustment – and including both the journey out and home" even if "its brand new set of Dunlop rubbers... was worn as bald as a coot in 2000 miles."[20]

Another rally car was the tourer of EW Hiskins, chassis 443-200 registered AHL 740 which he entered in the 1948 Alpine Rally, only

In the 1948 Alpine Rally, this 2-litre tourer was privately entered by its owner Hiskins but alas, the car had a serious accident. (Courtesy CTM)

BUILDING A RANGE

67

The big cars such as this 3-litre were not re-introduced after the war, when Rootes concentrated on Humbers in this class.

to finish upside down in a gully after going off the road. The Coventry City Police had a tourer chassis 661-200 registered GHP 353. The Northumberland Constabulary bought no less than ten saloons, replacing their pre-war Tens, and the 2-litre also found favour with their colleagues in Surrey who had eight.[21]

Together with the Ten, the 2-litre went out of production in May 1948 when it was replaced by the first 90. Post-war production was only 1124 cars, which must have been very disappointing to Rootes and was a fraction of Humber Hawk sales over the same period. This did not compare well with obvious competitors such as Alvis, Jaguar, Riley and Triumph, and was only around what the much smaller Lea-Francis firm could manage. Clearly the Sunbeam-Talbot had yet to find its feet.

Competitive appearances of the Talbot and Sunbeam-Talbot 3- and 4-litre:

Number	Entrant	Type	Reg. mark	Result	Notes
1939:					
Monte Carlo Rally					
131	T Abel Smith, E Smith	3-litre	ENK 345	64th overall	
RAC Rally, 25-29 April					
195	LG Wilkins	4-litre		21st of 42	
Scottish Rally, 29 May-2 June					
23	N Garrad	Saloon	FUV 6	5th of 24	"over 2200cc"
24	AG Douglas Clease	Saloon	FUW 860	12th of 24	"over 2200cc"
126	Miss K Whitelock	Drophead	FEL 408	23rd of 24	"over 2200cc"
Blackpool Rally, 9-11 June					
101	F Lye	Drophead		2nd class award	"over 16hp"
Welsh Rally, 19-22 July					
12A/32	N Garrad	Saloon	FUV 6 (?)	n/a	"over 15hp"

Notes: Where a second rally number is quoted (e.g. 12A/32), the second number applied to the coachwork competition. All results are in class unless otherwise indicated. This list is based on the late Donald Cowbourne's books *British Rally Drivers* 1925-1939 and *British Trial Drivers* 1929-1939.

1. *The Autocar* 15 Oct 1937
2. *The Motor* 13 Oct 1937
3. *The Motor* 22 Mar 1938; *The Autocar* 1 Apr 1938
4. *The Motor* 28 Oct 1942
5. Eden see Bullock *Rootes Brothers* p.104; information courtesy of Paul Walby; Noble *Milestones in a Motoring Life* pp.164-74 and photos pp.116-17
6. *The Motor* 30 May 1939
7. *The Motor* 11 Apr 1939
8. *The Autocar* 21 Apr 1939
9. Lem *Register* and information courtesy of Paul Walby
10. *The Motor* 12 Sep 1939; *The Autocar* 22 Sep 1939
11. *The Autocar* 1 Sep 1939
12. *The Motor* 5 Sep 1939
13. *Chassis Registers* for Ten and 2-litre models, in Coventry Transport Museum archive
14. *The Autocar* 1 Sep 1939
15. *The Motor* 8 Aug 1945
16. Healey *My World of Cars* p.79
17. Quotes from *The Autocar* 17 Jan 1947; *The Motor* 26 Nov 1947
18. *Motor Sport* Jul 1955; Frostick *Works Team* p.15
19. Letter from Garrad to the then owner of the car, *Stardust* no.57 Sep 1982, quoted in Lem p.83; Robson *Rootes Maestros* p.7
20. *The Autocar* 22 Aug 1947
21. *Chassis Register*

Chapter Four

Streamstyle and synchromatic: the 80 and 90

Someone ought to write a thesis on English as used in motor industry advertising, whether in Britain or the USA. In the early post-war period, Rootes made at least the two contributions recorded in the title for this chapter. "Streamstyle" was unique to Sunbeam-Talbot and referred to the new body styling launched with the 80 and 90 in 1948, whereas "Synchromatic" was used across the range and was jargon for the steering-column gear change introduced in 1947 on the Hillman Minx and the Humbers. In the following year this spread to the new Sunbeam-Talbots, which shared their transmission with the new Minx and Humber Hawk models of 1948.

Not that there was anything new about putting the gear lever on the steering column: famous examples were the de Dion-Boutons of the veteran era, and the original Rover Eight of 1904. In Britain, most 1930s cars with preselector gearboxes had the selector lever on the column, but the column change for ordinary gearboxes had begun to appear on late-1930s American cars. It was then used in conjunction with a bench front seat, to allow three-abreast seating in the front. Both of these features spread to Britain with the first generation of proper post-war cars. The pioneers were the Triumph 1800 – with its unusual right-hand column change – and the Jowett Javelin. Between 1947 and 1950 these features became commonplace even on quite small family saloons, despite the fact that such cars typically were not wide enough to accommodate three adults in the front seat, brochure illustrations notwithstanding. As a young child, however, the author often rode between his parents in the family Morris Oxford, something that would no longer be legal!

As far as the column gear change was concerned, one salesman at the time described

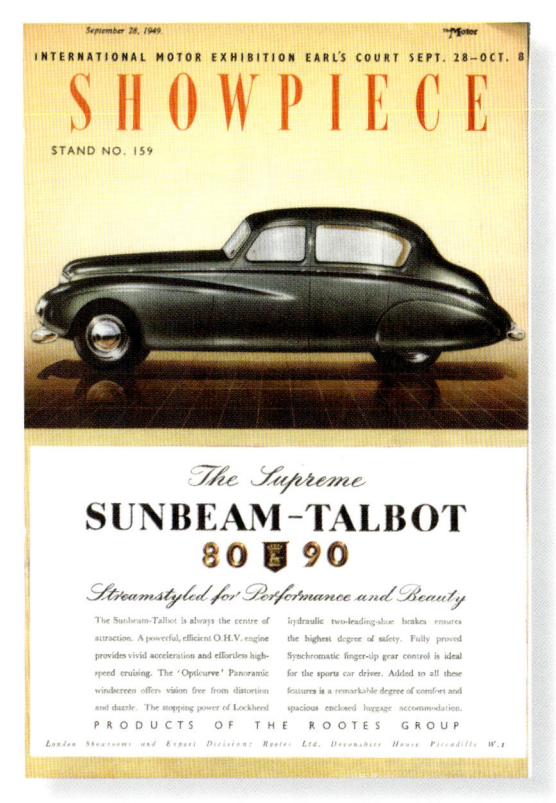

The artist who drew the car for this 1949 Motor Show time advertisement did perhaps not entirely capture the simple elegance of the lines, while the copywriter used all the catchphrases. (Courtesy Michael Scott)

SUNBEAM-TALBOT & ALPINE IN DETAIL

The 1948 brochure was the most lavish published for the Sunbeam-Talbots, and opened with this view of the front end.

The rear three-quarter view in the brochure was based on a photo of the prototype; it was quite accurate and showed the clean lines of the "streamstyling" well.

Much was made of the luggage accommodation but the drawing of a well-filled boot was rather exaggerated!

it as "just an ordinary lever turned on its side"[1] which was an oversimplification. It worked better with the three-speed 'boxes found on Fords, the Standard Vanguard and Vauxhalls, than with four speeds. Of the latter, Jowett had the best, since the gearbox on a Javelin was more or less at the bottom of the steering column. Most other systems necessitated very complex linkages, more so on left-hand drive versions, as the gear selectors on many British cars were on the right-hand side of the gearbox. The four-speed column change on Morrises and Wolseleys was memorably poor. The Rootes gear change had third and top closest to the driver with first and second further away, and the dog-leg reverse beyond and below the first-second plane: a pattern also used by Austin and Singer for their four-speed column changes, whereas three-speeders usually had first and reverse closest to the steering wheel.

Naturally there were many makers who stuck to a centre floor gear change, especially those who made sports or sporting cars – neither Jaguar nor MG ever made a manual gearbox car with a column change, but Riley and even Aston

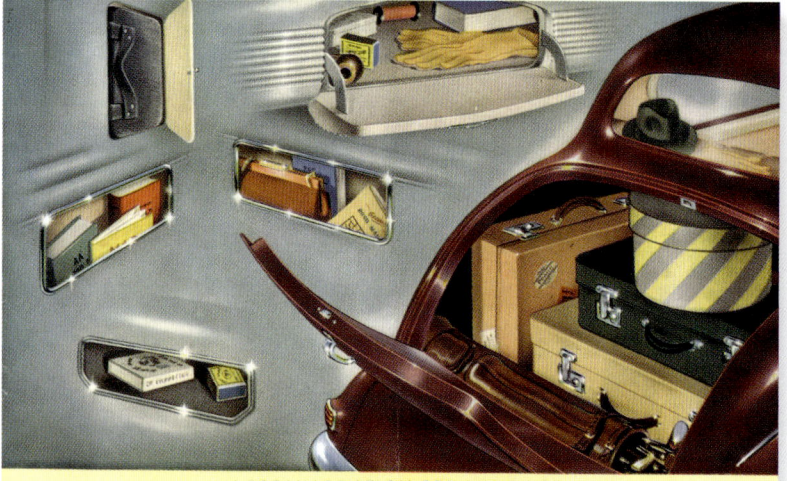

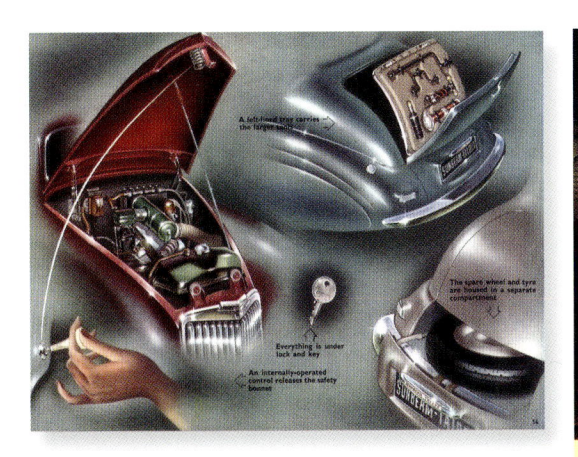

STREAMSTYLE AND SYNCHROMATIC

The brochure showed the 90 engine "in situ" and the tool and spare wheel compartments which were common to both models.

The "control panel" was similarly "streamstyled" and of perfectly symmetrical design, with well-arranged instruments and controls; only the wiper switch was in an odd position, on the right of the steering column below the fairing, with the bonnet release further to the right.

I am not sure that interiors on production cars were ever finished in a two-tone colour scheme, as suggested by this brochure illustration. The artist has rather glossed over the slides for the sunshine roof.

The 80 chassis drawing from the sales brochure reveals the relative simplicity of the design, with box-section side and cross members.

Martin did. The fashion for the combination of column change and bench seat was not confined to British cars, as it was found on many European family cars of the period. It continued to be used well into the 1960s, including on many cars made by American companies in Europe, before common sense prevailed.

In 1948 however, column change was the future, and no wonder that Rootes, which among British companies always had rather an American outlook, was keen to adopt it. Similarly, there was American inspiration behind the new "Streamstyle" body design for the Sunbeam-Talbot. As early as 1938, Rootes had signed a contract with the consultancy of the famous Franco-American industrial designer Raymond Loewy (1893-1986)[2], who by this time

71

SUNBEAM-TALBOT & ALPINE IN DETAIL

When the new Sunbeam-Talbots were introduced in 1948, Rootes issued a press release with a photo story of how the new cars were made, including this shot of an 80 on the assembly line. (Courtesy CTM)

This left-hand drive 80 is a little further down the assembly line, with two of the new Minxes in the background. (Courtesy CTM)

This photo is also from the press release issued to mark the introduction of the new cars, showing two examples leaving the factory at Ryton. (Courtesy CTM)

had an international practice with offices on both sides of the Atlantic. In automotive circles, he had attracted considerable attention with his 1930s designs, first for Hupmobile, then for Studebaker, and his post-war Studebaker of 1946 brought him real fame. This was a breakthrough in the process of developing a full-width, three-box shape of motor car: it was a common joke that you could not tell which was the front end and which was the rear end of a Studebaker. The contemporary Kaiser and Frazer by Howard Darrin struck a similar note, and it took a couple of years for the bigger American car manufacturers to catch up.

The influence of the early post-war American designs was just as important in Europe. In Britain, the Rover P4 75 was clearly inspired by the Studebaker, while the Singer SM 1500 imitated the Kaiser-Frazer design. Ford and Vauxhall followed their respective parent companies, and some of their design work was undertaken by American stylists. Rootes had the benefit of a similar input from the Loewy studio, and the new Hillman Minx and Humber Hawk models launched in September-October 1948 were undoubtedly American cars shrunk to fit British chassis sizes, never mind British garages and roads. Both were full-width designs, although with outlines of rear wing shapes, and both were three-box designs, even if the built-out boot on the Minx was rather stumpy. The Minx had a full-width horizontal grille, the Hawk a traditional vertical grille. Column change and a bench front seat were *de rigueur*, and in another step forward these two new models had independent front suspension with transverse wishbones and coil springs.

However, before either the Minx or the Hawk, in June 1948 Rootes had launched the new generation of Sunbeam-Talbots, the 80 and 90 models. These two cars were a curious mixture of ancient and modern. Unlike the unitary construction Minx – but like the Hawk – they retained a separate chassis, which was developed from the earlier Sunbeam-Talbot frame. Unlike both the Minx and Hawk, the 80 and 90 also still had a beam front axle with semi-elliptic springs. This seems almost perverse, when various independent systems were by now found on virtually every other proper post-war model. The 80/90 must enjoy the dubious distinction of being just about the last all-new British car to have cart springs front and rear. The few other cars which still had beam front axles were essentially pre-war designs such as AC, Alvis and Ford.

On the other hand, the 80 and 90 had Rootes's first overhead-valve engines, quite some time before either Hillman or Humber converted to ohv. It was generally conceded in the industry and by the journals that side valves

*In this retouched side view of a prototype 1948 convertible with the hood down, it may just be possible to see that the name badge still reads "Two-litre".
(Courtesy Leon Gibbs)*

were becoming old hat, but the jury was still out; Morris for instance introduced an all-new side-valve engine for the Oxford in 1948. A year later the new Triumph Mayflower had side valves, and Ford famously stuck with side valves for their small cars throughout the 1950s.

The body styling of the new Sunbeam-Talbot was a remarkable synthesis of British and American ideas, and is thought to have been influenced both by Clare Hodgman of Loewy's London office who oversaw the Rootes contract, and by Ted White and Ted Green, of Sunbeam-Talbot's own styling studio. White, born in 1905, had studied motor body engineering and joined Darracq Motors as chief body designer while still in his twenties, later being appointed to a similar position at Talbot and Sunbeam-Talbot. He also became chief engineer of British Light Steel Pressings and was the designer of the pre-war Sunbeam-Talbot sports saloon bodies (discussed in chapters 2 and 3). He eventually moved up to Coventry and in 1952 was appointed chief stylist for the Rootes Group, which by then had a very up-to-date styling studio in the Humber factory at Stoke. He stayed in this position even through the early Chrysler years until retirement around 1970.[3]

The joint Anglo-American effort to style the Rootes post-war cars could have made for an uneasy relationship but luckily there seems to have been complete harmony and co-operation. When interviewed later, Hodgman gave full credit to White for the exterior styling of the Sunbeam-Talbot, while he and other Loewy stylists concentrated on the interior – seats, instrument panel and steering wheel. On the other hand, quarter-scale clay models were made under Hodgman's supervision in the USA and shipped over to the UK for White's staff to translate into full-size models; the Rootes brothers were photographed admiring a scale

*In September 1948, a special British motor show was held in Copenhagen, and Harold Wilson as President of the Board of Trade paid a visit to look at the Sunbeam-Talbot; he is fourth from left. The Danish Rootes importer KW Bruun of Britmo is second from left, looking into the camera.
(Courtesy CTM)*

Pride of place on the Sunbeam-Talbot stand at the 1948 Motor Show was given to this sectioned 90. (Courtesy CTM)

At the 1948 Motor Show, Thrupp and Maberly displayed examples of the 80 and 90 convertibles, together with the Humber Pullman and Imperial. (Courtesy CTM)

model of the convertible, probably the same model that Rootes displayed at the Festival of Britain in 1951. Hodgman would have liked to introduce a modern, horizontal grille but the brief was to retain the classic grille. He remembered Ted White as "a very nice man, very co-operative. There was never any friction or any problems… It was a fine working combination". The whole styling process was supervised by engineering director Bernard Winter and inevitably by the Rootes family.[4]

The result was a remarkably elegant shape, which in a much modernised form echoed the by-now classic Sunbeam-Talbot lines. Ted White later said that he was inspired by aircraft drop fuel tanks for the wing shapes. The front wings with built-in headlamps swept into the front doors, but the body generally was built out to the full width of the car and it was one of the first British cars to have a flush-sided body, with not even a suggestion of separate rear wings – although in fairness, the Standard Vanguard launched a year earlier also had flush body sides, in its case all the way from front to rear. On both cars, the effect was heightened by spats fitted over the rear wheels, those on the Sunbeam-Talbot being of elongated teardrop shape, although they covered ordinary round wheel arches. Another modern feature was the one-piece curved windscreen, called "Opticurve" in Rootes PR speak, and the rear window was also curved.

If the lower part of the bodywork on the 80/90 was all new, apart from the traditional vertical Sunbeam-Talbot grille, the rest of the design made it instantly recognisable. The greenhouse retained that unique side window shape, with the pillarless reverse-angle rear quarter light. The front doors were front-hinged, but the rear doors were still hinged at the rear. A classic falling waistline was accentuated by a chrome strip which neatly incorporated pull-out door handles. The rear overhang was comparatively modest, with a falling line to the short boot. The whole design was commendably clean and free of ornamentation. It was up-to-date in 1948 but even so its proportions were not particularly modern, dictated by the traditional chassis layout, with a bonnet of near-vintage length, short cabin set well to the rear, narrow doors and an upright windscreen almost at mid-point between the axles. It has been stated that the roof panel was carried over from the previous generation; certainly the arrangement of the sunroof sliding back in full view inside was similar, and the tumble-home in the greenhouse confirms that the roof was narrower than the body.[5]

The only alternative body style was an equally handsome convertible coupé, with two wider doors, and small rear quarter lights for the rear seat passengers. Both these and the door windows had slim chrome-plated frames, in contrast to the saloon with its one-piece doors, and the convertible had front quarter lights, although these were fixed. The rear quarter lights were lowered in an arc, pivoting around their front bottom corner. The hood was of the three-position type allowing for the *de ville* position with just the front part folded back. There was naturally a little less rear seat room in the convertible model, but neither car really had any pretence at being more than a four-seater, with 41in (1041mm) across the rear seat between the armrests. The rear seat was right above the rear axle, and to allow reasonable legroom the rear cushion was 4in (102mm) above the front seat cushions, with a corresponding reduction in rear headroom.

The all-steel saloon body was made by British Light Steel Pressings at Acton, the convertible body by Thrupp & Maberly in Edgware Road, Cricklewood, also in London, so all bodies had to be transported up to Ryton for final assembly. On both cars the interior was nicely trimmed and appointed, with mostly unpleated leather upholstery, and centre and side armrests for rear seat passengers. The driving seat had adjustment for height and rake as well as reach, and there were quick-action levers for the front door windows, but the inside front door handles were uncomfortably positioned adjacent to your shoulder. An unusual feature was that the front ashtray was fitted in the transmission tunnel on the floor. The sunroof was standard on saloons, but a heater and demister were still extra, although there were built-in ventilation ducts. When a heater was fitted, it lived untidily in a bulky box under the dash.

American influence was particularly manifest in the facia layout, the work of John Reinhart of the Loewy office.[6] The symmetrical design facilitated building a version with left-hand drive, which was now increasingly important. The steering column and gear change were hidden under a domed shroud, with horizontal wings or buttresses either side. The shape of the shroud carried into the instrument panel with a semi-circular speedometer fitted so to speak around the column, flanked by two smaller instruments on either side: fuel gauge and clock, ammeter and oil pressure gauge, but no water temperature gauge yet, nor a trip meter for the speedometer. The instruments originally had attractive cream-coloured dials, matching the

The much-travelled Sir William Rootes in Buenos Aires in 1948 with Mr Fennell of Rootes Canada, apparently trying to get a left-hand drive version of the Synchromatic gear change to work. (Courtesy CTM)

steering wheel, gear lever knob and other controls.

Minor controls were mostly in the centre of the facia, together with a cubby hole where an HMV radio could be fitted. On the passenger side was a glove locker of the same size and shape as the instrument cluster; it had its own lamp which doubled as a map-reading light. Horizontal fluting ran across the facia, a motif continued in fluting on the door trims and across the seat backs. The near-vertical steering wheel with a light-coloured rim had three multiple-spring spokes in T-formation. Its hub carried the horn push, trafficator switch and, as was traditional for the brand, the headlamp dip

It was presumably the sectioned 90 from the 1948 Motor Show which drew the crowds at the 1949 Melbourne show as well. (Courtesy CTM)

SUNBEAM-TALBOT & ALPINE IN DETAIL

This 80 was built in 1950. The two-tone finish is not original but was found on some of the last Mark IIIs, and the owner has very sensibly fitted more up-to-date lighting equipment; the original headlamp dipping system is now in any case illegal.

Uninitiated observers some times think that "Supreme" is the model name, in fact it was the old Sunbeam catchphrase, whereas the heraldic beast was the original Talbot crest.

The front number plate hinges down to give access to the starting handle hole. These are the early type of bumper overriders. The badge is from the original Rootes-sponsored club.

The name badge on the side of the scuttle features the same art deco style typography as found on the radiator badge, and is supplemented by the model designation.

76

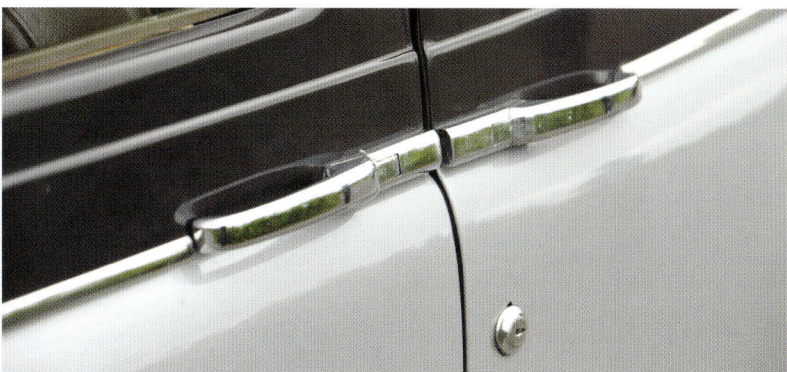

STREAMSTYLE AND SYNCHROMATIC

Similarly there are modern flashing indicators at the rear, and this car has lost its rear wheel spats. On a 1956 two-tone Mark III, the number plate panel would have been in the lower body colour.

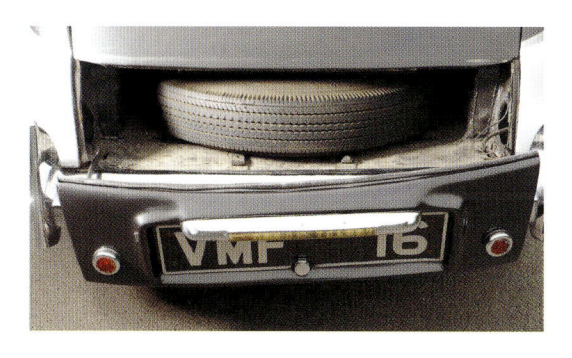

The pull-out door handles fit neatly into the chrome trim strip along the waistline. The driver's door has a separate key lock below.

The early cars through to 1952 with solid wheels have these large plain hub caps. The extra wheel trim rings, often called rimbellishers, were a popular period accessory.

The number plate panel below the boot lid swings down to give access to the spare wheel compartment. Note the Sunbeam Talbot name on the number plate lamp housing.

77

The fuel gauge is marked in both gallons and litres, here on the left of the clock in the instrument cluster. The light switch is fitted round the ignition lock and the red button is the ignition warning light. This car has an additional water temperature gauge (from a Wolseley?) and the switch next to it is presumably for an electric fan. The radio is a lovely original HMV unit, specially designed to fit the Sunbeam-Talbot facia.

This not very attractive box for the heater blower is fitted below the dashboard; the heater was of course still an extra.

Seat trim is mostly plain, with just a few horizontal pleats across the seatbacks. The little hand wheel protruding at the front corner of the driver's seat is for height and rake adjustment. On the passenger door we can see the interior door handle at the rear, and the quick-action window lift.

The rear seat style is similar. There is not a lot of room here, but it is an inviting and comfortable space, with three armrests. These rear quarter lights seem to have been fitted with a form of draught excluder!

STREAMSTYLE AND SYNCHROMATIC

This shot through the rear window gives a perfect impression of the symmetrical layout of the dashboard. The shape and size of the glove box is precisely the same as the instrument panel. The gear lever reaches well beyond the steering wheel rim to the centre of the car.

A close-up of the speedometer, with the additional "KPH" markings which were a Sunbeam-Talbot tradition, and as yet just a total distance recorder.

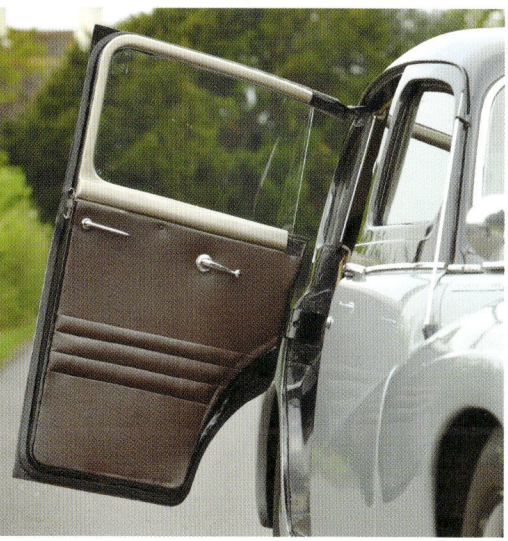

The horizontal flutes continue on the otherwise plain door trims. Because of the tumble-home in the body, the rear doors jut upwards at this angle when open, and the main hinge, just above the wheel arch, obviously has to be rather generously proportioned.

79

SUNBEAM-TALBOT & ALPINE IN DETAIL

Under the bonnet of an 80, with its unique overhead-valve engine; its lay-out is a mirror image of the better-known 90 engine, with the carburettor and manifolds on the left, here in the foreground. The oil filler cap is less handy than on the 90. The trunking at the top of this picture is for the interior ventilation.

From the ignition side of the 80 engine, the handily-mounted distributor can be seen, and the Sunbeam-Talbot name cast into the rocker cover. The oil filter is below the distributor in this photo.

switch. The pull-up handbrake was between the separate front seats; that separate front seats were fitted seems rather at odds with the column change! The rear view mirror was mounted below the windscreen.

The boot was improved in size but was still far from generous. The lid was hinged at the bottom, so it was possible to carry more luggage by having the boot lid open, if at the mercy of the weather or light-fingered individuals! Rally cars often ended up with roof racks. The spare wheel had its own compartment below the boot, with access through the swing-down panel which bore the built-in rear number plate. One peculiarity was that the rear jacking points were immediately below this panel, which meant that the spare wheel could not be taken out if the car already had been jacked up at the rear... The jack and other large tools were neatly stowed within the boot lid; the smaller tools were in a box in a compartment in the scuttle, accessible through a trapdoor to the outside of the left-hand foot well.

In mechanical terms the two models were closer than before. Both used the same chassis, with a wheelbase of 8ft 1.5in (2477mm) which was fractionally shorter than the old 2-litre. It had box-section construction for the side members and three of the cross members, with a fourth tubular cross member at the rear. There was no cruciform bracing, and the frame was still underslung at the rear. On the 90 the front springs had extra leaves. The front track was the same as on the superseded models but the rear track was 2in (51mm) wider. Burman-Douglas worm and nut steering gear was used, with about 2.75-3 turns lock to lock. Brakes were Lockheed hydraulic, of the twin-leading shoe type, with 10in (254mm) drums for the 90 but 9in (229mm) drums for the 80 – which seems penny-pinching. Another odd difference was that on the 80 the wheels were of the Minx type with three-stud fixing, but the 90 had five-stud wheels; both had 5.50-16 tyres. The car was fairly compact at 13ft 11.5in (4255mm) long and 5ft 2.5in (1588mm) wide but was no lightweight. An 80 tipped the scales at 23.25cwt (1182kg), a

At the 1949 Motor Show, Sir Reginald Rootes seems to have got Sir Stafford Cripps very enthusiastic about the Sunbeam-Talbot 90 engineering exhibit. Norman Garrad wears a rather resigned expression; he was presumably not a socialist. (Courtesy CTM)

90 was around 3cwt (152kg) heavier (kerb weights quoted).

The big improvement under the bonnet was that both cars now had overhead valves operated by pushrods. Engine dimensions were exactly as before, 63mm by 95mm and 1185cc for the 80, 75mm by 110mm and 1944cc for the 90. Compression ratios were still low in an age of low-octane Pool petrol: 6.88:1 on the 80, 6.57:1 on the 90. Power outputs had increased quite satisfactorily to 47bhp and 64bhp respectively. As a consequence of the conversion to

Rootes were very good at getting their cars into films, maybe because their backers, the Prudential, also had substantial interests in the film business. Here is a 1949 convertible with Stanley Holloway in The Midnight Episode. (Courtesy CTM)

The British Motor Show in New York in April 1950 was visited by HRH the Duke of Windsor, who is being shown the 90 convertible by FI Connolly of the curriers, who was then the President of the SMMT, and by Brian Rootes. (Courtesy CTM)

ohv, the new cylinder heads now had porting and manifolds on the opposite side to where they had been previously, so the 80 had its carburettor and manifolds on the left-hand side (nearside) of the engine, the 90 on the right-hand side (offside).

Otherwise the two engines were very similar in design, with a cast-iron combined cylinder block and crankcase extending well below the centre line of the crankshaft, which was carried in three steel-backed white-metal lined main bearings and was fully balanced with counterweights. The 90 had aluminium alloy con rods, on the 80 they were of steel, and both had Lo-Ex aluminium alloy pistons. The oil sump was a steel pressing. There was an external by-pass oil filter. A double roller chain drove the camshaft, mounted low down to one side of the engine; it had three bearings and a skew gear at its centre which drove a vertical shaft with the oil pump at the bottom, and the distributor handily mounted on top of the engine: a useful inheritance from the original side-valve layout. The 80 now had the benefit of a water pump which was still not found on the Hillman Minx. On both cars the pump was driven by belt, together with the fan and the dynamo, with the usual disadvantage that a broken belt stopped circulation.

The tappets on the 90 were of the barrel type, on the 80 of the mushroom type; they activated the overhead valves through hollow steel pushrods and rockers. The valves were set in line, at an angle of 5 degrees from vertical, in lozenge-shaped combustion chambers in the cast-iron cylinder head. Each cylinder had its own inlet port, while cylinders no.2 and no.3 had a siamesed exhaust port. The inlet manifold was divided internally to provide separate inlet tracts of approximately the same length, with a hot-spot where it met the exhaust manifold. Both cars had a single Zenith Stromberg carburettor with an automatic choke, regulated by a thermostat in the exhaust manifold. Fuel was fed by an AC mechanical pump from a 10-gallon (45-litre) tank. The engine was described as "a well-considered design on well-understood principles."[7] With nothing complicated, and of simple and straightforward design as one would expect from Rootes, the 90 engine certainly proved to be robust and to be capable of further development and tuning. The basic design lived on for nearly twenty years until the last Humber Hawk of 1967.

The gearbox, as well as the gear change, were from the standard Rootes parts bin, and were basically shared with the Minx and the Hawk, with the same internal gearbox ratios as on these cars, and indeed as on the previous Sunbeam-Talbots. However, the novelty was that the gearbox had been turned on its side so the layshaft was to the left rather than below the mainshaft, and the selectors to the right, rather than on top. This unusual arrangement was clearly adopted to suit the column change but also served to reduce the height of the gearbox tunnel. There was improved baulk-ring synchromesh on second, third and top. As the 90 was developed over the years, the gearbox increasingly struggled to cope with the extra power, and is now often felt to be a weak spot of these cars. There was an open Hardy Spicer prop shaft and final drive was by spiral bevel; the ratio was 5.22:1 on the 80 and 4.3:1 on the 90.

While the provision of twin built-in tail, stop and reversing lamps was welcome and not by any means universal yet on all British cars, the headlamp dipping system was not as up-to-date, in that dipping involved switching off both headlamps and switching on a single pass lamp mounted lower down next to the radiator grille. It was matched on the other side by a fog lamp which had its own separate control. Within a few years, the law was changed to make double-dipping headlamps mandatory. The side lamps were simply pilot bulbs built into the main headlamps. Twin wind-tone horns were fitted.

At introduction in 1948, prices (including Purchase Tax, to the nearest whole Pound) for the new models were £889 for the 80 saloon and £991 for the 90 saloon; convertibles were £953 and £1055 respectively. This meant that the 80 was very expensive for a car of its size – the new Hillman Minx of September 1948 cost £505 – and the 90 was similarly more expensive than the new Humber Hawk which cost £799. An MG Y-type, the most direct comparison with the 80 as one of the few quality 10hp cars left on the market, was much cheaper at £672. The 90 was bracketed by the two Rileys, the 1½-litre at £863, and the 2½-litre at £1135 (during 1949 Riley prices were increased to £912 and £1225).

The new cars were launched at a press reception hosted by the Rootes brothers on Tuesday 29 June at the Rootes premises at Ladbroke Hall (the old Talbot factory). The party then drove in some of the new cars to Woodcote Park, the RAC's country club, for luncheon. At this occasion, "It was stressed that the new models had been evolved largely for the Canadian and USA markets, where there is a distinct demand for British sporting cars. The first export models have, in fact, already been shipped to those countries…"

To publicize the new cars, an 80 and a 90 were entered in the Junior Car Club's Eastbourne Rally and Concours on 3-4 July, Norman Garrad in the 80, Tommy Wisdom in the 90, and Garrad got a first-class award, but neither figured in the Concours. Also present was Peter Harper with a 2-litre saloon.[8]

Both the 80 and the 90 were tested by both *The Autocar* and *The Motor*, with briefer road impressions also appearing in *Motor Sport*. The same 80 was tested by both weekly magazines; this was HNX 80, chassis number 2800080HSO. *The Motor*'s 90 was GWD 669, chassis number not certain, and *The Autocar* used GWD 100, chassis 3800005HSO, which became a rally car. The comparative performance figures from the leading magazines were as follows:

Clearly, "streamstyle" had a beneficial effect on top speed, since the 80 was now as quick as the 2-litre had been, but an additional 2 or 3cwt (100-150kg) seems largely to have negated the potential for lower fuel consumption. Acceleration was noticeably improved, more so in case of the 90, whose performance was now much more comparable with cars such as the Jowett Javelin or the Riley 1½-litre, and it was usefully quicker than the new Humber Hawk which had a top speed of 71.4mph (114.9km/h) and took 19.8sec to get to 50mph (80km/h). "You pays your money and takes your choice" – for an extra £200 the Sunbeam-Talbot 90 owner got less *Lebensraum* but more urge than the Hawk owner.

Generally the road tests were very positive about both the 80 and the 90. It is clear that the conventional front suspension raised some editorial eyebrows, thus *The Autocar* testing the 80: "A driver now accustomed to independent front wheel suspension would be able to tell, even if the fact had been concealed from him before handling the car, that it had half-elliptic springs all round… there are occasions when greater lateral firmness would be appreciated for the fast cornering which the car's performance encourages." That the car rolled was confirmed by *The Motor*, writing again of the 80: "some pitching was noticed when travelling fast over indifferent roads with a full complement of passengers… the car rolls more than its low build might lead one to expect."[9]

Curiously the 90 had passed muster in these respects, thus *The Motor*: "Only when the car is flung into an acute turn with vastly more enthusiasm than discretion, can any cause for criticism be found; in these circumstances, some trace of roll is apparent and one feels a slight suggestion of independence between axles and chassis frame… general road holding is good, with a commendable absence of pitch." Bill Boddy in *Motor Sport* of the 80: "There is rather too much up-and-down movement over bad surfaces,

		Weight	Top speed	0-50mph (0-80km/h)	10-30mph on third	20-40mph on top	Standing ¼ mile	Fuel cons.
80	*The Autocar* 18 Feb 1949	2485lb (1128kg)	73-74mph (118km/h)	22.2sec	9sec	14.8sec	n/q	26-36mpg
80	*The Motor* 27 Apr 1949	2604lb (1182kg)	70.9mph (114km/h)	19.4sec	9.4sec	14.9sec	24.4sec	28.8mpg
90	*The Autocar* 2 Jul 1948	2828lb (1284kg)	80mph (129km/h)	17.6sec	7.6sec	11.7sec	n/q	22-28mpg
90	*The Motor* 30 Jun 1948	2940lb (1335kg)	76.6mph (123km/h)	15.9sec	7.2sec	11.3sec	23.1sec	23.2mpg

At the British Motor Show in New York in April 1950, Alec Guinness and fellow actor Robert Flemyng also tried out the convertible. They were appearing together in TS Eliot's play The Cocktail Party *on Broadway. (Courtesy CTM)*

when quite appreciable return-motion occurs through the steering-wheel. The wheels can be felt negotiating undulations and the more severe bumps (or tram lines) tend to deflect the car and provoke steering reaction. – The car rolls considerably when cornering… mild tail-slides tend to develop rather unexpectedly."[10]

John Eason Gibson, writing of the 80 in *Country Life,* echoed the main journals: "An experienced driver would have little difficulty in observing that independent suspension was not fitted… at higher speeds it would be an advantage to have greater stability, both on corners and on the straight. This fault is first revealed in the necessity to steer consciously on any other surface than very smooth ones." He of course had greater experience of the 80 than most other road testers, since he had been one of the Sunbeam-Talbot 80 team drivers in the Monte Carlo rally earlier that year.[11]

The other possible point of contention, to wit the column change, surprisingly merited unstinted all-round praise. *The Motor* went so far as to say, rather prophetically, that "The rally driver who requires a transmission which will stand a real snatch change without hesitation or protest will find in this system the answer to his prayer". *The Autocar* writing of the 90 also praised the gear change but disagreed slightly with their rival as they found it "works lightly, and fairly fast, but is not at its absolute best for the very quick movement necessary when making acceleration tests. For ordinary handling it is excellent."[12]

Eason Gibson, quoted above, felt that the change pattern with third and top, the most frequently used gears, closest to the steering wheel made "it unnecessary to remove the hand from the wheel when changing gears" – was it really such a finger-tip operation? Let *The Motor* have the last word on the subject: "In writing of every recent product of the Rootes Group, one automatically finds oneself singing the praises of the steering-column gear change and the fool-proof system of engagement incorporated in the gearbox. …the Synchromatic gear change has now become synonymous with all that is easy and quick in gear changing".[13]

Michael Sedgwick was blunter in his assessment: "…the boot was a bad joke. The facia was too like that of the Humber Hawk for comfort, and there was no excuse for the dreadful Synchromatic column shift. Another unwelcome survival was the beam front axle, which gave a ride comparable to a lodging-house bedstead. …the sports veneer was thin and the gear ratios agricultural."[14]

In their original form, the 80 and 90 had a production life of little more than two years, from June 1948 to September 1950. Production figures proved their greater popularity compared to their predecessors, as 3500 80s and 4000 90s were made. Of the 7500 cars built, in round figures 2000 were exported, not exactly a high figure by contemporary standards when for instance Jaguar in one year hit an 80 per cent export rate. At this time Australia and Switzerland were the best export markets, but from 1950 onwards quite a number also went to the USA. There is some discrepancy between the figures of Sunbeam-Talbot supposedly shipped from Britain and the numbers actually sold in the USA, as follows:[15]

Exports and sales USA

	1948	1949	1950	1951	1952	1953	1954	Total
Exports to the USA	49	34	175	339	379	1304	179	2459
Actual sales in the USA	13	17	120	133	281	809	553	1926

The discrepancy cannot be accounted for simply by delays in shipping and distribution States-side; some cars may have been re-exported, or returned to UK. Unlike Nuffield, Rootes shipped cars on consignment, so dealers did not have to pay until a sale was made, and could return unsold cars. By August 1953, Rootes had an inventory of unsold cars in the USA worth $4,500,000 at retail prices, spread over 450 dealers.[16] There is also no doubt that the British motor industry generally had a roller-coaster ride in the USA in the early years. The devaluation of the Pound in September 1949 enabled British car makers to lower their prices but this fillip was short-lived. With the outbreak of the Korean War in June 1950, the new car market in the USA went into a decline: some British makers had to ship cars back home and others cut production of left-hand drive models for the American market, which did not completely return to more normal conditions until 1952.

As early as 1949, Rootes had set up a wholly-owned subsidiary in the USA to handle sales, the first British manufacturer to do so.[17] Norman Garrad helped Brian Rootes to establish the New York operation, which incidentally for some years also handled Rovers and Land Rovers, and John Dugdale, formerly a journalist with *The Autocar*, looked after sales and marketing until he joined Jaguar in 1954. The most important model in the American market was the Hillman Minx, since British market leaders in the USA were at first small cars such as the Austin A40 or the Ford Anglia and Prefect, only overtaken by MG from 1951 onwards. Some prices for British cars in the USA in July 1950 were as follows:[18]

A left-hand drive 90 saloon clearly photographed in North America, which was an important export target. (Courtesy CTM)

	Price in New York, duty and federal taxes paid	Equivalent price in £ at £1 = $2.80	Ex-factory retail price in UK, before Purchase Tax	Variation between US and UK price
Morris Minor	$1295	£463	£299	+55%
Austin A40 Devon	$1480	£529	£392 (fixed head)	+35%
Hillman Minx	$1495	£534	£395	+35%
Morris Oxford	$1750	£625	£427	+46%
MG TD Midget	$1850	£661	£445	+49%
Humber Hawk	$1997	£713	£625	+14%
MG Y-type saloon	$2250	£804	£525	+53%
Austin A90 Atlantic	$2345	£838	£645 (convertible)	+30%
Sunbeam-Talbot 90	$2395	£855	£775	+13%
Riley 2½-litre	$3250	£1161	£958	+21%
Jaguar Mark V 3½-litre saloon	$3750	£1339	£988	+36%
Jaguar XK 120	$3945	£1409	£988	+43%
average	$2317	£828	£622	+33%

At least this photo shows that Rootes also handled Rover in the USA. On a snowy April day in 1950, the Rover gas turbine car arrives outside the Rootes showroom in Park Avenue, New York, before going on to the British Motor Show, and "Billy" Rootes has jumped behind the wheel. (Courtesy CTM)

This put the 90 close to the price of the most expensive Pontiac ($2411) or Studebaker ($2328) while the cheapest Cadillac was $2761, and unless Rootes had wrought a miracle so that their costs were substantially less than those of other manufacturers, one draws the conclusion that they were subsidising American prices of Humber and Sunbeam-Talbot, as was Nuffield of the Riley, probably in their efforts to generate sales. It should be added that shipping costs would add proportionately more to the price of the cheaper, smaller cars.

Only the 90 was available in the USA and it generally sold better abroad than the 80, while under the new flat-rate tax system in the UK there was inevitably a declining market for the smaller-engined car. The preserved sales ledgers unfortunately do not show the actual destinations for export cars (they are simply marked Export) but for home market cars names of distributors and often also of customers were added. Now, sixty years later, the names of many owners, even if they were celebrities in their day, have become meaningless, but titled owners are usually easier to trace on websites. The following are a small selection of first owners who might be of interest; their cars were all 90 saloons:

Chassis 3800753HSO was owned by the eighth Earl of Antrim (1911-77) whose mother's maiden name was *Talbot*... Chassis 3801159HSO was owned by Viscount Errington (1918-91), who succeeded as third Earl of Cromer in 1953. He was then the managing director of the family firm Barings Bank but was Governor of the Bank of England from 1961-66 and British Ambassador to the USA from 1971-74. He became a Member of the Privy Council and was made a Knight of the Garter in 1977.

Chassis 3801414HSO, later the Mark II A3000029HSO and finally the Mark III A3502087HSO, were all owned by Lord Willingdon, second Marquess (1899-1979), a director of the Rootes Group; his father the first Marquess had been Governor General of Canada and later Viceroy of India. The second Marquess, whose family name was Inigo Brassey Thomas, succeeded to the title in 1941. His maternal grandfather Lord Brassey had owned a yacht called *Sunbeam* – actually a substantial three-masted schooner – which during the First World War became a hospital ship on which the young Inigo served an apprenticeship.[19]

Chassis 3802101HSO was owned by the fourteenth Duke of Hamilton (1903-73). As Lord Clydesdale he was a pioneer aviator who flew over Mount Everest in 1933, and he was even

Illustration from the 1948 brochure

more famously the man that Rudolf Hess allegedly flew to Scotland to meet. Chassis 3802488HSO and later the Mark II convertible A3007078HCO were owned by the sixth Lord Bolton (Nigel Amyas Orde-Powlett, 1900-63).

A few 90s were delivered to some of Rootes's suppliers in the motor industry, including Triplex Safety Glass, Connolly Bros. (Curriers), and Joseph Lucas. In June 1950, six 90s were sold to the Constabulary of Northumberland; the only other Police car I have come across went to the Surrey Constabulary. Both forces had previously used 2-litres. Some names of rally drivers can also be found in the sales records, including Murray-Frame who had both a 90 (3800119HSO) and later a Mark II (A3000232HSO), Perring (3802215HCO, believed to be registered OPA 6 which was later also seen on a Mark II), and JPS Slatter (3803202HSO, probably registered OPF 300).

When the time came to update the model in 1950, the less-popular 80 was unceremoniously ditched, but since it had no successor it was produced for a little longer than the original 90. Surprisingly, both the ohv engine sizes from the original 80 and 90 models remained unique in the Rootes range; the Minx continued with side valves for its larger engine of 1265cc from 1949, and only acquired ohv when it was fitted with the all-new square 1390cc engine in 1954. At the same time the Humber Hawk switched to ohv, but its engine was by then of 2267cc.

---

1. Montagu with Sedgwick *Lost Causes of Motoring, Europe* vol.1 p.126
2. Jodard *Raymond Loewy*; Langworth *Tiger, Alpine, Rapier* pp.20-21
3. *Who's Who in the Motor and Commercial Vehicle Industries* (1965 ed.) p.534; BB Winter "Fashioning a Car for Rootes" in *The Times Survey of the British Motor Car Industry* Oct 1951 pp.21-22, 28; Robson *Sunbeam Alpine and Tiger* pp.18, 29-32
4. Langworth pp.22-25; Pressnell "Fruits of the Rootes" in *Classic and Sportscar* Jul 1988; *The Times Survey of the British Motor-Car Industry* Oct 1949 p.25
5. Pressnell "Fruits…"; Roy Axe quoted in Robson p.18
6. Langworth p.26
7. *The Autocar* 2 Jul 1948
8. *The Autocar* 2 Jul 1948, 9 Jul 1948
9. *The Autocar* 18 Feb 1949; *The Motor* 27 Apr 1949
10. *The Motor* 30 Jun 1948; *Motor Sport* Sep 1949
11. *Country Life* 12 Aug 1949
12. *The Motor* 30 Jun 1948; *The Autocar* 2 Jul 1948
13. *The Motor* 27 Apr 1949
14. Sedgwick *The Motor Car 1946-56* p.222
15. Exports from Nuffield Exports statistics, BMIHT archive; US sales 1948-52 from Dugdale *Jaguar in America* pp.18, 29; 1953-54 from *The Motor Industry of Great Britain*; the 1953 and 1954 figures will include Alpines
16. *Time* magazine 31 Aug 1953 on Rootes in the USA, courtesy Derek Cook
17. Dugdale p.25
18. Whisler *At the End of the Road* p.197; UK prices from *The Autocar*, *The Motor*, Jul 1950
19. A picture of the yacht *Sunbeam* had featured on the menu cover for the lunch at the introduction of the Sunbeam Thirty in 1936; *The Autocar* 16 Oct 1936 p.722

Chapter Five

Developing a winner: 90 Mark II to Mark III

I am not quite sure of the occasion or who these visitors to the production line at Ryton were, but I think it must have been in 1950 when the Mark II was just going into production, as we can still see the front wing of a Mark I in the foreground on the left. (Courtesy Guy Woodhams)

Over its two-year production period, the 90 had carved a niche for itself as a compact sporting saloon, offering good looks as well as good performance, but the absence of independent front suspension meant it was clearly behind the times in terms of chassis design. Road holding, handling and ride did not measure up to the rest of the car, or to the opposition, in spite of which it had begun to make an impression in rallying – clearly there was nothing wrong with the ruggedness or stamina of the 90.

It was a much-welcomed step forward when the Rootes engineers produced a new version of the 90 which was launched as the Mark II in September 1950. The new model incorporated an almost completely redesigned chassis with independent front suspension, using double transverse wishbones and coil springs. In principle the layout was the same as that which had been found on the Minx and the Hawk since 1948. It was much more modern and vastly better than the 1930s "Evenkeel" system which still persisted on the top-of-line Humber models. There was an anti-roll bar at the front, and the shock absorbers were changed to the Armstrong lever-arm type.

To go with the new suspension, the revised chassis had substantial cruciform bracing which made it far more rigid. The chassis side members were still underslung at the rear. The rear springs were longer and wider than before, and there was a Panhard rod to help with lateral axle location. The Sunbeam-Talbot now fell into line with other Rootes cars by adopting a final drive of the hypoid bevel type, which allowed a lower line for the prop shaft tunnel; the rear axle was a narrow-track version of that found on the Humber Hawk. Another change was that the steering gear was of the Burman Douglas recirculating ball type, at first rather low-geared for the period with over three turns from lock to lock.

To take full advantage of the new suspension and chassis, the engine size was increased to 2267cc by opening up the bore to 81mm, and although the compression ratio was still a modest 6.45:1, power output was improved to 70bhp at 4000rpm. At the same time the

Humber Hawk was also given a 2267cc engine, but on that car it still had side valves and so developed only 58bhp at 3400rpm. On the new 90, the gearbox and gear change were left unchanged but the more powerful engine allowed a higher final drive ratio of 3.9:1.

The Mark II was easily identified by its revised front end. The front wings were reshaped, the headlamps were mounted three inches higher and a little further apart; it is probable that the original headlamp position was too low for legal requirements in some export markets. The headlamps used the double-dip system instead of the single pass lamp, so this and the fog lamp were deleted. On the other hand there were now separate side lamps below the headlamps. Where the auxiliary lamps had been there were extra air intakes which served the ventilation ducts, or the heater if this were fitted. The front end actually looked much better than before, with according to *The Motor* "a more commanding and business-like air." This magazine clearly liked the styling, as they later wrote: "...probably the greatest virtue of the Sunbeam-Talbot 90 is – handsome appearance. Very modern and very British, it is certainly one of the best-looking small cars on the road."[1]

There were no other changes to the exterior, and very little was done to the interior, except that on the saloon the mirror was now of a somewhat anachronistic oval shape. Early Mark IIs still lacked a water temperature gauge but this was introduced in 1951 when it displaced the clock from the instrument cluster. Instead, on saloons the clock migrated to a position above the windscreen, where it was not at first illuminated at night. On the convertible it was incorporated in the rear view mirror, which on this model was still rectangular and fitted above the windscreen. Those awkwardly-positioned interior front door handles were moved to the front, and passenger doors were locked by buttons on the window sills.

The Mark II was introduced at the price of £775 (£991 including Purchase Tax) for the saloon, and £825 (£1055 including Purchase Tax) for the convertible, but in February 1951 factory prices went up so that the saloon now cost £820/£1049 and the convertible £875/£1119. Then Purchase Tax was increased from one-third to two-thirds of the wholesale price in April 1951, and with a further factory price rise by September 1951 the saloon cost £845/£1316, and the convertible £895/£1394.

When the Mark II (a saloon registered KNX 603) was road tested by the journals, the improvement in performance was obvious, with the top speed up from 77-80mph (124-129km/h) to around 85mph (137km/h) and a few seconds shaved off acceleration times from standing start through the gears, even more so the higher the speed. In 1948 the journals had measured 0-70mph (0-113km/h) times averaging 38.8sec; in 1951 this was down to an average 34.7sec, and in 1952 *The Motor* actually measured 29.1sec for a convertible.[2] The more powerful engine and the higher gearing probably cancelled each other out as far as fuel consumption was concerned, and there was also a weight increase

Probably in 1950 or 1951, Sunbeam-Talbot cars including this Mark II Convertible were featured in a Honeyman photo shoot for Vogue *magazine. (Courtesy CTM)*

SUNBEAM-TALBOT & ALPINE IN DETAIL

Typically, there were six cars, four saloons and two convertibles, plus a sectioned unit, squeezed on to the 1950 Motor Show stand. (Courtesy CTM)

claimed to be "no more than 84lb" (38kg) – in practice at least 100-130lb (45-59kg) – so 21-24mpg was still the norm.

The Autocar was generous in praising the changes: "General handling is markedly improved over that of the earlier model. With the new suspension the wheels feel better tied down to the road, and the steering has gained in accuracy, and the car feels safe at speed. A still more positive feel in the steering would be appreciated, however. It is lower geared than is ideal for precision", and *The Motor* also found that steering "feel is somewhat disappointing." They concentrated on the improved ride comfort offered by the new suspension, perhaps understandable since much of their test was carried out on *pavé* roads in Flanders, and in the depths of winter, which led to a eulogy in praise of the heating equipment. The only snag was that the driver's right foot was rather left out in the cold, and *The Motor* made a similar comment in the later test of a convertible; this was LHP 988, chassis number A3004927HCO. Here the steering came in for further criticism: "frankly, [it] is not up to the same high level as other performance characteristics, there being a distinct deadness which, coupled with some springiness in the linkage, makes steering a conscious function under certain conditions."[3]

The gear change still met with approval but *The Motor* commented that it was "unfortunate… that the steering column gear control is not arranged in accordance with the internationally accepted standard so far as gear positions are concerned." In the later convertible test, they did however make amends: "the standard set is appreciably higher than that of many contemporary cars." *The Autocar* felt that "Operation of the steering-column gear change is quite good of its kind for general purposes, though it does not lend itself well to really fast

A nice publicity shot of a 1950-51 Mark II saloon. (Courtesy Leon Gibbs)

90

changing" and Bill Boddy in *Motor Sport* thought it was "quite nice".[4]

The slightly curmudgeonly road tester in the Scottish *Motor World* begged to differ: "The under-wheel gear change is not so light as on other cars of the Rootes Group, neither does it give a rapid change." This however was his only serious criticism. "RNC" in *Motor Industry* struck a similar note: "The gear change on the steering column is light but on a sports car of this type the majority of drivers prefer the now old-fashioned short central lever. As the handbrake is in this position, and separate seats are provided, there seems to be no reason why this type of simple and effective lever could not be used. A fly-off handbrake could be accommodated elsewhere." While it was generally acknowledged that the 90 was a sporting car, a fly-off handbrake was probably too much to expect from Rootes, and floor-mounted gear levers were equally off the corporate menu.[5]

Douglas Clease of *The Autocar*, who had competed in a 90 in the 1949 Alpine Rally, now used a 90 Mark II convertible (KNX 606, chassis A3000022HCO) to cover the same event for his magazine in July 1951 and afterwards wrote of the car in glowing terms: "Between the earlier models and the present version… there is no comparison. Climbs which were hard going in 1949… were romped up in the 1951 edition. Descents were easier and faster, too, the brakes being more adequate, the steering lighter and more decisive."[6]

In the USA, G Thatcher Darwin of *Motor Trend* borrowed a 90 Mark II convertible which was the personal car of Timothy Rootes, Sir Reginald's son, who in 1951 was the company's regional director on the West Coast, operating out of an office in Beverly Hills. Based on the rally successes of the make, Darwin expected "a vehicle with all the gentle attributes of an army bulldozer" so was pleasantly surprised "to discover instead a trim convertible… with very attractive lines". He was impressed by the combination of comfort and performance, and praised the suspension, steering and brakes, but found that "the transmission control… [was] quite stiff going into and out of low gear." Average top speed was 81.08mph (130.49km/h) with a one-way best run of 84.34mph (135.73km/h), very similar to the figures measured by British journals.[7]

Of notable owners, first mention must go to Sir William and Sir Reginald Rootes, who in February 1951 took delivery of a new Mark II each. William had a Satin Bronze saloon chassis A3000315HSO, and Reginald a Gunmetal convertible chassis A3000316HCO, "for Lady N Rootes", his wife. They were registered under KHP 703 and KHP 704 respectively. The famous comedian Arthur Askey had chassis number A3000293HSO, while A3002007HSO went to

If the registration mark KYO 104 is real on this Mark II convertible it must be quite an early car of its type, built in 1950. (Courtesy Leon Gibbs)

SUNBEAM-TALBOT & ALPINE IN DETAIL

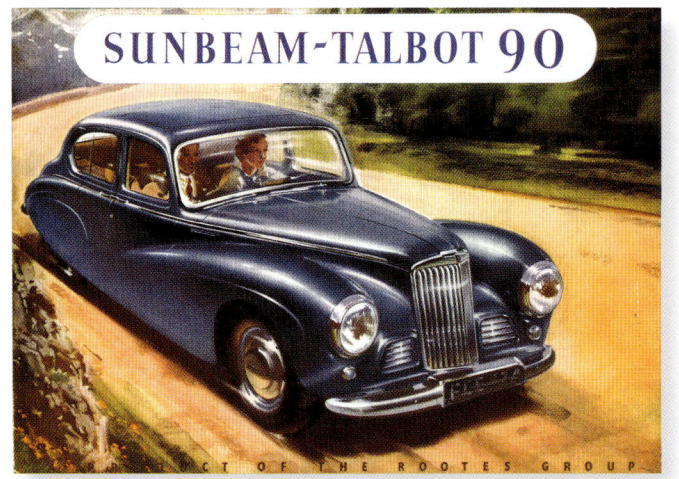

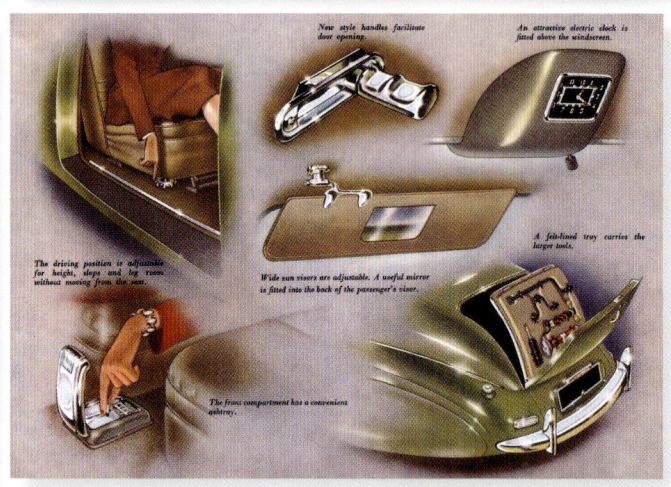

Artist's impression of side view of saloon, used in the Mark II brochure. This rendering is better than the one used in the 1949 advertisement seen in the previous chapter.

Among the new features on the Mark II were the interior door handles, and the clock positioned above the windscreen.

The brochure artwork of the chassis had to be much modified for the Mark II, and now showed the independent front suspension as well as the cross-bracing of the chassis, and of course the 90 engine.

The major improvement over the Mark I was the independent front suspension with unequal length wishbones and coil springs.

92

The brochure illustrations consistently exaggerated the rear seat room, as will be evident by comparing with photos elsewhere in this book. (Courtesy Leon Gibbs)

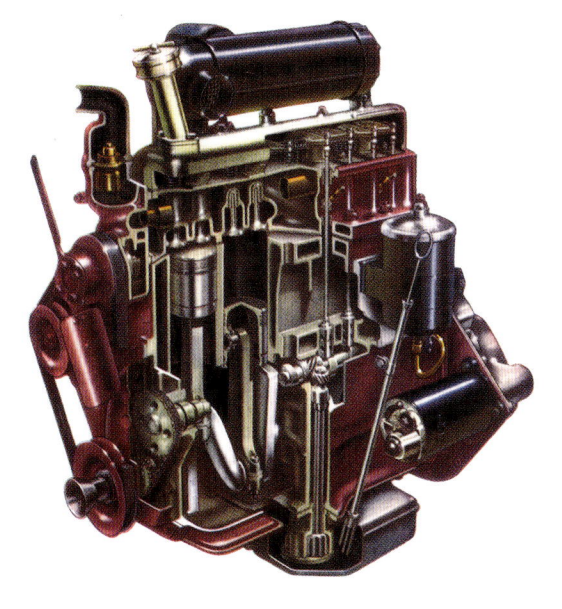

The sectioned Mark II engine drawing from the Mark II brochure shows most of the important features of the design, and gives a good idea of the undersquare cylinder dimensions.

Quite early in Mark II production, if not from the start, a water temperature gauge was added to the instrument cluster. On this car, there also seems to be a non-standard map light under the edge of the dashboard. (Courtesy Leon Gibbs)

Lord Tedder, Marshal of the Royal Air Force who as Eisenhower's deputy had received the German surrender in 1945. He later became chairman of Standard-Triumph and was involved in the abortive 1955 talks about a merger between this company and Rootes.[8]

A number of cars were sold to members of the aristocracy. A3005843HSO was owned by the Duchess of Westminster; it is not clear whether this was "Nancy", the second Duke's fourth wife (born Anne Winifred Sullivan, 1915-2003), who later owned the famed steeplechaser Arkle, or the Duke's third wife Loelia (born Ponsonby, 1902-93), author of the memoir *Grace and Favour*. A3007884HCO was owned by Lady Brocket (1906-75), grandmother of the third Lord Brocket, the classic car collector who turned insurance fraudster.

A3008050HCO was owned by Lady Elizabeth Montagu (1917-2006), daughter of the ninth Earl of Sandwich who became a celebrated novelist in the 1950s: "Montagu had great style: she tore around in a yellow open-top Sunbeam."[9] A3009660HSO was owned by the seventh Earl of Wilton, Seymour John Egerton (1921-99), some time owner of Ramsbury Manor in Wiltshire, which he sold to Sir William Rootes in 1958.

Among company owners were Dunlop, Tecalemit, Smith & Sons (the instrument makers), GKN, Vandervell (bearings), Alfred Herbert, the Coventry machine tool maker, and the *Daily Herald*. A3007461HSO was bought by Temple Press Ltd, the publishers of *The Motor* magazine. The West Suffolk Constabulary had two saloons and the Lanarkshire Fire Brigade had one; this, too, was Black! Coventry City Police bought a black convertible A3009137HCO registered MHP 402 in July 1952. A3008611HSO went to Ferodo of Chapel-en-le-Frith and is likely to have been registered MVM 797, the test car that they entered in the 1952 Alpine Rally and the 1953 Monte Carlo Rally.

A number of other private rally cars can again be identified in the sales records. A3003140HSO went to Dr AW Lilley in Cheshire and was

On the Mark II and later models, the interior door releases are sliding catches at the front, and there are normal winders for the drop glasses. Front doors have these useful pockets. The front quarter lights on convertibles are fixed.

The spats slot into the rear wheel arch at the front and are held by a single fastener at the rear, and the built-in trafficator can also be seen here.

The new front end of the Mark II was considered to be an improvement over the original. This convertible has its hood folded back in the "de ville" position.

DEVELOPING A WINNER

From this angle, the Mark II is all but identical to its predecessor. The spats which were fitted until 1952 suit the shape of the car well. The rear window in this convertible hood may be larger than the original. This car again has modernized rear lighting.

A detail of the hood partly folded back, where it is held in place by two straps. The convertible has chrome-plated window frames attached to the drop glasses.

To get access to the spare wheel, you need to unlock the number plate panel with this coach key.

95

A vanity mirror was usually found on the back of the passenger sun visor, while this 1952 convertible has the clock built into the rear view mirror…

…since the clock in the instrument cluster has been replaced by this water temperature gauge, which oddly enough is marked only in Fahrenheit, and not Centigrade as well, whereas other instruments have both Imperial and Metric markings. Instrument dials were now black.

This is the boxed tool kit that lives in the cubby hole in the foot well.

Seat trims were revised on the Mark II, with vertical flutes for the seat backs. The front passenger got an armrest. This car has a not uncommon floor change conversion, and a rev counter has been added – not a Sunbeam-Talbot instrument but in the central position below the dashboard as on the 1953-54 Alpines.

DEVELOPING A WINNER

The 90 Mark II under-bonnet view will be more familiar to Sunbeam-Talbot enthusiasts. The inlet manifold is divided internally. The heater blower in the foreground takes in air from the right-hand side grille, while the air cleaner is connected to the left-hand grille.

The rear seat on a convertible is a little narrower than on a saloon. The new-style seat trim is evident. Note the position of the interior lamp, and the winder for the rear quarter light.

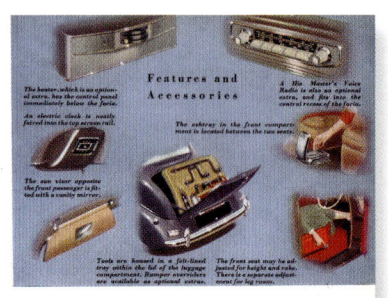

The Mark IIA brochure published in late 1952 used rather impressionistic renderings of the cars, but this convertible looked quite effective against a motor racing background. The vignette of the interior was more accurate, probably drawn from a photograph.

presumably his rally car NTC 400. A3004366HSO was owned by Sir Charles Kimber (1912-2008), the mildly eccentric Baronet, who used this car registered FBW 545 in national rallies in 1954-55. RW Merrick of Birmingham had A3004598HSO which was probably his rally car registered LOV 4 and which he used on three successive Monte Carlos from 1952 to 1954, and Alan Fraser in Kent had a convertible, A3004886HCO, although this does not appear to be his rally car MEL 63 which was a saloon. A3004906HSO registered LLJ 900 was rallied by George Hartwell and Dr Slatter. F Downs of Andover had A3004959HSO, which must have been JOU 898 with which he won the 1953 MCC Rally.

That the 90 appealed to those of sporting inclination who might seek to improve the performance of their cars was confirmed when in early 1952, the Rootes agent (and rally driver) George Hartwell of Bournemouth offered a range of tuning kits for the model. The Stage I kit included a modified cylinder head with a 7.24:1 compression ratio and a few other changes which resulted in 77bhp at 4500rpm. Stage II involved more extensive engine modifications including a lighter flywheel and the compression ratio was raised to 7.5:1, with an output of 80bhp at 4700rpm. On a Stage III engine there were in addition special cast-alloy inlet manifolds and two downdraught carburettors, producing 84bhp at 4800rpm; this would make the car go from 0-50mph (80km/h) in 9.5sec, compared to the 14-16sec of the standard model. Hartwell also offered a range of speed equipment including close-ratio gears, stiffer springs, special shock absorbers and competition brake linings, and various comfort and coachwork modifications, "even special coachwork". *Motor Sport* already a year earlier had hinted that he was "experimenting with four carburettors on a Sunbeam-Talbot engine and with a three-abreast convertible body on this chassis."[10] (See also chapter 7.)

The next set of official modifications was directly inspired by experiences with the car in rallying. In September 1952, the 90 became the Mark IIA. The most important improvement was that the brake drums were wider, with linings now 2.25in (57mm) rather than 1.75in (44mm), while drum diameter remained at 10in (254mm). The friction area was increased by 28 per cent from 134 to 172sq.in (865 to 1110 sq cm). Brake linings were by Mintex rather than Ferodo as before. At the same time, to improve brake cooling ventilated disc wheels were fitted, and the rear spats were deleted, as they had already often been on rally cars. A higher-geared steering box was fitted, reducing the turns from lock to lock from over three to around 2.5. Mud shields were fitted inside the front wings to protect the steering and gear linkages. A trip meter was added to the speedometer, and interestingly an override for the automatic choke became available as an optional extra. The saloon price was now £865/£1347, but the convertible remained at £895/£1394.

When the Mark IIA saloon MRW 201 (chassis A3009797HSO) was road tested by *The Autocar*,

The colour and composition of this advertisement from September 1951 cannot be faulted, even if the car appears wider and lower than it really is. The mountain background was more than justified in view of the car's successes in the Alpine Rally. The phrase "Craftsman Built" was a recurring theme in publicity. (Courtesy Michael Scott)

Although we see only three cars here, again there were supposedly six cars and a sectioned unit on the 1951 Motor Show stand; it seems less crowded so I guess the stand was bigger than before. (Courtesy CTM)

Pride of place on the 1951 Motor Show stand went to an Ivory convertible, in which these girls from the Windmill Theatre posed during a preview visit. (Courtesy CTM)

curiously enough the mean top speed was only 81.4mph (131km/h), rather less than had been achieved by the Mark II model tested earlier. The performance test was still carried out on Pool petrol. Economy was on the other hand rather better at 28mpg overall, and acceleration times were not much different. "The steering column gear change is an average example of its kind; it is fully able… to cope with 'snatch' changes", and the synchromesh was "effective and seldom beaten". They found some improvement to handling and steering, even if "Rather more pronounced under-steer would perhaps be desired by some drivers… the general precision of the steering enables the car to be placed and to maintain a straight course despite a tendency to deadness. In this respect the current Mark IIA shows appreciable improvement in comparison with earlier versions." The ride was both comfortable and well controlled, with very little in the way of either pitching or roll.[11]

John Eason Gibson road tested a convertible for *Country Life* and agreed with *The Autocar* that the handling of the car had been much improved, specifically "by modifications to the spring rate, the hydraulic damper settings, and the stiffness of the anti-roll bar" – none of which changes had been mentioned in the motoring journals. "Corners could be taken at the fastest possible speed without the car's showing any tendency to roll or wander, and one felt that it could be accurately placed even when one was driving at the limit." He did better than *The Autocar* when it came to top speed, which he measured to 85.8mph (138km/h), and his acceleration times were very similar, but he got an overall fuel consumption of only 23mpg, which he actually felt was very good since he had been driving the car very hard. He added "I should think that if one drove normally the consumption could be considerably improved… I think, however, that few Sunbeam-Talbot owners are likely to drive very slowly."[12]

If any did, they would presumably not have included those Mark IIA owners who used their cars for rallying. Thus the first owner of A3009825HSO was Miss J Slatter of Cirencester and this must have been her rally car registered MLJ 492, which she took on a number of events

LHP 820 was actually issued to one of the works rally saloons in 1950, yet here it has migrated on to a Mark IIA convertible. We can just see what is probably the standard size and shape of the rear window. (Courtesy Leon Gibbs)

As we have seen some Labour politicians before, in the interests of balance here is the Conservative Foreign Secretary Anthony Eden with Sir William Rootes at the 1952 Motor Show. Eden had owned a 3-litre before the war. (Courtesy CTM)

including the 1953 and 1954 Monte Carlo rallies. Another woman rally driver was Guernsey-born Patricia "Tish" Ozanne (1923-2009) who had A3012904HSO, with which she took part in two RAC Rallies, despite apparently never having passed a driving test.[13] In another category of owners unlikely to drive very slowly, the Coventry City Police had a second black convertible A3014045HCO registered OHP 972 in October 1953, as part of an all-Rootes fleet, and the Essex Constabulary had two saloons. Many Police forces apart from the Metropolitan however stuck with their traditional Wolseleys; a 6/80 might not have been as quick as a 90, but it was cheaper and roomier. In fact I think that of the Rootes cars Humbers always did rather better for Police sales.

Sir Alliott Verdon-Roe (1877-1958) owned A3010274HSO. He was a pioneering pilot, said to be the first Englishman to make a powered flight, at Brooklands in 1908. He founded the AVRO aircraft company in 1910, and later Saunders-Roe. He also from time to time dabbled in car design and manufacture, notably with a two-wheeled monocar in the 1920s, an idea he revived with the "Bicar" in 1956. Geraldo Orchestras Ltd owned A3010419HSO; this was the company of the dance band leader Geraldo, alias Gerald Walcan Bright (1904-74).

Of other notable owners, the Viscount and Viscountess of Arbuthnott in Kincardineshire had a matching pair of saloons, A3010663HSO and A3015768HSO, supplied a year apart in June 1953 and June 1954 respectively. John Ogilvy Arbuthnott (1882-1960) was the fourteenth Viscount. The third Earl Kitchener (born

Norman Garrad was of course the sales manager as well as the competitions manager. In 1952 he and Sheila Van Damm got roped in to help out with the Sunbeam-Talbot show and service week at Holmes & Smith, Westcliffe on Sea. Here they are possibly trying to get to terms with the Synchromatic on a left-hand drive sectioned show unit. We can get some idea of the extra complications in the linkage... (Courtesy CTM)

Apart from Hillman Minxes, the West Suffolk Constabulary had these two 90 Mark II saloons in 1952, and ran them without spats. (Courtesy CTM)

The display plinth from the 1951 Motor Show was later installed at Devonshire House, the Rootes showroom in Piccadilly. Here it is occupied by a Mark IIA convertible in 1952. The trophies in the showcase in the background had originally been displayed at Barlby Road; many of these were won by Sunbeams and Talbots in the pre-Rootes days, but Garrad's team would add substantially to the collection. (Courtesy CTM)

A 90 Mark IIA saloon in a typical publicity photo. The registration mark LVC 623 had in fact been issued to a Mark II convertible but the photographers regularly swapped number plates. (Courtesy CTM)

The Coventry Police operated an all-Rootes fleet; barring the motorcycles, I guess. In this 1954 line-up there are two 90 convertibles, five Humbers and three Hillmans. (Courtesy Guy Woodhams)

1919), great-nephew of the famous field marshal, had a convertible, A3011068HCO, and another convertible, A3012203HCO, was supplied through Rootes in Birmingham to TD Rootes who was Timothy David; by 1953 he had returned from the USA to become general manager of Rootes's Birmingham branch.[14]

Iliffe & Sons Ltd, the publishers of *The Autocar* magazine, bought A3014005HSX in November 1953, although it is not clear what was "non-standard" about it, as suggested by the final suffix letter X. An interesting owner was Pedro or Peter, also known as "Bobby", Marquis de Casa Maury (circa 1895-1968). He was a Cuban playboy who had occasionally been an amateur racing driver in his youth. He later founded the Curzon cinema in Mayfair and was a friend of Louis Mountbatten; in 1937 he married Freda Dudley Ward, formerly the mistress of the Prince of Wales, but they divorced in 1954, the year after he bought A3013486HCO. The Hon Mrs David Astor, wife of the editor and publisher of *The Observer*, was the owner of A3014569HSO.

Other well-known owners included Raymond Glendenning, the plummy-voiced BBC sports commentator (1907-74); Charles Hawtrey, the comedy actor who starred in many *Carry On* films (1914-88); Richard Todd, the actor and film star who played the role of Guy Gibson in *The Dam Busters* (born 1919), and Bruce Woodcock, the heavyweight boxer, who was at one time

In the autumn of 1953, Her Majesty Queen Elizabeth II and the Duke of Edinburgh undertook the first major tour of her reign, starting in Bermuda in November, where Rootes seemed to have monopolised the Royal transport, including these three Sunbeam-Talbot convertibles of which two were of the latest Mark IIA model, and the third a little earlier. (Courtesy CTM)

British and empire champion (1921-97).[15] Perhaps the most famous of all owners was Sir Edmund Hilary (1919-2008), the conqueror of Mount Everest, who took delivery of a Mark IIA saloon registered NYO 591 at the end of 1953 and planned to use it for a lecture tour of North America.[16] Sadly I have not found his name in the sales ledger.

After only a year, the 90 Mark IIA was updated yet again. In the meantime the Alpine had been introduced (see chapter 6) with a mildly-tuned 80bhp engine, and in October 1953 the cylinder head from the Alpine with a higher compression ratio of 7.42:1 and other changes was introduced on the 90 saloon and convertible models, for which output was now quoted as 77bhp at 4100rpm, 3bhp less than on the Alpine due to minor variations in specification. A slightly longer drop arm also from the Alpine was fitted, effectively giving a higher-geared steering; however on this point the workshop manual and the contemporary journals do not entirely agree. The revised model had redesigned bumpers where the front number plate now hung below the bumper, and some internal factory documents refer to it as the "Mark IIB".[17] Prices were actually reduced, to £825/£1170 for the saloon and £855/£1212 for

Sir Edmund Hilary bought this Mark IIA at the end of 1953, supposedly for a planned lecture tour of North America; so why did he not have a left-hand drive car? (Courtesy CTM)

Stirling Moss explains the engine of a 1954 Mark IIA to a KLM pilot; who knows, may be the Dutchman was buying this left-hand drive car. (Courtesy CTM)

SUNBEAM-TALBOT & ALPINE IN DETAIL

The biggest visual change on the Mark IIA was that the spats were deleted, and there were new ventilated wheels with smaller hub caps.

The new ventilated wheel, and hub cap with the Talbot crest. Whitewall tyres are a lovely touch on a car of this period.

The correct original tail lamp unit, and a detail of the later type overrider.

DEVELOPING A WINNER

The rear wheel arches in themselves were not changed. This 1954 car displays the later style bumper overriders; they were in fact an optional extra.

With the new bumpers and front number plate, the starting handle hole was hidden behind this cover.

This was the solution adopted for the top hinge of the rear door, very "streamstyled"! We can also see the small overlap of door glass and rear quarter light.

The saloon rear window did not change during the production period; like the windscreen, it uses curved glass.

105

SUNBEAM-TALBOT & ALPINE IN DETAIL

A detail of the steering wheel; it's that Talbot beast again on the horn push. The trafficator switch above and the dip switch below are of identical and rather intricate design.

All cars have the handbrake sensibly mounted between the front seats, with the ashtray set into the low transmission tunnel in front of it.

The choke was automatic on all models before the Mark III but the Mark IIA could be fitted with this override control, here hiding under the steering column where you can't read the instruction labels! Above it to the left is the wiper control, and to the right a Tudor windscreen washer push and the bonnet release.

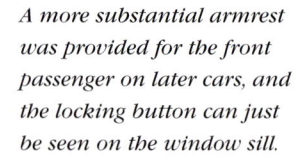

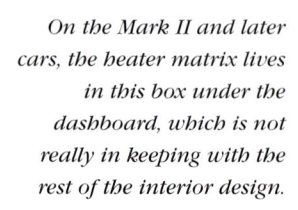

A more substantial armrest was provided for the front passenger on later cars, and the locking button can just be seen on the window sill.

On the Mark II and later cars, the heater matrix lives in this box under the dashboard, which is not really in keeping with the rest of the interior design.

DEVELOPING A WINNER

No real change for the Mark IIA interior, but here we see the oval shape of the mirror – slightly old-fashioned by this time.

As far as they can be traced in the records, these two Mark IIA cars have their genuine registration marks, issued in August 1953 to cars which were part of a batch of works demonstrators. (Courtesy Leon Gibbs)

the convertible, and also benefited from the reduction of Purchase Tax to 50 per cent earlier in the year.

Finally, the process of almost constant development reached its happy conclusion in October 1954, when the Mark III model was introduced. As was already the case for the Alpine, the car was now simply called Sunbeam, and the name Talbot was laid to rest – until briefly brought back in the 1980s under the Peugeot regime. The 90 designation had also disappeared. The Mark III could immediately be identified by its new front end where bigger side grilles surrounded the side lamps, which now incorporated flashing direction indicators. The wheels were fitted with slotted wheel discs, which were supposed to assist brake cooling; one wonders whether they did.

Then a set of three Buick-like portholes appeared on either side of the bonnet towards the rear. They were intended to let hot air escape from the engine compartment, something the bonnet louvres on the Alpine had failed to do. The portholes displaced the model script, which was replaced by a shield-shaped badge at bottom rear of the front wing, where the words "Rootes Group" and "Sunbeam" appeared together with the old *Talbot* crest! This was also still found on the radiator badge, on which the Sunbeam name now appeared twice, as already seen on the Alpine.

Mechanically, the cylinder head was now the same as that used on the new ohv Humber Hawk, with eight ports and larger inlet valves, but the compression ratio of 7.5:1 was higher than the Hawk, which had 7.42:1, and there was a corresponding increase in power output to 80bhp at 4400rpm. There was a new Zenith Stromberg D1 36 carburettor with a manual choke. A Laycock de Normanville overdrive could now be fitted as an optional extra, and overdrive cars had a shorter prop shaft, as well as a lower final drive ratio of 4.22:1. The overdrive was engaged electrically and operated only on top gear; with a 28 per cent reduction ratio it gave an overall ratio of 3.28:1 in overdrive top. The switch was on the steering wheel boss, finally displacing the time-honoured dipswitch to the floor, where it was built into the driver's left foot rest.

The dashboard layout was re-arranged to give space for a centrally-placed rev counter. By now standard on the Alpine, it was an option on the Mark III, and if not fitted, the space was covered by a circular blanking plate with a central S motif. There were centre and side armrests for the front seats, which featured more curved backrests for greater lateral support. Two-speed self-parking wipers were fitted. The prices were further reduced, so that a saloon now cost £795/£1127 and the convertible £845/£1198, with in either case £45/£64 extra for the overdrive. The heater was still an extra, as was the radio, and the options list now also included a windscreen washer.

The new model was road tested by *The Autocar* and *The Motor*. Both journals used PRW 318 (chassis A3500132HSO). It was fitted with the overdrive, which *The Autocar* praised, while at the same time expressing regret that the lower final drive ratio "reduces the third gear maximum to a little over 60mph [97km/h], and it would be better if a little higher speed could be used in that gear." The gear change still passed muster, as did the handling, steering and brakes. When it came to packaging, the goal posts had apparently moved slightly, since *The Autocar* observed that "In designing the Sunbeam, the aim has been to provide a car with good all-round performance and compact overall dimensions – as a result there is less passenger space than in some saloon cars of comparable engine size." It was noted that the clock was now illuminated.[18]

The Motor took the car to Italy for their visit to the Turin Motor Show and covered altogether more than 2000 miles (3200km). It opened its road test report by a comparison of the performance of the Mark III with the earlier Sunbeam-Talbot 90s, to demonstrate "the sensible benefits which can be derived from constant attention to the details of a design" while "running in international rallies… is also a powerful stimulus towards developments which will enhance roadworthiness and all-round performance."

It was only four years earlier that *The Motor* had praised the handsome styling, but now, like *The Autocar*, they found aspects of the car old-fashioned, such as the bonnet "which is high and rather long by modern standards" while "the luggage locker is of smaller capacity than is normally to be found on a car of this size and price" and "the steering wheel is rather nearer to the chest than is desirable", but another traditional feature, the sliding roof, now acknowledged to be a rarity, was found "exceedingly useful… particularly valuable when touring". They summed up, "the basic layout of the car itself falls in some particulars behind the times. Those who have experienced… the latest cars would certainly find as a first impression that the body interior of the Sunbeam Mark III seems narrow, the scuttle high, the window area limited, and the doors exiguous." *Exiguous* by the way means "scanty or slender; meagre". Somehow I don't think that this is a word you would find in many road tests these days!

Bill Boddy found very little to criticize in his report on PRW 318 in *Motor Sport*. He acknowledged that the car was really only a four-seater, with indeed not too much room in the rear seat, and the door area was somewhat cramped, not to say exiguous, but he felt that the boot was reasonably large. The 10-gallon (45-litre) fuel tank, on the other hand, was insufficient for high-speed long-distance motoring, when fuel consumption fell to around 15mpg, but the performance and handling of the car encouraged fast driving. Boddy was especially lavish in his praise of the handling, which in turn was described as "safe", "vice-free", "truly excellent"

This Mark III brochure, issued at the end of 1955, featured the new two-tone colour schemes which were then being introduced on production models, and naturally the Monte Carlo win was given a prominent mention

PWK 605 was one of the final batch of Mark III works rally cars, built in late 1954. It was Peter Harper's car in 1955 and 1956; he finished third overall in the 1956 Monte Carlo rally. Oversize rain/snow/bug deflectors were all the rage at the time!

The radiator badge on the Mark III was changed, as it already had been on the Alpine. As "supreme" as ever, clearly the car was now so good they had to name it twice…

…but instead there were new badges at the bottom of the front wings. Like the radiator badge they still displayed the Talbot crest, regardless of the fact that the car was no longer a Talbot

These portholes appeared on either side of the Mark III scuttle, displacing the name and model script…

DEVELOPING A WINNER

This rear view of the Mark III shows up the rear jacking points particularly well, and it is just possible to make out the name on the number plate lamp housing which is now simply "Sunbeam". On these later cars the tail lamps incorporated flashing indicators, and the reversing lamp was built into the number plate lamp housing.

111

SUNBEAM-TALBOT & ALPINE IN DETAIL

The internal rear door releases are the same sliding type as found on the front doors, again with a locking button on the window sill above.

The driver's door on the rally car has not only the large armrest but a knee pad.

This gives some idea of how high the rear seat is relative to the front seats, and in the roof above can be seen one of the two channels where the sunroof slides back in full view.

The clock was in this position above the windscreen from 1951 onwards, and the sunroof was standard equipment on all saloons.

112

DEVELOPING A WINNER

There was a new horn push on the Mark III with a larger badge, and the switch below it operated the overdrive if this was fitted; the dip switch was now floor-mounted. No rev counter on this car but another extra instrument, while the Halda speed pilot below the glove box is rally equipment, like the additional electric demisters for the windscreen.

Generally on Mark III cars, the front seat backrests were more curved, but this reclining passenger seat with a headrest is special rally equipment. The cut-outs in the seat backs are there to accommodate a removable centre armrest.

SUNBEAM-TALBOT & ALPINE IN DETAIL

Very little changed under the bonnet of the Mark III but a new rocker cover with transverse flutes is a recognition point. The ventilated box at bottom right is the radio receiver and amplifier.

That the Mark III engine had a new eight-port cylinder head may not be obvious, but from this side the new four-branch inlet manifold can just be made out.

The larger tools are fitted in a felt-lined compartment within the thickness of the boot lid, including the enormously long starting handle, wheel brace, foot pump, jack and grease gun.

The boot was never very roomy, and was increasingly criticized towards the end of production. Finish is rather stark, but at least there is a rubber mat for the floor.

and "very impressive", while brakes and steering also got full marks. "An enterprising driver will like the Sunbeam better and better the faster he drives it… it becomes more endearing the further and faster it is driven… It is a saloon car you really can throw about… [it is] a very fast car from place to place".[19]

According to all of the road tests, the Mark III was easily capable of over 90mph (145km/h), Eason Gibson in *Country Life* even measured 94.5mph (152.1km/h) in direct top and 95.8mph (154.2km/h) in overdrive, a useful improvement over previous models, and its acceleration was similarly improved, both in gear and through the gears.[20] Despite the overdrive, fuel consumption was no better than that of earlier cars, even worse according to some testers, but it is evident that Bill Boddy, and probably his fellow journalists, preferred to exploit the performance in full rather than trickle along in overdrive. Boddy stated that the overdrive was "really an economy gear, as it kills performance under the give-and-take of English roads." He went on to suggest that appreciable use of the overdrive would "lift the fuel consumption above 20mpg", so economy was obviously a relative term. It is an interesting reflection on prevailing standards fifty-odd years ago that 30mpg was considered an excellent figure for a 1.5-litre family car with a top speed around 75mph (121km/h).

There was a final face-lift to come. At the 1955 Motor Show which also saw the debut of the Rapier, the Mark III saloon – the convertible had been discontinued that summer – appeared in a choice of additional two-tone colour schemes, divided along the waistline chrome strip. Rootes had begun to adopt the then-fashionable two-toning with the Minx-based Californian hard top coupé in 1953 and it now spread to other models. They actually called it the "Gay Look"… On the Sunbeam, the choice was quoted as Cactus Green over Pine Green, with Light Green trim; Dawn Mist over Corinth Blue, with Blue Grey trim; or Dove Grey over Claret, with Ascot Grey trim (a few other combinations are found in the sales ledgers). Embassy Black, Claret or Thistle Grey monotones were also available, but the last of the classic metallic finishes had disappeared. The basic price was now £835 and with an increase in Purchase Tax, by November 1955 the retail price had gone up to £1254.

Quite soon into the Mark III production run, the practice of writing the owners' names in the sales ledger was discontinued, but it is worth noting that Lady Rootes (but which one?) had A3500351HSO registered PWK 549; Lord Willingdon had A3502087HSO registered RHP 966, his third 90; and the Coventry City Police had A3505000HSO, registered TVC 14.

The Mark III survived for another year or so, and the price saw a final reduction in September 1956 to £765/£1149. Saloon production finally came to an end in December 1956, by which time the car had almost become a classic in its own lifetime. It still had a market niche and a following, and continued to be rallied almost to

In the 1955-56 Mark III brochure, the dashboard illustration showed a car equipped with both the rev counter and overdrive.

the end. There is however ample evidence in the sales ledgers that the last cars took an awfully long time to sell, with many cars only being despatched in 1957 and new cars being available from stock for most of that year. After production had ended, in 1957 the magazines carried news of a special model, called the Mark IIIS, which had a floor-mounted gear lever. In fact these were private conversions by the Rootes dealer Castles of Leicester – one way of using up unsold stock.

Initially, for £22 10s Castles had supplied a kit to convert both the Mark III and earlier models to floor change. The full-blown Mark IIIS followed a little later. This model also incorporated a tuned engine with an 8:1 compression ratio, a Stromberg D1 42 carburettor, and a claimed 92bhp; this seems to be the specification of the tuning kit offered by Rootes generally for Mark III and Alpine models, discussed in the chapter on the Alpine. The overdrive, heater, and windscreen washer were all standard, and so was a Halda Speed Pilot, which usurped the position of the rev counter. Externally the cars could be identified by an air intake on top of the bonnet, while the boot lid was hinged at the top. The car was described as "not a conversion applied to existing models… [but] an additional new model produced with the full co-operation of the Rootes Group", which must have rung a little hollow with those who knew that production had ceased. The price quoted including Purchase Tax was a steep-ish £1350 when the final list price for a standard Mark III had been reduced to £1149 and £1465 would buy you a 2.4-litre Jaguar. Michael Sedgwick suggests that some 30 cars were converted to this specification, a figure which is difficult to verify from the sales ledger.[21]

In later years, the Sunbeam-Talbot and the Mark III sold predominantly in the home market. In the previous chapter, I quoted export and sales figures for the USA which in 1953-54 are likely to include more Alpines than saloons. Similar comparisons between exports and sales are also available for the Australian and New Zealand markets, which over the years were the second and fourth best markets; Switzerland came in as number three but took relatively few

Of course Sheila Van Damm drove Sunbeam-Talbots privately. Her Mark III saloon registered PWK 396 was built in September 1954 and was an early two-tone car, finished in Crystal Green and Dark Green, here with Sheila at her place of work, the Windmill Theatre in Soho. (Courtesy CTM)

cars after 1951. The figures for Australia dropped dramatically after 1951 as the Australian government introduced significantly higher tariffs on fully-assembled cars in 1952 to protect their own emergent car industry, in other words the Holden. Foreign manufacturers were encouraged to set up plants for local assembly of CKD (Completely Knocked Down) cars with increasing Australian content, and while Rootes did so they concentrated on the Hillman Minx. There were also import restrictions in New Zealand but the figures which are available suggest that in 1951 Rootes made a large batch of CKD kits for this market which fuelled their sales through 1952. Admittedly, I have not found any CKD cars in the sales ledgers but I speculate that such cars, if they existed, had a different chassis number series.

The 90 seems to have been well liked in Australia. The New South Wales magazine *Wheels* carried out a road test of a Mark IIA saloon in 1954, this model at that time costing £1598 in Sydney. Their comments broadly speaking echo those of British road testers, but the steering was criticized for its heaviness and its strong self-centring action. The car was summed up as "A specialist's four-passenger touring saloon with high performance" and was equally praised for its docility in city traffic and its capability for comfortable long-distance touring, described as "a real ten hours to Melbourne job"; the distance from Sydney to

Exports to, and sales in, Australia and New Zealand, 1947-54[22]

	1947	1948	1949	1950	1951	1952	1953	1954	Total
Exports to Australia	114	232	434	164	333	76	57	97	1507
Actual sales in Australia	17	291	343	262	157	145	116	89	1420
Exports to New Zealand	30	9	1	12	358	25	5	38	478
Actual sales in New Zealand	4	22	5	15	144	230	15	38	473

Melbourne is now quoted as 882 kilometres or 548 miles but I do not think there were any motorways in 1954. Mean top speed was measured at 84.5mph (136km/h) with a "highest recorded" of 92mph (148km/h) which may have been a speedometer reading.[23]

The lineage that had begun with the Talbot Ten in 1935 effectively came to an end in 1956-57. The final Mark III had become a far better car than any of its predecessors and still had many attractions for the enthusiast, but the styling and more pertinently the packaging were now out-of-date. The Rapier (which I shall discuss in a later chapter) was a successor, but not really a replacement.

At the 1956 Motor Show the Sunbeam stand was not surprisingly dominated by Rapiers at their second show, but there was also a single Mark III saloon making its final Earls Court appearance. (Courtesy CTM)

Comparative performance figures for Sunbeam-Talbot 90 Mark II and Sunbeam Mark III:

	Weight	Top speed	0-50mph (0-80km/h)	10-30mph on third	20-40mph on top	Standing ¼ mile	Fuel cons.
Mk II							
The Motor 7 Feb 1951	3052lb (1386kg)	84.5mph (136km/h)	14.6sec	7.1sec	11.7sec	22.4sec	23.7mpg
Mk II							
The Autocar 23 Feb 1951	3068lb (1393kg)	86mph (138km/h)	16sec	8.2sec	11.8sec	n/q	21-24mpg
Mk II conv.							
The Motor 9 Jan 1952	3052lb (1386kg)	85.2mph (137km/h)	13.9sec	8.0sec	12.9sec	22.2sec	22.5mpg
Mk IIA							
The Autocar 6 Mar 1953	3122lb (1417kg)	81.4mph (131km/h)	14.4sec	7.7sec	12.1sec	22.2sec	28.1mpg
Mk III o/d							
The Autocar 11 Mar 1955	3122lb (1417kg)	91.12mph (147km/h)	12.6sec	7.3sec	11.4sec	21.4sec	20.8mpg
Mk III o/d							
The Motor 25 May 1955	3108lb (1411kg)	93.6mph (151km/h)	12.4sec	6.5sec	10.1sec	21.2sec	22.1-24mpg

1. *The Motor* 20 Sep 1950, 7 Feb 1951
2. *The Motor* 9 Jan 1952
3. Quotes from *The Autocar* 23 Feb 1951; *The Motor* 7 Feb 1951, 9 Jan 1952
4. *Motor Sport* Jul 1951
5. *Motor World* 22 Jun 1951; *Motor Industry* May 1951
6. *The Autocar* 10 Aug 1951; also quoted in Robson *Rootes Maestros* p.28
7. "Sports Trial" in *Motor Trend* Jul 1951
8. Bullock *Rootes Brothers* pp.200-02
9. Obituary in *The Times* 10 Feb 2006; her car was actually Bronze
10. *Motor Sport* May 1952 for Hartwell tuning kits; ditto Apr 1951
11. *The Autocar* 6 Mar 1953
12. *Country Life* 18 Jun 1953
13. Obituary in *The Times* 7 Mar 2009
14. *Who's Who in the Motor and Commercial Vehicle Industries* (1965 ed.) p.512
15. Information courtesy of Leon Gibbs
16. Photos in Coventry Transport Museum archive
17. Files of chassis numbers in ditto
18. *The Autocar* 11 Mar 1955; *The Motor* 25 May 1955
19. *Motor Sport* Aug 1955
20. *Country Life* 2 Jun 1955
21. *Autosport* 25 Jan 1957; *The Motor* 30 Jan 1957, 12 Jun 1957; Sedgwick *The Motor Car* 1946-1956 p.222
22. Exports from Nuffield Exports statistics; sales from *The Motor Industry of Great Britain*
23. *Wheels* Oct 1954

Chapter Six

"Bred in the Alps": Sunbeam Alpine

Rootes had no tradition at all for making sports cars, disregarding the Hillman Aero Minx if this qualifies for that description. The last proper sports car from Sunbeam had been the 3-litre of the 1920s, and while there had been Talbot sports cars in pre-Rootes days, they were in a sense the by-products of a range which always concentrated on high-performance touring cars. Indeed, when Rootes brought out their new Talbot and Sunbeam-Talbot cars in the late 1930s, there were amazingly few sports cars on the market. In the popular and affordable sector, the choice was practically between the MG Midget and the SS 100, with Morgan and HRG on the sidelines. Riley, Singer and Triumph all pulled out of the sports car market.

This was to change radically after the Second World War when it was discovered that the American market had a seemingly limitless appetite for British sports cars. The pioneers were MG and Jaguar, but there was a huge gap in the market between, say, a TD and an XK 120, both in Britain and in the USA. Several British manufacturers saw a ready-made opportunity for making sports cars which would out-perform the small MG and come closer to the Jaguar, at a price which was less than an XK and hopefully not totally out of reach for the potential MG buyer. There were a number of surprising entrants in this market sector, some from companies such as Jowett or Daimler which had never before made a sports car. The one factor that they all had in common was that their sponsors entertained high hopes for these cars in the USA.

This is a fascinating photo of an Alpine prototype, if we believe the number plate it is the Jabbeke car, but this picture was taken before that famous run and the wheels and bonnet are different. Unlike some prototype photos published in other books, the car has a rev counter, rear overriders and a fishtail exhaust. It says Sunbeam-Talbot on the number plate lamp housing, and it is of course Garrad on the right, but who is the chap on the left? (Courtesy Leon Gibbs)

The car that begat the Alpine; two shots of the original Hartwell Special taken on the occasion of the Alpine Rally in 1951, showing its many unusual features, as described in the text. (Courtesy CTM)

In the end, the two most successful attempts at bridging the gap between MG and Jaguar came from well-established mass-producers, Austin (BMC) with the Austin-Healey 100, and Standard-Triumph with the Triumph TR2. Both were 1952 Motor Show debutantes, the Austin-Healey 100 simply as the Healey 100 until the deal was done between Donald Healey and Austin's Leonard Lord, the TR2 in half-baked prototype form which needed a lot of sorting to get right. Rootes, however, also wanted a piece of the action. They had enjoyed reasonable success with the Hillman Minx in the American market, but by 1952 the MG was the biggest-selling British car in the USA, and Jaguar was doing similarly well.[1] The simplest answer was to take the most sporting Rootes product, the Sunbeam-Talbot 90, and develop a sports car from it.

So, if it is reasonable to suppose that the impetus for a Rootes sports car came from the American market, the means to achieve the desired goal came from a completely different and perhaps unexpected source. This was the Rootes distributor in Bournemouth, George Hartwell, who had already driven for the Rootes works team in some of their early rally appearances, starting with the 1949 Monte Carlo Rally. In April 1951 *Motor Sport* noted that he had been "experimenting with four carburettors on a Sunbeam-Talbot engine and with a three-abreast convertible body on this chassis."

The multi-carburettor experiment may not have borne fruit – although it is interesting that in the 1951 MCC National Rally, Hartwell is listed as having entered a *supercharged* 90 with which he won his class – but the "three-abreast" convertible did appear. This car was registered under LEL 333 (issued in Bournemouth, 20 March 1951), and was first entered by Hartwell in the 1951 Alpine Rally. He unfortunately retired with broken rear suspension, and the car retired again in the 1952 Alpine, with a broken con rod. LEL 333 was driven by Sherley-Price in

When the Jabbeke car was hoisted off the ferry on arrival in Belgium, it still had the standard windscreen, although the front bumper fairing was already in place. (Courtesy CTM)

The car during the run at Jabbeke, zooming past the timing van of the Belgian automobile club. A coloured version of this image featured on the cover of the one-page leaflet later produced for the Alpine Special. (Courtesy CTM)

the 1953 RAC Rally, when it finished.[2] I should add that it *could* have been LEL 333 which Hartwell raced at Silverstone on 5 May 1951 – none of the contemporary magazines are specific about his car in this race – but it is unlikely that it was LEL which was supercharged for the 1951 MCC Rally, since Hartwell ran in the closed car class in that event.[3]

In the 1953 Alpine Rally, there were two Sunbeam-Talbot "Hartwell coupés", Fraser and Sherley-Price in MRU 666 (Bournemouth, 18 February 1953), and Hartwell himself with Scott in VRE 690, curiously a 1951 Staffordshire registration. That car was also seen at the Ibsley racing circuit together with another Hartwell special, and Alan Fraser did occasionally race such a car at this venue in 1953-54.[4] We have now got three Hartwell specials identified, but it is not known whether there were others. It is unlikely that any more were made after the Alpine became available in 1953. Hartwell later went back to rallying saloons.

It is rather difficult to decide what the first Hartwell car LEL 333 had started life as, and the Bournemouth registration records do not quote chassis numbers. Lewis Garrad, Norman's son, says that it was originally a convertible, which seems logical, but as re-bodied by Hartwell it had some unusual features. It had the body-colour integral windscreen frame of the convertible, and there were quarter lights in the front doors, but these were not quite of the standard shape and size, and remarkably the top line of the front door skins had been re-worked – it was lower but curved up at the front. Even more oddly, the external door handles were sliding catches fitted towards the front of the doors, while later there were additional normal handles at the rear but lower down than on the standard model.[5]

The cockpit was strictly for two, with separate seats and a centre partition, and immediately aft of the seats there was a long tail panel which flowed smoothly all the way down to the rear bumper. Towards the front of this tail panel there was a sizeable boot lid, hinged at the rear; could it have concealed a dickey seat? The bonnet had a front air scoop and louvres towards the rear. By 1953, there was an addi-

In this rear view taken at Jabbeke, Leslie Johnson is at the wheel, Raymond Baxter to the left at the rear of the car, and Sheila Van Damm on the right by the driver's door; it still says Sunbeam-Talbot on the rear of the car. (Courtesy CTM)

The three drivers Johnson, Moss (typically in a woolly hat), and Van Damm gathered over the car at Jabbeke. (Courtesy CTM)

The official time sheet which confirmed that Sheila Van Damm was indeed one fast lady. (Courtesy CTM)

tional fuel filler cap centrally above the rear number plate, suggesting an extra tank. The Hartwell cars never had rear spats, and LEL later acquired the ventilated Mark IIA wheels. There was a large rev. counter in the centre of the dashboard, and Hartwell rallied his cars with additional external trumpet horns.

The second car, MRU 666, was probably chassis A3010159HXO which was despatched to Hartwell in chassis-only form (note the second letter X in the suffix code) on 18 February 1953, the same day that it was registered; by the way, to the best of my belief this was the *only* example of a chassis delivery of any of the Sunbeam-Talbot 80/90/Alpine models. MRU shared most of the features of the first car, including the well-rounded shape of the wind-down door windows. A slightly different car was photographed in mock-up form, and this must surely have been the work of Ted White's styling studio, or possibly Thrupp & Maberly. Compared to the original Hartwell cars the line of the long tail was more elegantly curved, and normal Sunbeam-Talbot door handles were fitted.[6]

There is a reasoned argument for concluding that Rootes saw the original Hartwell car, liked it, and decided to put a modified version into production. Norman Garrad, however, has provided a further insight into the Alpine story. He remembered that the idea of making a sports version of the 90 came out of a "brain-storming" session between him and Rootes directors in New York in 1949, but when Rootes apparently procrastinated, Garrad suggested to Hartwell that he should build a "prototype" *pour encourager les autres*, and LEL was the result.[7]

We must not overlook the possibility that the final styling of the Alpine had some input from the Loewy studios. Langworth tells the story that a scale clay model was prepared by Loewy designers in South Bend, Indiana. As it was urgently required for a viewing by Rootes executives in New York, designer Robert Bourke and a colleague put the model in the back of a Studebaker convertible and set out. Unfortunately, during the journey Bourke's colleague Kurt Boehm was car sick after having had a few beers and as the top was down, some of it blew over the model. They washed it down with beer and then tried to cover up the beer smell with perfume. When Loewy inspected the model before the presentation he commented that it looked fine but smelt a little funny…[8]

Whatever the Loewy clay model looked like, always assuming that it was of an Alpine, there were certainly differences between the original Hartwell cars or the mock-up referred to above, and the final production version. Most prominently the convertible-type windscreen frame was replaced by a slimmer chrome-plated channel frame, and the quarter lights were now fixed to this rather than to the doors. This type of windscreen was readily detachable for competition work if required. The front shut line of the door was more curved, the door top was straight and there were no external handles at all. Loose sliding Perspex side screens were fitted, and the doors were opened in time-honoured sports car fashion by sliding open the side screen and reaching inside for the door release. The boot lid was further back and the tonneau panel consequently longer. It is entirely possible that the overall shape was designed with the memory of the short-lived 1939-40 Sunbeam-Talbot Ten and 2-litre two-seaters in mind.

Rootes awarded the contract for making the Alpine body to Mulliners of Bordesley Green in Birmingham. This company had made some short-run bodies for Hillman and Humber before the war but the Alpine was the only post-war body they supplied to Rootes. Around the same time, Mulliners obtained the contract to supply the TR body to Standard-Triumph, which turned out to be a bigger and more important job. In 1954, Mulliners agreed to undertake new work only for Standard-Triumph, and they were later taken over by this company. The swift demise of the Sunbeam Alpine must therefore have been rather convenient to them! Alpine bodies were in fact based on incomplete units supplied from British Light Steel Pressings, sent up to Birmingham to be finished with their distinctive rear end, and painted and trimmed, before being sent on to Ryton for final assembly. In both 1953 and 1954, there was an Alpine on Mulliners' stand at the Motor Show.

There were comparatively few modifications to the mechanical specification of the 90. The chassis was stiffened up with extra side plates at the front, and there was an additional tubular cross member bolted in below the engine. There were stiffer front springs and a thicker front anti-roll bar, as well as harder shock absorbers. According to *The Autocar*, the ratio of the steering box was altered so the number of turns from lock to lock was reduced from 2.75 to 2.63, but the actual difference seems to have been in the length of the drop arm. A higher compression ratio of 7.42:1 was used, and with other small changes output was up to 80bhp at 4200rpm, with torque of 124lb.ft at 1800rpm. The choke was manual and there was even a manual ignition control.

Other features included a sports ignition coil, a new air cleaner, and a different exhaust silencer. A larger four-row radiator was fitted, and there were two rows of louvres in the bonnet which under normal conditions were blanked off. With the aid of a feather duster, Norman Garrad established that these louvres were of no help at all in helping hot air to escape, which also made nothing of the entertaining suggestion that the rearmost louvres would help to keep the windscreen clear in

The cast and crew moved to Montlhéry the day after the Jabbeke run. Here, Johnson is at the wheel and behind the car are David Humphrey, Sheila Van Damm, Stirling Moss, unidentified, David Hodkin of ERA, Garrad and unidentified. (Courtesy CTM)

No wonder that Stirling Moss jubilantly sent his hat flying in the air while jumping up and down as Johnson brought the car in after its run at Montlhéry. (Courtesy Derek Cook)

SUNBEAM-TALBOT & ALPINE IN DETAIL

Proudly displaying the (reproduction) rally plate and number from the 1954 Alpine Rally, MKV 21 was Stirling Moss's car in the 1953 and 1954 events, and the car in which he won the Gold Cup.

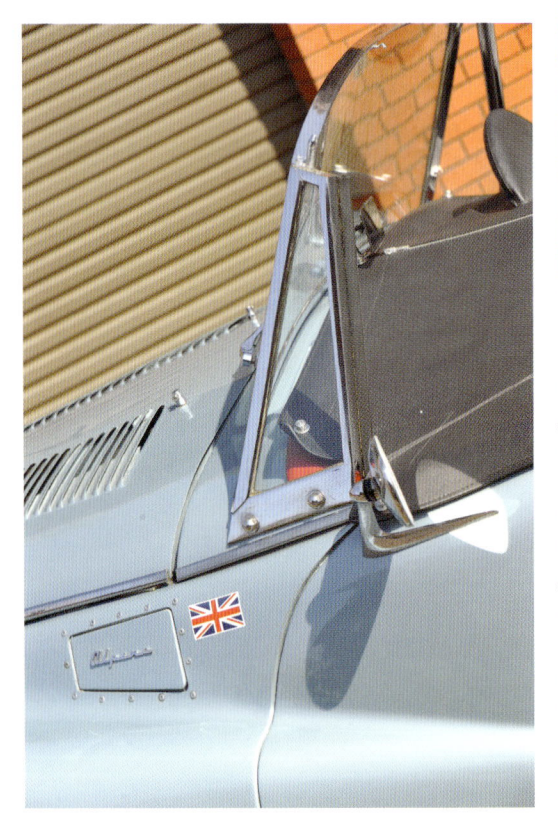

The windscreen is readily detachable, and has these fixed quarter lights attached. This feature meant that the front shut line of the door had to be changed. The ventilation flaps on each side of the scuttle were fitted to the works rally cars to provide air extraction from the engine bay. The Alpine never had portholes but kept its model name script here.

Naturally a cockpit cover was available for the Alpine. On the panel behind are some of the fasteners for the hood.

Even with the hood up and side screens in place, the Alpine loses very little of its elegance. The rally-type side exhaust can just be seen in front of the rear wheel.

The hood on this car has a generously-sized rear window.

Unlike the saloons and convertibles, the Alpine has a top-hinged lid for the boot, which is usefully larger than on the sister cars. Spare wheel accommodation is identical. We can just see the "Sunbeam" name on the number plate lamp housing.

MKV 21 is a very early 1953 Alpine, but this car has the revised dashboard introduced for the 1955 Mark III models, with the minor controls rearranged to provide space for this central rev counter. To the right of this is the manual ignition control found on the Alpine, and the knob below also marked "I" is actually the choke.

The bonnet leather strap was fitted to the works rally cars, but the bonnet was louvred on all Alpines…

…even if the louvres were more for show, since they were normally blanked off as seen here. They were not very efficient anyway.

"BRED IN THE ALPS"

The Alpine speedometer reads to 120mph (or 200kph) and, like all 1953 and later models, has a trip recorder. On the Alpine, the top of the dashboard is padded in leather to match the trim rolls of the cockpit surround.

With the seats tipped up, we get a glimpse into the hood stowage area; the hood frame is attached and moves up and down within a vertical slide on each side. Note the centre armrest which is fixed to the tunnel. The round receptacles on either side just behind the door are for holding thermos flasks and were found on the rally cars.

The simple door trim of the Alpine, with armrest and knee pad as seen on the saloon rally car, a padded trim roll at the top, and the two mounting points for the side screen.

A detail difference is that the glove box on the Alpine is lockable (since the car is not), and the passenger has a grab handle. The extra horn button on the left is rally equipment

127

SUNBEAM-TALBOT & ALPINE IN DETAIL

In addition to MKV 21, Leon Gibbs also owns the sister car MKV 26. It is still being restored and was photographed in chassis form. It has been jury-rigged with a battery, fuel canister, etc, to get it running.

Basically the Alpine chassis is the same as the other models in the range, so all have the chassis passing under the rear axle, with hypoid-bevel final drive and simple leaf spring suspension. Just behind the axle is the Panhard rod. The outriggers in front of the rear wheels serve as body mounting points.

"BRED IN THE ALPS"

On the ignition side of the engine, the mechanical fuel pump combined with a transparent filter bowl is at the front, and the large externally mounted oil filter at the rear. The red-painted frame at the front of the engine is the engine steady which is also found on the convertible; the saloon has a much simpler steady bracket between the rear of the cylinder head and the scuttle.

The actual gear selector mechanism is on the right-hand side of the gearbox, together with the oil filler and dip stick. The brake master cylinder is in the foreground, rather exposed on the outside of the chassis side member and seemingly very close to the outboard exhaust pipe used on the rally cars. The brake fluid reservoir is remote, under the bonnet.

The independent front suspension employs two unequal length wishbones on each side and coil springs, all mounted on a detachable cross member. The front shock absorber is mounted on the chassis behind the suspension unit and is not visible from this angle. The linkage for the anti-roll bar is in front of the coil spring. The steering box is prominent to the right in this photo; it is mounted almost at the front end of the chassis. The steering drop arm points forwards to a transverse drag link which in turn operates a central swinging arm or relay lever which acts on an equally-divided track rod behind the front axle line.

The Rootes Synchromatic gearbox was effectively turned on its side, and this gives some idea of the complex linkage for the column change. This car has an overdrive unit behind the gearbox. To the left of the transmission is the front part of the cruciform box member.

129

One can, on the whole, rather forgive Rootes for putting this stylized imaginary and very dramatic rally scene on the cover of the original Alpine brochure.

winter! Instead, he had rally cars fitted with ventilation flaps on either side of the scuttle, below the rear of the bonnet. The gearbox had slightly closer ratios but of course still the column change. The final drive ratio was the standard 3.9:1 but a 4.22:1 ratio was available, and was fitted to cars with overdrive.

The interior was little changed, except that the top of the facia was padded, the glove box was lockable, and there was a rev. counter which was at first very much an afterthought, fitted in a pod untidily suspended below the centre of the dashboard – and originally quoted as an extra: it was missing from the car road tested by *The Autocar*.[9] The speedometer now read to 120mph. There was a centre armrest and detachable side armrests, and the passenger had a grab handle below the glove box. There was some space behind the seats, where the hood and side screens were stowed, but more importantly the boot was of course much larger than on the 90 saloon, of 14cu.ft (396 litres). The double-texture cotton hood had a rear window which could be zipped out.

Apart from items already mentioned, the list of options included radio, heater, whitewall tyres, tonneau cover, petrol tank filter, badge bar, long-range driving lamp, cigar lighter, exterior mirror, bumper overriders, a half-height racing windscreen and windscreen washer. In addition there were unspecified "kits to provide improved performance" – which just might have had something to do with George Hartwell, see chapter 5 for a discussion of the tuning kits he offered for the 90. It was suggested at the launch of the car that there would be two versions – a standard production model, and a super-tuned model for competition. This came to fruition with the Alpine Special.[10]

The name chosen was a natural, to commemorate the successes of Sunbeam-Talbots in the Alpine Rallies; indeed, "Bred in the Alps" was at one time a by-line in their advertisements. The idea that the new sports model should be called the Alpine apparently came from John Dugdale, formerly of *The Autocar*, now working for Rootes in the USA, who wrote to Brian Rootes making this suggestion.[11] Another piece of the jigsaw puzzle is an internal factory memo from early 1953 which clearly refers to the construction of the two first pre-production Alpines, and where the new model is called the *Chasseur*; did somebody at Rootes with a sense of humour recall the French army's elite mountain infantry, *les Chasseurs Alpins*, the Alpine hunters?[12]

It is perhaps less clear why at this time, in March 1953, Rootes should decide to jettison the Talbot part of the moniker. One possibility is that the Alpine was originally intended for export only, and many markets already knew the cars simply as Sunbeam anyway. Another was that they considered the name Sunbeam to have the stronger heritage for a sports or competition car, or that they felt that "Sunbeam-Talbot Alpine" was a bit of a mouthful – or that they were simply beginning to think of "Talbot" as a model name of Sunbeam. The name change by and large passed without comment, but there were those publications which still managed to refer to the new car as a "Sunbeam-Talbot". *The Autocar* seemed on the whole to approve of the name change, as they wrote that a "famous name assumes a justified appendage".[13]

There was a "teaser" or controlled leak in *The Autocar* a month before the launch, when it was reported "that Sir William Rootes has been showing to interested parties in New York pictures and details of a new Sunbeam-Talbot sports two-seater… which should have a special appeal in North America" and the magazine made a direct connection between the original Hartwell special and the new car.[14] Perhaps as a result of Sir William's visit, *Road and Track* quickly published a slightly exaggerated artist's impression of the new car.[15]

Exactly four weeks later on 20 March 1953,

the Alpine was introduced with a fanfare of publicity, resulting from a prototype being taken across to Belgium for an attempt at a record run on the stretch of motorway near the village of Jabbeke, just inland of Ostend. This had become a favourite spot for British car makers to test their sporting models, ever since Goldie Gardner had first used it in 1948 for a run with his MG EX.135, then fitted with a 2-litre prototype Jaguar XK engine. Jabbeke had seen a run by the prototype Austin-Healey 100 in October 1952 where Donald Healey had recorded 111.7mph (179.8km/h). Apparently Sir William Rootes, not one to miss a trick when it came to publicity, latched on to this and instructed Norman Garrad to do a similar run which had to beat the Healey's speed: the aim was 120mph (193km/h).[16]

To achieve the required 25mph (40km/h) improvement over the top speed of a standard Alpine, Garrad enlisted the help of his friend Leslie Johnson and of David Hodkin, both of ERA. The engine was tuned, with among other changes two twin-choke Solex carburettors, a compression ratio of 8.5:1, a "hotter" camshaft and a four-branch exhaust which pushed power output up to 125bhp. In a "first" for any Rootes car, a Laycock-de-Normanville overdrive was fitted to ensure that the engine would not rev at unhealthy figures at top speed. The car had many aluminium panels including a non-louvred bonnet, doors, and boot lid, and ran without windscreen and front bumper, which was replaced by a shaped panel. A metal cover was fitted over the passenger seat and a wind deflector in front of the driver; a full undershield was fitted, but no rear wheel spats. The overdrive and the body changes probably made the greatest contributions to the eventual result.[17]

For the actual run, Stirling Moss and Leslie Johnson were on hand as drivers, but so was Sheila Van Damm, the up-and-coming woman member of the Rootes rally team (see chapter 7). On 17 March 1953 (which apparently was Garrad's birthday), after running out of petrol on her first attempt, she accomplished a two-way run over the flying kilometre at an average of 120.135mph (193.340km/h), which was a new national Belgian record in the 2- to 3-litre class and gained her the title of the fastest woman in Europe. Stirling and Leslie chivalrously declined the opportunity to improve on her result; Stirling in fact had been slightly faster on an earlier one-way run. Afterwards, the team went on to the Montlhéry race track near Paris, where on the following day Johnson drove for an hour at 111.20mph (178.96km/h) and Moss lapped at 115.85mph (186.44km/h).[18]

After much nail-biting, Garrad's relief at achieving the desired result at Jabbeke must have been enormous, especially as Raymond Baxter was on hand to record the proceedings for the BBC, together with other journalists. The car was a right-hand drive prototype painted light metallic blue (i.e. Alpine Mist) with red wheels and registered MWK 969, which according to the Coventry registration records had chassis number EXP.006/3 and engine number EXP.146. It was sold to ERA in late 1953 and then for many years disappeared in Northern Ireland, but was eventually found in a pitiable state by Graham Wilson in 1969 and restored by him over a ten-year period. He sold it in the mid-1980s and MWK 969 now survives in Switzerland, having been restored as near as possible back to Jabbeke specification.[19]

Unfortunately for Sunbeam, in May 1953 Ken Richardson in a specially modified prototype Triumph TR2 recorded a speed of 124.095mph (199.712km/h) over the same stretch of hard-used Belgian motorway, which was a world speed record for a 2-litre production sports car. Since the Alpine's engine was over 2 litres, the Triumph run at least left the Alpine's record intact! Of course the top speed of a normal

The official debut of the Alpine followed at the 1953 New York motor show, where Lord Montagu of Beaulieu stopped by and was photographed in the car surrounded by a bevy of local beauties. According to Rootes, his lordship had just completed a 10,000 mile tour of North America in a Humber Hawk. Note the half-height windscreen and the covers over the trafficator slots. (Courtesy CTM)

SUNBEAM-TALBOT & ALPINE IN DETAIL

I think this publicity photo of a "fake" MWK 969 with left-hand drive and racing windscreen is faintly comical. "Bye-bye, dear, have a nice day at the office." Or at the motor races? This is probably the car displayed at the launch at Devonshire House in London. (Courtesy CTM)

Another picture of the "fake" MWK 969 with left-hand drive but this time the standard windscreen, showing its capacious boot; note the Sunbeam name at the rear, and the added-on rev counter under the dashboard. (Courtesy Derek Cook)

Alpine was at best 95-96mph (153-154.5km/h), that of a TR2 around 103mph (166km/h).

The car that was shown to the press at the launch party at Devonshire House on 20 March was a left-hand drive example, and is likely to have been the same car that figured in the Rootes publicity photos at the time, with whitewall tyres on body-colour wheels, a radio aerial on the left-hand front wing, fitted with the rev. counter and sometimes the half-height racing windscreen. In the photos it bore the number plate MWK 969, to capitalise on the successful record run. At the time, only Bill Boddy in *Motor Sport* chided Rootes for displaying the same number plate on two different cars.[20] The car displayed at the launch and photographed could have been the first production car, chassis A3011393LRX, a left-hand drive export car in Alpine Mist, built in early January and despatched on 26 February 1953; presumably this car eventually went to the USA, as it still exists in that country.

While it has been said that Sir William Rootes took the actual record car to the USA immediately after the Jabbeke run, the car that went to the USA may have been the LHD car with the MWK 969 number plate.[21] It has indeed been speculated that there may have been a few replicas of MWK 969 made for show purposes. It is believed to have been the real MWK 969 that Sheila Van Damm drove for a number of demonstration laps at a Brands Hatch meeting on 17 May 1953; the car was now in standard road trim but still had those red wheels.[22]

Whatever, the new model made its public debut at the New York International Motor Sports Show which opened on 4 April 1953. Sir William, Sir Reginald and Geoffrey Rootes were all in New York for the show. From contemporary reports and photos there were two Alpines on the Rootes stand, one in Ivory (with the half-height racing windscreen) and one in Red. These colours match the fourth and fifth Alpines, A3011908LRX and A3011992LRX, although the latter was only despatched from the factory on 2 April. I have not found any photos showing either the actual or a replica MWK 969 at this show, but a 90 rally car was displayed.[23]

The New York launch was premature as production was rather slow to build up, with substantial numbers only coming off the line towards the end of May and cars being despatched from June onwards. It is likely that there were further delays in distribution in the USA, and my conclusion is that the new model missed the main summer sales season in this market – a stumble which may have proved crucial to its prospects of success. The first six home market cars were built during May and June and were the cars entered for the Alpine Rally, at least three of them being to the "Special" specification (see below), and home market production generally got under way in July.

The new model was politely, if not over-enthusiastically, received in the USA. In summing up, *Road and Track* felt the Alpine offered "an excellent combination of proven durability, more comfort than is usual, excellent quality of finish and reasonable price" – in fact $3000, which was more than the obvious competitors, never mind the fact that the first Ford Thunderbird came on the market in 1955 at just under this figure. *Motor Trend* eventually published a brief road test, in February 1954. Almost the first comment of editor Walt Woron was "I wouldn't make the mistake of calling the Sunbeam Alpine a sports car, and I'm glad that the builders don't either. I think it falls more closely into the touring car category..." He was not happy about the awkward gear change, especially as the 'box needed to be used to get the best performance out of the car, which was "somewhat lacking in power." He criticized the steering which was heavy at low speeds in traffic: once on the move, it was much quicker, fast and precise. He would have liked external push-button door handles. Plus points were flat cornering although the car would break loose a little too soon – around 45mph (72km/h) which sounds rather worrying – the high-speed cruising ability, the good ride, and the comfort, with much praise for the seats. He also liked the amount of luggage space – and the rugged construction coupled with excellent finish.[24]

As the Alpine was initially reserved for export, a home-market price was not quoted at launch in March 1953, although it appeared in the price lists in August 1953 at £895 or £1269 including Purchase Tax. It took even longer for road tests to appear in the British press, *The Motor* in fact never road tested the model and *The Autocar* only published their report on an

The Alpine appeared for a second time at the New York show in 1954, when the American racing drivers and occasional Sunbeam-Talbot rally drivers Sherwood Johnston and John Fitch were photographed sitting in the car, which by now had the new style front bumper. (Courtesy CTM)

This is a simpler and nicer publicity shot and has the advantage that we can identify the car, as the registration mark was issued to an Alpine in August 1953; only thing is, that car was Coronation Red, not Ivory. It still has the early front bumper and overriders. (Courtesy CTM)

"BRED IN THE ALPS"

133

At the Brighton concours in 1954, this Alpine was entered by Harrington, the local Rootes dealer at Hove. Miss Harrington was apparently dressed in colours to match the car. (Courtesy CTM)

At the 1954 Motor Show, where the Mark III made its debut, the only update to the style of the Alpine was the new wheel trims. Two Windmill girls were photographed in the car. (Courtesy CTM)

Alpine (OWK 805, chassis number A3013978HRO) in April 1954. In their view the Alpine was "not an out-and-out sports car, but rather a sports roadster." They praised the refinement and comfort of the car, which had interior fittings "up to a standard generally associated with drophead coupés" rather than sports cars, but pointed out the inevitable concomitant of a weight increase compared with "a more stark vehicle". Actually, the root cause of the Alpine's kerb weight of 2968lb (1347kg) lay not in its fittings and equipment but in the solid construction of its chassis and engine, and its saloon-like dimensions. Both the Austin-Healey 100 and the Triumph TR2 tipped the scales at less than a ton.

With a slight front weight bias, the Alpine was an understeerer; the steering generally merited praise but the large turning circle of 36ft 6in (over 11 metres) was on occasion found inconvenient. There was little roll on corners and the brakes were above reproach. The only adverse comment on the gear change was that "it would be even better if the neutral position were a little more defined" but "The synchromesh is effective and is not easily beaten even if fast gear changes are made." The ride was comfortable, even with tyre pressures increased to 30lb, as recommended for fast driving.

The Autocar took the car to Belgium and measured top speed over the same Jabbeke motorway that had witnessed the model's debut performance. The flat-out top speed of 96mph (154.5km/h) was disappointing compared to the obvious competitors – the Austin-Healey and the Triumph would easily exceed 100mph (161km/h), and both had significantly faster acceleration (see table below) – but *The Autocar* put the best gloss on it by praising the Alpine's ability to cruise at 75-80mph (121-129km/h), "with a useful degree of performance in hand." Fuel consumption of 24.6mpg overall when driven fairly fast was similarly described as "useful" but was higher than the bigger-engined Austin-Healey, and the two TR2s tested by the same magazine got a remarkable 31-32mpg overall.[25]

Rootes had one further shot in its locker and fulfilled the prediction made in *Precision* (see above) that there would be a tuned Alpine for competition. This was the Alpine Special, also described as a replica of the works rally cars. This had a larger twin-choke downdraught carburettor on a special inlet manifold, one side of the carburettor feeding cylinders 1 and 4, the other cylinders 2 and 3. In addition there were enlarged valve ports, bigger inlet valves with stronger valve springs, the compression ratio was raised to 8:1, and a new exhaust manifold and straight-through silencer were fitted. Output went up to 97.5bhp at 4500rpm. Overdrive was standard. An example (OKV 899, chassis number A3015663HROS) was lent to John Bolster of *Autosport*, who recorded a top speed of 104mph (162.5km/h) in overdrive with the ignition fully advanced. However acceleration was still less than competitive, as will be clear from the figures below. There was also a penalty in the form of increased fuel consumption, down to 15.5mpg when driven hard, and Bolster reckoned that 20mpg might be a more typical average for a fast driver.[26]

Bolster declared that the column gear change "was the best example of its type that I have yet encountered" and was generally happy with the car although "The Sunbeam has far greater luxury and is much more heavily constructed than most modern sports cars... its weight prevents the Alpine Special from equalling the acceleration of lighter, super-sporting cars" and he concluded wistfully "Should the manufacturers ever consider building a lighter car, they will at once have a very high performance machine. They already have a most remarkable engine, and if it had a moderate load to pull, it would certainly show most of the others the way." The price of the Alpine Special was £970 plus Purchase Tax of £405 for a total of £1375, but even if this included the overdrive, it was not particularly good value for money in terms of "bang for the buck" – a Jaguar XK two-seater cost around £1600 in 1954 and would easily do over 120mph (over 190km/h).

Unsurprisingly, production of the Alpine

The original exuberant brochure artwork gave way to a much more sober rendering on the front of the leaflet for the 1955 Alpine, although the proportions were a little distorted. (Courtesy Derek Cook)

Comparative performance figures for the Alpine and its main competitors:

	Sunbeam Alpine	Sunbeam Alpine Special	Austin-Healey 100	Triumph TR2	Triumph TR2 hard top with overdrive
Road test	*The Autocar* 23 Apr 1954	*Autosport* 3 Sep 1954	*The Autocar* 11 Sep 1953	*The Autocar* 8 Jan 1954	*The Autocar* 18 Feb 1955
Kerb weight	2968 lb (1347kg)	2884 lb (1309kg)	2100 lb (953kg)	2100 lb (953kg)	2184 lb (992kg)
Top speed	95-96mph (153-154km/h)	104mph (167km/h)	103-108mph (166-174km/h)	103-105mph (166-169km/h)	103-107mph (166-172km/h)
0-50mph	12.9sec	12sec	7.6sec	8.2sec	8.8sec
0-60mph	18.9sec	16.8sec	10.3sec	11.9sec	12.6sec
0-70mph	26.7sec	24sec	13.4sec	15.9sec	17.1sec
Std ¼-mile	21.1sec	20sec	17.5sec	18.7sec	18.8sec
Fuel consumption	24.6mpg overall; range 18-26mpg	Range 15.5-20mpg	24.5mpg overall; range 24-27mpg	32mpg overall; range 28-38mpg	31mpg overall; range 28-38mpg
Price, basic/incl. PT	£895/£1269; later £855/£1212 (including o/d)	£970/£1375 (including o/d)	£750/£1063 (including o/d)	£595/£844 (o/d: £40 extra)	£670/£950 (o/d: £40 extra)

Figures from *The Autocar* have been chosen, where available, in order to be directly comparable with each other, however the only test of the Alpine Special was the one published in *Autosport*. Tests of the Austin-Healey 100 in *The Autocar* and other British magazines were of prototypes or specially tuned lightweight cars, *The Autocar* for instance measured an average top speed of 111mph (178.6km/h) and a one-way best of no less than 119mph (191.5km/h) with driver only and a single aeroscreen; the figures quoted above are their mean and best top speeds with hood and side screens in place, and carrying a passenger. *Road and Track* in July 1954 measured a top speed of 102-106mph (164-171km/h) and slightly slower acceleration than *The Autocar*; their figures are acknowledged by Healey experts to be the most realistic published performance figures for the production 100.[27]

To mark the AA's Golden Jubilee in 1955, there was a parade in Regents Park which included this Alpine. That's Sheila at the wheel, and Norman beside her. (Courtesy CTM)

Special was very limited, and one published figure suggests that only 120 of these cars were made.[28] Having gone through the original sales ledgers, I have found a total of 90 cars with the additional chassis suffix letter S which indicates this model, 43 for the home market, and 47 left-hand drive export cars, of which probably 42 were for North America. Most of these were built in the first half of 1954 and I have not found any Specials in the Mark III chassis number range from 3500001 upwards. It is quite possible that Rootes at this time decided not to persevere with the Special, but I accept that some cars may be missing the S suffix in the records. In support of the lower production figure, I have found an internal factory memo dated 29 March 1954 issued jointly by Hancock and Winter which states that an initial sanction of 25 cars had been released on 5 March, a further sanction of 31 cars was now being released and that the sanction may be closed at 56 cars rather than the 100 cars originally authorised.[29]

When the Sunbeam Mark III saloon was introduced in October 1954, the Alpine also underwent a few minor modifications. While it did not adopt the new radiator side grilles of the saloon, the dashboard was re-arranged to give a central location for a built-in rev. counter which was now standard on this model, the new wheel trims were fitted, and overdrive became standard at least in the home market. The extra equipment notwithstanding, the price was reduced to £855 basic or £1212 including PT, in line with the reduction of the saloon price. The revised 1955 model is usually referred to as the Alpine Mark III. It had a production life of less than twelve months, as it was discontinued in July 1955 around a month after the Mark III convertible. However it continued to figure in the price lists in the weekly magazines until the Rapier was introduced the following October.

For both the Sunbeam Mark III and for the revised Alpine, a tuning kit became available, including a replacement cylinder head, an inlet manifold with separate branches for each cylinder, a new distributor, and a Stromberg D1 42 carburettor. The head had larger inlet ports and the compression ratio was increased from 7.5:1 to 8:1. Power output was up from 80bhp at 4400rpm to 92bhp at 4600-4800rpm, and torque was improved from 124lb.ft at 1800rpm to 130.8lb.ft at 2800rpm. The specification was not quite that of the Special, and the resulting power output was lower. The ignition hand control was no longer a standard fitting but was quoted as a separate extra.

The Alpine did not succeed in establishing

This 1955 Wolverhampton-registered Alpine is not in its first flush of youth but has been included to show that somebody made a purpose-built hard top for the car, with three-piece wraparound rear window. It also has the Mark III-type wheel trims. (Courtesy CTM)

Rootes in the sports car market, despite notching up some excellent results in rallying, appropriately enough in the Alpine Rally from which it had taken its name, as will be recounted in the following chapter. As far as performance was concerned, its weight was a built-in handicap, and its rallying successes owed more to its sheer strength and stamina than to its performance. I feel it had little appeal to those who had cut their teeth on an MG Midget and eyed the Jaguar XK 120 enviously; such drivers were more likely to graduate to an Austin-Healey or a Triumph. However good the steering column change was of its kind (and opinions differed), sports car drivers on either side of the Atlantic expected a central remote lever.

Despite being announced as primarily intended for the North American market, even early in its production life the car failed to catch on in the USA; only 13 were sold in the USA in the first half of 1953 (allegedly 1000 cars had been shipped but this figure must include saloons, see also chapter 4)[30], and total production was less than 1600 cars (see appendix) over a run of little more than two years, from May 1953 to July 1955, far fewer than Austin-Healey or Triumph over the same period. In its favour, the Alpine had the comfort, refinement and equipment of its saloon sister, coupled with a striking and attractive appearance. John Bolster had "never driven any vehicle which excited so much female admiration", helped by the cream and red colour scheme which apparently exuded sex appeal![31]

How important this factor was to Alpine buyers must remain a matter for speculation. Owners of more than usual interest include Lord Trevor (Charles Edwin Hill-Trevor, fourth Baron,

The story here is that in 1955, Dirk Bogarde was making a film called The Naked Flame *which included a car racing sequence, where he was driving an Alpine (Rootes product placement at work again) and Sheila Van Damm was asked to teach him how to drive it. I'd love to know more! (Courtesy CTM)*

This is a lovely shot of a 1954 Alpine in the unusual colour of black, taken by its first owner Patrick Vanson in New York state in 1956. Apart from the obvious extras, he fitted a bonnet leather strap and tells me that his car was in fact a Special. It is part of the story that Mr Vanson now owns another Alpine which he is restoring! (Courtesy Patrick Vanson)

In this studio shot the Alpine has for a change been fitted with aero screens, rather than the half-height windscreen.

1928-97), who had chassis A3013925HRO in Ivory, and the seventh Earl of Lonsdale (James Hugh William Lowther, 1922-2006) with chassis A3013992HRO in Alpine Mist, both in early 1954. This Earl clearly did not share the preference of the famous fifth Earl (his great-uncle) for the colour yellow! Two of the 1955 models also found distinguished owners, A3500983HRO in Severn Blue went to the ninth Earl of Guilford (Edward Francis North, 1933-99), and A3501538HRO registered PKV 940 in Crystal Green to Lady Rootes; but *which* Lady Rootes?

A Sapphire Blue Alpine famously featured in Hitchcock's 1955 film *To Catch a Thief*, driven along mountain roads above the French Riviera by Grace Kelly as the daughter of a wealthy American widow, with Cary Grant as a supposedly reformed ex-jewel thief in the passenger seat. For plot reasons too complicated to go into, this turns into a high-speed attempt at escaping from pursuing Police, during which Kelly handles the Alpine with complete insouciance while Grant grows increasingly tense, until the Police car behind crashes. The Police drove a Citroën Traction Avant: not as quick as the Alpine, but with excellent road holding! So I still wonder how realistic the scenario was – but the point is that the elegant Alpine was the perfect vehicle for the equally elegant Grace Kelly!

---

1. Dugdale *Jaguar in America* p.29
2. Photo in Langworth *Tiger, Alpine, Rapier* p.43
3. Silverstone race: *The Autocar* 20 Apr, 11 May; *Autosport* 4 May, 11 May; *The Motor* 2 May, 9 May; *Motor Sport* Jun 1951; MCC Rally: results in *Autosport* 16 Nov.
4. Information and photo from Chris Derbyshire
5. Bournemouth registration records in Dorset History Centre, Dorchester; Lewis Garrad quoted in Langworth p.46 and Robson *Sunbeam Alpine and Tiger* p.20
6. Photo Frostick *Works Team* p.30
7. Garrad quoted by Graham Wilson, former owner of MWK 969, in *Stardust* no. 111, Apr 1994; also Cook "Sunbeam Alpine at Jabbeke" in *The Automobile* July 2005
8. Langworth p.47
9. *The Autocar* 23 Apr 1954
10. *The Motor* 25 Mar 1953; *Precision* May 1953; a magazine which belied its title by wildly over-estimating the new car's top speed as 120mph
11. Dugdale p.27
12. In file of Sunbeam-Talbot chassis numbers, Coventry Transport Museum archive
13. *The Autocar* 20 Mar 1953; not so Bill Boddy, *Motorsport* May 1953
14. *The Autocar* 20 Feb 1953

15. *Road and Track* Mar 1953
16. Robson *Rootes Maestros* pp.85-92
17. Wilson and Cook, quoted above
18. Van Damm in *Modern Motoring* Jun 1953 and *No Excuses* pp.108-09; Frostick pp.30-32
19. Wilson and Cook, quoted above
20. *Motor Sport* May 1953; Cook, quoted above
21. Van Damm p.109
22. *Motor Sport* Jun 1953; Cook, quoted above
23. John Bentley in *The Autocar* and Ruth Sands Bentley in *Autosport* both 17 Apr 1953; they were of course Mr and Mrs Bentley
24. *Road and Track* Jul 1953; "Driving around with Walt Woron" *Motor Trend* Feb 1954
25. *The Autocar* 23 Apr 1954
26. *Autosport* 3 Sep 1954
27. Piggott *Austin-Healey 100 in Detail* pp.146-49
28. *Beaulieu Encyclopaedia* p.1548
29. In file of Sunbeam-Talbot chassis numbers, Coventry Transport Museum archive
30. *Time* magazine 31 Aug 1953; Langworth p.49 says "by the autumn of 1953"
31. *Autosport*, quoted above

Chapter Seven

Excuses not needed: the competition story

As the manager of the Rootes works rally team, Norman Garrad's standing orders to his drivers were "Keep your mind on the job, the car on the road, and remember – there are no excuses." *No Excuses* therefore was the title adopted by Sheila Van Damm for her memoir of rallying with Rootes, and I make "no excuse" for using a variation for this chapter. The Rootes team indeed had nothing to apologise for, and much to be very proud of.[1]

Norman Garrad (1901-92) was born in Yorkshire of Scottish stock and had begun his career with the Arrol-Johnston company of Dumfries in 1919, but after this company went into liquidation in 1929 he joined Crossley, and soon after Talbot, eventually becoming their sales manager for Scotland. He had already taken part in rallies, trials and even the TT race while with Arrol-Johnston; in fact near the end of his career with Rootes, he reckoned to have taken part in 200 rallies since 1923. His autobiographical fragment suggests that he drove in the Scottish Six-Day Trial where Galloway cars, built by Arrol-Johnston, took part in 1922 and 1924; although Garrad is not listed as an entrant he could well have been a co-driver.[2]

His first experience of a major international rally was in the 1929 Monte Carlo as Leverett's co-driver of an Arrol-Aster. Starting from Riga, they got stuck in the snows of East Prussia. In 1931 Garrad entered a Crossley in the Monte and finished 23rd in the large car class, and appeared with this car in a number of other

Norman Garrad photographed at his desk, probably around 1960. (Courtesy CTM)

events. He was Humfrey Symons's co-driver in a Talbot in the 1931 Alpine, where they won a Glacier Cup, and again in the concours-winning Sunbeam in the 1932 Monte. After this, Symons described Garrad as "one of the finest road drivers I know". Garrad's best-known exploit of this period was that he drove one of the works Talbot 105s (with John Playford as co-driver) in the 1932 Alpine Trial, where the team of three Talbots won an Alpine Cup.[3] As discussed in chapter 2, he became more involved with competition activities after the Rootes takeover. In the post-war period he became sales manager of Sunbeam-Talbot and spent a period in New York helping to set up the American Rootes subsidiary, but continued to run the

Garrad spent many years in retirement in the USA where his son lived, but came back to the UK in the 1980s and was then photographed with a Mark III. (Courtesy Chris Bryant)

competitions department.

To the young and impressionable Sheila Van Damm, "he was one of the most experienced rally drivers in the country... Tall and broad-shouldered, with a face like a boxer... with a pair of cold blue eyes": a pardonable expression of hero-worship. Garrad in fact was of medium height with a receding hairline and tended towards portliness – he was after all in his fifties – but his nose at least could have graced the face of a boxer! Incidentally, Garrad later returned Sheila's compliments when he stated "her driving ability was something I have not come across since". Before the war, "Sammy" Davis had shared a Talbot Ten with Garrad on the Monte Carlo Rally and he remembered Garrad's reputation for being "a mite temperamental" although they got on well.[4]

Normally maintaining strict discipline in the team, he was an early practitioner of what later became known as "bonding", with team members, drivers and mechanics, spending time together before rallies, often in a comfortable hotel and eating in the best restaurants, reflecting Garrad's undoubted taste for the good things in life![5] On such occasions, he did tolerate a certain amount of "high jinks" and horseplay among his drivers.[6] However, Graham Robson, who joined the Rootes team as a youngster in the early 1960s, remembers Garrad not only as businesslike and extremely serious about motor sport, but also as a humourless martinet who insisted on getting his own way – and usually did. It must be remembered that Garrad was then in his early sixties and was no doubt under pressure from the powers within Rootes to continue to pull rabbits out of the hat. By 1963 the team's fortunes were on the wane and their cars falling behind the times. Soon after, Garrad was effectively sacked (see also chapter 9).

This was an undeserved finale to an otherwise illustrious career. Garrad can take all the credit for establishing Rootes at the forefront of rallying. He had plenty of self-confidence, and clearly possessed the ability to inspire others with his conviction. As a long-serving, trusted employee, he was close to Sir William Rootes, and was able to persuade "Billy" that success in competition had enormous value in terms of publicity, apart from improving – and selling – the cars.[7] From a very modest beginning, fortunately a major success came Rootes's way early on in the 1948 Alpine Rally, and after that first Alpine Cup one imagines that the Rootes brothers were happy to support an ongoing involvement in motor sport. From all accounts they took a close interest – and much pride – in the competition achievements. They also footed the bill, which was considerable; Garrad later spoke of an annual budget of £110,000.[8]

Since Garrad was not only the team manager but also continued to take part in rallies, he effectively led by example. He created the first truly professional competitions department in the British motor industry. At the high point of Garrad's career, he had displayed remarkable persuasive powers and was able to entice many leading drivers into joining the Sunbeam-Talbot team, at least for "guest" appearances in selected events. The three most talented young British racing drivers of the day – Stirling Moss, Mike Hawthorn and Peter Collins – all drove for Norman Garrad, reputedly for a flat fee of £50 a time if even that, and so did Ronnie Adams and Maurice Gatsonides, both Monte Carlo winners, though neither in a Rootes car. Garrad fully realised the publicity value of having women drivers and encouraged the career of Sheila Van Damm, who became the leading lady of the team, with co-drivers Anne Hall and Françoise Clarke, but Nancy Mitchell and Elsie "Bill" Wisdom also drove for Rootes. Even two of the leading American racing drivers, John Fitch and Sherwood Johnston, occasionally appeared behind the wheel of a Sunbeam-Talbot.

The press and media were represented by Raymond Baxter of the BBC, John *"Autocar"* Cooper, AG Douglas Clease also of *The Autocar*,

Joe Lowrey of *The Motor*, Tommy Wisdom of the *Daily Herald*, Basil Cardew of the *Daily Express*, John Eason Gibson of *Country Life* and Charles Fothergill of the *News Chronicle*. Company staff members were often enlisted into Garrad's team as co-drivers, including WR "Chippy" Chipperton, John Cutts, "The Boy David" Humphrey, Ron Kessel and Peter Miller. The Rootes dealer George Hartwell was a core member, as was Leslie Johnson of ERA and Jaguar fame who had rallied a BMW 328 before the war. Peter Harper was a Garrad discovery. Behind the scenes, workshop manager Jim Ashworth, chief mechanic Gerry Spencer and engine wizard Ernie Beck, as well as their team, were equally as important to success. And then there were all the privateers who used Sunbeam-Talbots, including a certain young Scotsman called Jim Clark who at the age of 19 began his career in club events, running his own Mark III (BSH 510) during 1955-56.

1947: A hesitant start

The very first appearance of a Sunbeam-Talbot works car[9] in a post-war rally occurred at Easter 1947, when Norman Garrad managed to take a Ten across the Irish Sea to take part in the Circuit of Ireland Trial, and finished third in class. Apparently the Irish government had allowed extra petrol coupons for the event! No such gestures were made by the British government, but in spite of rationing the first post-war rallies, even if in truncated from, got under way in June 1947. At the Blackpool Rally on 6-8 June a certain PCE Harper appeared with a new Sunbeam-Talbot 2-litre but broke his gearbox during the final tests. Garrad turned up for the Junior Car Club's Eastbourne Rally on 28-29 June in another 2-litre, "which showed excellent acceleration", and he got a first-class award.[10]

Better known – and far more significant – is the tentative exploit with the 2-litre in the Alpine Rally of July 1947 where Douglas Clease of *The Autocar* finished sixth in class, but where, much more importantly, Garrad attended as an observer and reporter for the Rootes magazine *Modern Motoring* in a similar car, and afterwards wrote his famous report on its deficiencies, which is widely credited with having kick-started the rally career proper of the Sunbeam-Talbots (see chapter 3).

1948: First major success

Whether or not Garrad's report had an immediate effect on the design of the new models, which were less than a year away from production, is now difficult to determine and is in any case a rather moot point. Clearly the 80 and 90 represented an improvement over their predecessors, and Garrad was sufficiently confident to arrange for an entry of a three-car team of 90s in the Alpine Rally in July 1948, only a few weeks after the introduction of the new car. They were registered consecutively in Warwickshire under GWD 100, 101 and 102. Garrad and Horton drove one of the cars, another was entrusted to Tommy Wisdom, who was an experienced rally driver apart from being motoring correspondent to the *Daily Herald*, and the third car was driven by George Murray-Frame and LJ Onslow-Bartlett.

It was the last pair who scored the marque's first notable success in a major international event, by winning the 2-litre class and receiving the coveted award of a *Coupe des Alpes*. Garrad was fourth in class, despite damaging the engine sump on a rock, while Wisdom and Mrs Elsie "Bill" Wisdom retired with gearbox problems. In the same rally, Hiskins's privately-entered 2-litre tourer locked its brakes, went off the road and ended upside down in a gulley, with serious injury to his co-driver Marsden.[11]

Murray-Frame was typical of the semi-professional drivers of the time; he was an

The first serious competitive appearance for the new 90 came in the 1948 Alpine Rally. Garrad and a very natty-looking Wisdom with the team cars at Marseilles before the start. (Courtesy CTM)

SUNBEAM-TALBOT & ALPINE IN DETAIL

It was Murray-Frame and Onslow-Bartlett who won that first Alpine cup in 1948. Here they await post-rally scrutineering. (Courtesy CTM)

unassuming Scot who ran a tobacconist's business (he was usually photographed smoking a pipe) in Glasgow's Queen Street and had been much involved with Singers before the war, as well as the "Highlanders" trials team of MG T-types. He treated the Alpine Rally as his summer holiday and did five Alpine Rallies with the Sunbeam-Talbot team, missing out only in 1949, and in 1951 when he was recovering from an accident, but rarely appeared in other events, although he did the 1953 and 1954 Monte Carlos, the latter in a Humber, and the 1952 MCC Rally. His Alpine record was remarkable, with three Alpine cups; had he won a fourth in the 1954 event, he would have got a gold cup for winning three in a row.

1949: 80 or 90?

Following the initial success and bearing in mind that the more powerful 90 would seem to stand a better chance of a good result in any form of competition, it is rather odd that for the next outing of the works team three examples of the 80 model were chosen. The occasion was the first post-war Monte Carlo Rally in January 1949, where there was also a privately-entered Ten tourer. On this occasion, Garrad was not among the drivers – he was probably away in New York – but one of the crews included two future Jaguar XK 120 drivers, Leslie Johnson and Nick Haines, while in another of the cars George Hartwell made his debut with the works team. Maybe the smaller-engined car was chosen with an eye to a class win, but such a hope was frustrated as the best result was fourth in the 1100-1500cc class (and four other even smaller cars also finished ahead), together with 34th overall for Peter Monkhouse and Brown. The two other works cars finished but further down. A small consolation was a team award in the *Concours de Confort* competition.

Cutts and Pearman took GWD 101 on an "unofficial" outing to win their class in the Circuit of Ireland in April 1949, with local man Ronnie Adams second in the first of his Sunbeam-Talbot 90s, MZ 2496. In July the team was back with four 90s for the Alpine Rally, the three GWD cars and HUE 509, and Monkhouse now with Hartwell again got the best result, third in the 2-litre class and fifth overall. Three of the works cars finished (Haines was the only

Afterwards, their car went on show with its trophies. (Courtesy CTM)

142

The 1949 Monte Carlo Rally saw a rare appearance for the 80 in rallying. Although not greatly successful, at least all three cars arrived at Monte Carlo. (Courtesy CTM)

The three GWD cars were used again in the 1949 Alpine Rally. The drivers from left to right were Cutts, Douglas Clease, Monkhouse, Hartwell, Garrad and Horton. Missing from the line-up is Haines's car HUE 509 which retired. (Courtesy CTM)

A delightful photo of George Hartwell (left) and Leslie Onslow-Bartlett (right) with their 1949 Monte Carlo car. I doubt Onslow-Bartlett would win any prizes for sartorial elegance. (Courtesy CTM)

retirement) and won the "Foreign Team Challenge Trophy"; a well-meant gesture on behalf of the organisers but a somewhat hollow one, as the team award proper went to Citroën, and no other teams finished intact anyway. The other team drivers were Douglas Clease/Cutts, and Garrad/Horton. Murray-Frame was included in a provisional list of entrants but did not appear on this occasion.[12]

1950: Sheila makes her debut

At the time, the Alpine and Monte Carlo rallies were practically the only major international events of their type, so there was another six-month break before the three works GWD-registered 90s from the Alpine appeared again, in the 1950 Monte Carlo Rally. Despite being delayed by blizzards in France, all three cars finished but not particularly well: Hartwell and Monkhouse were highest in 46th place overall. However, this rally saw a works Humber Super Snipe finish a remarkable second in the hands of the famous Dutch rally driver

And they appeared again in the 1950 Monte Carlo Rally, now fitted with decent fog and spot lamps, here together at the Hague control. (Courtesy CTM)

The GWD cars were still entered in the 1950 Alpine Rally, fitted with the standard lamps again, and came away with a lot of trophies. Here are the drivers, Hartwell, Chipperton, Garrad, Cutts and Pearman; only Murray-Frame is absent. Note the unusual wheel trims on Garrad's car GWD 101. (Courtesy CTM)

Maurice Gatsonides. With co-driver Barendregt, he was one of only five entrants to come through to the finish of the road run within the time limit, but lost narrowly to the Hotchkiss of Becquart and Secret on the regularity run.[13] The three GWD team cars were then entered for the Circuit of Ireland in April but this time they were all beaten by Ronnie Adams who finished third in class. The Rootes team stayed away from Ireland for the next ten years!

Peter Monkhouse, born in 1912, was tragically killed on 23 April 1950 while a passenger in a Healey in the Mille Miglia. He had been one of the founders of Monaco Engineering at Watford in 1935, and had co-driven Stapleton's Aston Martin DB1 at Le Mans in 1949. After his death, there was a reshuffle of driver pairings for the 1950 Alpine Rally. As well as three works 90s there were three private entries, including Maurice Gatsonides in a Dutch-registered 90, and DH Perring's 90 convertible registered OPA 6. Together with other privateers such as Downs, Elliott, Fraser, Offley, Sherley-Price, Slatter, Sneath and Whatmough, Perring became one of the "Sunbeam-Talbot irregulars", one of the more frequent private entrants; he had already trialled a Ten back in 1938. Although the team carried home no *Coupes des Alpes*, five of the 90s finished first, second, fifth, sixth and seventh in the 2-litre class, with Murray-

Frame/Pearman leading the pack, and the three works cars won a team award based on a performance index. The only retiree was none other than Gatsonides, whose car stripped its crown wheel.

The first large national rally organised in Britain after the war was the Motor Cycling Club's rally to Torquay held in November 1950, sponsored by the *Daily Express*. The event was dismissed by Bill Boddy in *Motor Sport* as being far too easy, with a low average speed for the road sections, but I feel that Mr Boddy rather missed the point: as the first event of its type for more than ten years, it was probably one aim of the organisers to attract newcomers to the sport, and they succeeded magnificently with over 470 cars entered.[14] The list naturally included a number of Sunbeam-Talbots, of which Dr Slatter's car finished twelfth overall, but just as importantly, this rally witnessed the debut of a certain Miss S Van Damm, who despite having received no tuition for the special tests was third in the Ladies' Award section, in a works Sunbeam-Talbot 90 lent by Norman Garrad. This must have been one of the GWD cars but at least on this occasion it was fitted with a Mark II 2267cc engine.

Sheila Van Damm (1922-87) was born into a Jewish family of Dutch descent as the daughter of Vivian Van Damm, who was the proprietor of the Windmill theatre in London's Soho. He initially dreamt up the rally entry as a publicity stunt for the theatre; the car was emblazoned with the words "Windmill Girl" and Sheila was crewed by her sister Nona. If the words Windmill Girl led spectators to expect a scantily-clad beauty at the wheel, they were disappointed; Sheila was by all accounts a charming, vivacious and jolly-hockey-sticks sort of person, but rather plain, dumpy, and inclined to dress sensibly. She was also a complete tomboy who "would go off and do fairly butch boys' things" together with her friend Joan ("Jonnie") Werner Laurie, the founder editor of *She* magazine, until Joan and her partner Nancy Spain were killed in an air crash in 1964.[15] During her years with the Rootes Competitions Department, Sheila established the remarkable record of finishing every single event that she started, including the 1952 RAC where she was disqualified for changing co-driver, bar one: her swansong, the 1957 Mille Miglia, where her Rapier crashed early on.[16]

This Swedish registered convertible started the 1951 Monte Carlo Rally from Stockholm. (Courtesy CTM)

1951: More events beckon

When Garrad found that Tommy Wisdom was unable to shake off Sheila during the 1950 MCC Rally, he was sufficiently impressed with her performance in this first rally to offer her a place in the works team proper. For the next six years, she was to be a regular member of the Rootes team, attracting publicity in equal measure for her undoubted ability and her achievements, and the fact that she was a woman. Her first event was the 1951 Monte Carlo where she crewed with Elsie "Bill" Wisdom and Georgie Fotheringham-Parker in a Hillman Minx, for a 159th place of 281 finishers. Garrad's growing

Maurice Gatsonides with his second 90 rally car, a Mark II with the same registration as his Mark I. (Courtesy CTM)

SUNBEAM-TALBOT & ALPINE IN DETAIL

The best-placed Sunbeam-Talbot in the 1951 Monte Carlo Rally was this new works Mark II, driven by Wisdom and Humphrey into a 27th place overall, here at Monte Carlo. (Courtesy CTM)

team included Hillmans and Humbers, apart from a mixed bunch of 90 Mark I and Mark II models. Starting from Lisbon in a 90 Mark II (KUE 90), Tommy Wisdom was the highest-placed Rootes driver to finish, in 27th place overall, and Garrad himself with Basil Cardew of the *Daily Express* was 51st in the old 90 Mark I, GWD 101. Soon after the Monte Carlo, in February 1951 Garrad was seriously injured when his car collided with a lorry at night, and he took a long time to recover fully. Garrad was still walking with the aid of a stick when he (and Sheila Van Damm) attended the Alpine Rally in a support car, and the next time he drove a competing rally car was in that autumn's MCC event.

The 1951 season saw Sunbeam-Talbots in an increasing number of events including the Tulip Rally and even, unusually, the BRDC Production Car Race at Silverstone on 5 May, where George Hartwell was completed out-classed in a field of sports cars dominated by XK 120s and ended up 25th and last overall, well behind assorted Healeys and Allards apart from the Jaguars. More importantly, June saw the first post-war RAC Rally, where Hartwell was second in the class for closed cars over 1500cc and Major Sherley-Price ran the old works car GWD 101, as the works team was now completing the change-over to the 90 Mark II. There were no Rootes works cars in the RAC, so Sheila Van Damm entered her own Hillman Minx, with Elsie "Bill" Wisdom as her co-driver.

The 90 Mark II was prominent in the Alpine Rally in July 1951, where John Cutts and John Pearman were third in the 3-litre class with KUE 90. Perring and Griffiths were fourth in the 2-litre class with their 90 (Mark I) convertible, while Hartwell was best in the Mont Ventoux hill-climb test but later retired with broken rear suspension. This was the first occasion when Hartwell rallied his special two-seater registered LEL 333, which is credited with having inspired the Sunbeam Alpine (see chapter 6). In the MCC *Daily Express* rally to Hastings in November 1951, Hartwell drove a supercharged 90 to win his class, and the Offleys were second in their class. Of the three works 90s, Van Damm was again third in the ladies' awards, crewed by Chris Hornby.

George Hartwell (1911-75) was the Rootes distributor in Bournemouth and his name is still found on Peugeot dealerships in the area. He was close to the Rootes family and served as the company's home sales director in the 1960s. He had begun motor racing before the war in MGs, including the ex-Earl Howe Mille Miglia K3 Magnette, and in 1938 appeared at Brooklands in a 4.3-litre Alvis. After the war, he was one of the pioneers of 500cc racing but soon concentrated on rallying, while in the 1960s he sponsored Team Hartwell which raced Hartwell-tuned Hillman Imps in the saloon car championship, and he also for a time ran the Harrington coach-building company (see chapter 9).

1952: Moss makes his mark – and Hawthorn, too

Much better was to come. The 1952 Monte Carlo Rally saw no less than seventeen Sunbeam-Talbot 90s entered: a mixture of works and private cars. Garrad had succeeded in persuading the up-and-coming racing driver Stirling Moss to join the Rootes team. At just 22, he had already won a number of important races, including the Tourist Trophy for Jaguar in 1950 and 1951. Together with Lance Macklin, Moss had taken part in the 1950 MCC *Daily Express* Rally in an Aston Martin but this was his first winter rally; he was joined in LHP 823 by John Arthur Cooper, sports editor of *The Autocar*, and Desmond Scannell, secretary of the British Racing Drivers Club (BRDC).

It was the most difficult Monte so far in the post-war period, with blizzards in France, but

Before the 1952 Monte Carlo Rally, some of the drivers visited the Ryton production line and were given the VIP tour. Left to right Sheila van Damm, Garrad, Stirling Moss, Geoffrey Rootes, Nancy Mitchell and (possibly) Sir Reginald Rootes. (Courtesy CTM)

Moss showed himself master of everything the weather could throw at him, and finished an amazing second overall, close behind Sydney Allard's Allard. To quote Frostick, "No one who saw them would like to choose the better man; Allard was the rougher of the two, literally bouncing his car off walls of snow (and occasionally brick) to get round the special test in time – indeed, most of the marks he lost were for dents. Stirling was only a fraction slower but a great deal neater and the Rootes competitions department was not faced with so much panel beating at the end of the event."[17]

Cooper, being sports editor of *The Autocar*, naturally wrote up the story of their "Very Great Adventure" for his magazine. He and Moss looked very professional and ready for anything in flying suits, in Moss's case with a natty fur collar, only slightly spoilt by different head gear: Moss wore a bobble hat, Cooper a beret. Old sober-sides Scannell preferred a jacket and tie. They elected to start from Monte Carlo so as to do some practising on the way down and were rewarded by heavy snowfall; the oft-reproduced photo of two oxen dragging their Sunbeam-Talbot out of a snowdrift was taken during this practice run...

During the rally itself Moss chose to drive the most difficult sections, of which there were plenty; he decided that the car was so slow that he had to go flat out, even over snow or rutted ice. Theirs was one of only fifteen cars to arrive at Monte Carlo without penalty points. During the final regularity run, they briefly went off the road and lost time, yet they finished 28 seconds too early. As Cooper commented, "Had we slowed and lost just five seconds more, we would have won the rally..." He expressed the hope "that some day we can do it all over again." His wish was granted in 1953 and 1954.[18]

The next Sunbeam-Talbot was Sneath's privately-entered car in 24th place, then Hartwell and Chipperton in a works car in equal 28th place. Garrad and Cutts retired while Nancy Mitchell, Elsie Wisdom and Van Damm were in 129th place and fourth among the ladies, after the as yet inexperienced Sheila had been scared out of her wits by Nancy's fast driving on ice.[19]

Sunbeam-Talbot results in the RAC Rally were less impressive, although Sneath was tenth and Offley eleventh. Of the works cars Garrad was 30th, Hartwell retired and Sheila Van Damm was disqualified for changing her co-driver during the rally, while Rootes PR man John Bullock and Charles Fothergill of the *News Chronicle* were 73rd overall.[20] Sheila's original co-driver was Margot, Viscountess Erleigh, who had never been on a rally. Clearly unwell at the start, her

John Cooper and Desmond Scannell accepting presents at the Hague control during the 1952 Monte Carlo Rally (not tins of spam, we hope). A bleary-eyed Moss peers out from the back seat. (Courtesy CTM)

1952 Monte Carlo rally: Moss (LHP 823) at La Turbie

It was customary for Police motorcyclists to guide Monte Carlo cars through Paris, here with the private entry of Milton, Done and Leaman in 1952, while a Rootes service truck is also in attendance. (Courtesy CTM)

condition probably deteriorated further from Sheila's driving, and when they reached Blackpool she "was nearly in a state of collapse, and a doctor appeared and glared at me [i.e. Sheila] and forbade her to go on". Sheila found a new co-driver, Molly Hardman, who with her husband won the 1952 MCC Rally, but despite their belief that this had been permitted by the Clerk of the Course, protests were made and Sheila was disqualified. In a parting shot the unhappy Viscountess remarked to Basil Cardew, "That woman is so tough that if you threw a brick at her it would bounce off." I suspect Sheila felt more flattered than chastened![21]

The Alpine Rally brought a much happier outcome. Moss was again part of the team and so was another up-and-coming young racing driver, Mike Hawthorn – his only drive in a Sunbeam-Talbot. Of the works cars, three finished eighth, ninth and tenth overall – Murray-Frame/Pearman, Hawthorn/Chipperton and Moss/Cutts in that order – and each pair brought home a *Coupe des Alpes*, as well as the two team prizes between them. It was only the second full racing season for Mike Hawthorn (1929-59) and this was his sole foray into

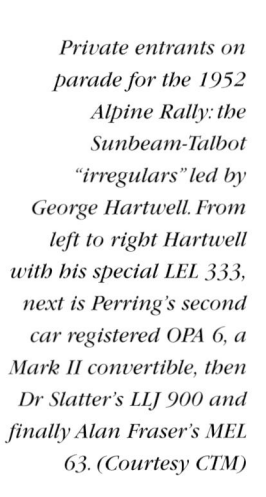

Private entrants on parade for the 1952 Alpine Rally: the Sunbeam-Talbot "irregulars" led by George Hartwell. From left to right Hartwell with his special LEL 333, next is Perring's second car registered OPA 6, a Mark II convertible, then Dr Slatter's LLJ 900 and finally Alan Fraser's MEL 63. (Courtesy CTM)

148

Hawthorn and Chipperton with their 90 Mark II after the 1952 Alpine Rally. (Courtesy Tony Bailey and Paul Skilleter)

One of the more unusual drivers in the 1952 Alpine Rally was the Polish Count Kolaczkowski, here at Monza. The countess sitting in the car apparently just came along for the ride. (Courtesy CTM)

rallying; it merits a two-line entry in his 1958 book *Challenge Me the Race* where he spells Garrad's name wrong. The photo of him and Chipperton with their Sunbeam-Talbot finally appeared in *Mike Hawthorn Golden Boy* published to mark the fiftieth anniversary of Hawthorn's death.[22] In 1952 he had just graduated from running pre-war Rileys to a Cooper-Bristol Formula Two, but his talent was so obvious that he was given a Ferrari works drive in 1953. After driving a variety of cars – including the Jaguar D-type with which he won Le Mans in 1955 – he returned to Ferrari and became the Formula One World Champion in 1958. He had officially retired from racing when he was killed in a road accident in January 1959.

Apart from Hawthorn, this Alpine Rally saw two unusual recruits to the team. The Polish Count Wojciech Kolaczkowski (1908-2001) had driven in rallies before the war, when he was a Citroën agent in Warsaw. He became a pilot in the Polish Air Force, and escaped after the fall of Poland in September 1939. Eventually he found his way to England where he joined the Polish no. 303 Squadron of the RAF, which he commanded in 1941-42. He ended the war as a Wing Commander and Air Attaché of the Polish Embassy. He emigrated to the USA in 1948, where he worked as a sales representative for several British car manufacturers, and sporadically took part in motor sport. His notable achievement in this Alpine Rally was to drive apparently single-handed to a 21st place overall.[23]

The other newcomer was the American driver John Fitch, who retired when his hub bearing broke, but unlike Kolaczkowski, Fitch would drive for Sunbeam-Talbot again. Fitch (born 1917) was a Rootes dealer[24]; he had cut his teeth on an MG TC in American sports car racing but quickly graduated to better things and joined the Cunningham team in 1951, winning the

The Murray-Frame Alpine cup winning car was displayed on the Sunbeam-Talbot stand at the 1952 Motor Show. (Courtesy CTM)

Sebring race in 1953. He drove a variety of cars in many different events, and as a Mercedes-Benz works driver in 1955 was the designated co-driver for Pierre Levegh at Le Mans but did not get a drive before Levegh's tragic accident. In 1956 he joined the new Corvette racing team but also continued to race for Cunningham. He retired in 1966 but took up racing again in his eighties! His best result for Sunbeam was in the 1953 Alpine Rally, where he and Peter Miller won a *Coupe des Alpes* for a penalty-free run.

In the 1952 MCC *Daily Express* rally, this time finishing at Brighton, the most important Sunbeam-Talbot result was that Sheila Van Damm, now partnered by Françoise Clarke, won the Ladies' Prize. The result in the Alpine Rally was sufficient reason for Sunbeam-Talbot to be awarded the Dewar Trophy by the RAC for that year's outstanding achievement in motoring; as much as anything else I feel this award was to honour the Rootes Group's and Garrad's commitment to international rallying, since this was as yet the only major such effort by a British manufacturer.

1953: Alpines for the Alpine

That a Sunbeam-Talbot 90 was by now the car to have for rallying was best demonstrated by the fact that 31 examples were entered in the 1953 Monte Carlo Rally, including nine works or works-supported cars, although two failed to start, including the car entered for Mike Hawthorn, who had bigger fish to fry at the Argentine Grand Prix. The trio of Moss, Cooper and Scannell could not quite repeat their 1952 success but finished a still-impressive sixth overall, and Peter Harper, still a private entrant, was seventeenth. All the works cars finished; next highest-placed were AG "Goff" Imhof, better known for his involvement with Allards, and the BBC broadcaster Raymond Baxter who finished 24th, while Garrad, Murray-Frame and Pearman were 26th, and a team of drivers from the Metropolitan Police were 29th.

John Cooper again wrote his personal account in *The Autocar*. They followed the same itinerary as in 1952; he and Scannell drove down through France for a bit of practice on the way to their starting point at Monte Carlo, where they were met by Moss. The rally itself was "fairly uneventful"; there was some snow in the *Massif Central* but generally speaking the organisers were let down by the weather, so 253 crews arrived unpenalized and everything hung on the special tests at the end of the rally. At the end of the regularity test only three seconds separated the winner Gatsonides in a Ford Zephyr from the second-placed Jaguar of the Appleyards; Moss and Co. could not do quite as well. Cooper was however full of praise for their Mark IIA compared to their car of the previous year: "[it] proved just as robust and reliable, while the steering and brakes were a definite improvement on those of the 1952 model."[25]

Sheila Van Damm had now settled with Françoise Clarke and Anne Hall as her crew and came in 90th, narrowly losing the *Coupe des Dames* to Madeleine Pochon and Irene Terray in a Renault 4CV, after being delayed by a puncture on the final regularity test over the Col de Braus. They changed the wheel in two minutes and twenty seconds, beating their best practice time of three minutes... Anne Hall (born Newton, 1919-2003) is some times referred to demeaningly as a "Yorkshire housewife": in fact she was a competent rally driver in her own right with a Jaguar XK 120, often with her sister Mary, and was a director of the family motor business, Newton of Huddersfield. Like Sheila, she had made her rallying debut in the 1950 MCC event, and after the three "must-get-theres" (Sheila, Anne and Françoise) broke up in 1956, Anne carried on rallying, sometimes in works Fords. She continued to be involved in motor sport,

At a ceremony in 1953, Sir William Rootes accepted the ornate Dewar trophy from Wilfred Andrews of the RAC, with Geoffrey on the right. The RAC still award this 100-year old trophy. More recent winners have been JCB for the Dieselmax record car, and Lotus.
(Courtesy CTM)

The episode that cost Sheila Van Damm the ladies' prize in the 1953 Monte Carlo Rally: a puncture and wheel change during the regularity test. (Courtesy CTM)

latterly in classic rallying, until she was over 80. Yes, she was also a housewife and a mother of three – and a Yorkshirewoman to her core![26]

Raymond Baxter (1922-2006) had begun rallying while stationed in Germany soon after the war and had joined Imhof in his Allard on the 1950 Lisbon Rally. As often as not, he combined competing in rallies with commentating on the event for the BBC, and he was to have a long association with the Rootes Competitions Department.[27] Another young racing driver, Peter Collins, made his first appearance with the team in the 1953 Monte; he shared a car with John Fitch and John Cutts and they finished 112th overall. Collins was born into the motor trade in 1931 as his father ran a dealership at Kidderminster. Starting out in 500cc racing he got his first Formula One drive for HWM in 1952 and in 1956 joined the Ferrari team, coming third in the Drivers' Championship after Fangio and Moss. He was killed when his car went off the road in the 1958 German Grand Prix.

Of the works cars, Moss/Cooper/Scannell, Imhof/Baxter/Pearce, and Leslie Johnson with David Humphrey and John Eason Gibson in 58th place won the Charles Faroux award for a nominated team, the first time this was won by Rootes, and the privately-entered 90 of Dutch drivers Proos Hoogendijk and Seitz carried off the main award in the *Concours de Confort* contest. The event was marred when a privately-entered Sunbeam-Talbot was in collision with a lorry in Belgium, resulting in the death of co-driver Alistair S Buchanan.

In the 1953 RAC Rally there were 22 Sunbeam-Talbots and this year saw one of the best results for the works team in this event, as the Ulsterman Ronnie Adams and Pearman were second overall to Appleyard's Jaguar XK 120 and won the touring car category. Sheila Van Damm and Françoise Clarke were 23rd overall and won the Ladies' Cup. There were at least fifteen Sunbeam-Talbots in the Tulip Rally, driven by British as well as Dutch entrants, but three of them including Peter Harper were disqualified as their cars were not quite to standard specification, which deprived Elliott and Wright of a class win. Harper drove an ex-works car, KNX 955 re-registered HUR 1, which had been fitted with non-standard rear brake drums.[28]

Ronnie Adams (1916-2004) was the first Ulsterman to be successful in international rallying and had the distinction of having won, with Clarke and Holmes, the first Circuit of Ireland Trial in 1936. He enjoyed a long and varied career in motor sport, and took part in classic car events even in his eighties. In the early post-war period he competed in two

Also from the 1953 Monte Carlo Rally, the two Dutch Sunbeam-Talbot drivers who carried off the main prize in the Concours. (Courtesy CTM)

Three of the works cars which were entered for the 1953 RAC Rally, with drivers Adams, Pearman, Hartwell, Garrad, Scott and Cutts. Sheila Van Damm and Anne Hall and their car are missing. (Courtesy CTM)

The team of six Alpines and the Commer service van lined up at the Humber sports club before the 1953 Alpine Rally; in the centre, Humber's general manager EW Hancock and Garrad, with the staff of the Competitions Department. (Courtesy CTM)

Sunbeam-Talbots of his own. The second place in the RAC was his best result so far, although topped by his win with a Jaguar Mark VII in the 1956 Monte Carlo. He had also raced the big Jaguar at Silverstone and took part in two of the TT races at Dundrod, but never enjoyed any similar success and finally retired from rallying in 1963.[29]

For the 1953 Alpine Rally, Garrad's team had a new toy to play with, the Sunbeam Alpine. The works team consisted of six Alpines consecutively registered MKV 21 to MKV 26.

The best individual result was Moss/Cutts in fourteenth place overall and fourth in class. They won a *Coupe des Alpes*, as did Murray-Frame/Pearman in eighteenth place and Fitch/Miller who finished 20th overall. Van Damm/Hall in 24th place won the Ladies' Cup and brought home a fourth Alpine Cup, only the second time a woman crew had won this award. On this occasion, Peter Collins was paired with Ronnie Adams, but when Collins refused to let Adams drive, the offended (and prickly) Ulsterman walked out. David

Humphrey, who had been co-driver to Leslie Johnson until engine problems forced his retirement, then joined Collins but they would have been disqualified because of the change; as it was, the car retired with rear axle and gearbox problems. Understandably, Adams fell out with Garrad over his treatment in this rally, but later did drive for the Rootes team again.[30]

Sheila Van Damm side-swiped a rock which tore the fuel filler pipe away from the tank. This caused them to lose petrol and made re-fuelling almost impossible, but they were rescued with a bodged repair by a local garage on the last day of the rally. Several works cars had problems with wheel nuts working loose, as the new too-thick paint on the wheels flaked away around the stud holes. However, the four survivors took the team prize. There were altogether fifteen Sunbeam-Talbots in this rally, including two of the Hartwell specials, which both retired. Incidentally, 1953 was the all-time record year for the number of Alpine Cups awarded: no less than 25 competitors came home with clean sheets. Murray-Frame was awarded a silver cup for having won three Alpine cups in non-consecutive years.

After winning two Ladies' Awards and coming second in the Monte Carlo *Coupe des Dames*, Sheila Van Damm was in with a good chance of winning the 1953 Ladies' European Touring Car Championship; her only possible rival was the experienced Swedish driver Greta Molander in a SAAB 92. The outcome would be decided in the Lisbon Rally in October. This was not deemed to be a particularly important event otherwise, so apart from Van Damm and Clarke, the only other works Sunbeam-Talbot was that of "Goff" Imhof and John Suter. After the final tests in Estoril, it was actually Nancy Mitchell who won the ladies' award, Van Damm was second and Molander third, putting Sheila and Greta equal on points, but since the Swedish driver had more wins, she was awarded the championship title.

The 1953 MCC *Daily Express* National Rally to Hastings saw an overall win for the privately-entered 90 Mark II of Frank Downs with Bartley and Heagren, but the works team did not

The Alpines often ran with bonnets released, only held by the leather strap, to force more cooling air through the engine bay; Van Damm and Hall in the 1953 Alpine Rally.

figure, as some of them were on the other side of the Atlantic taking part in the first Great American Mountain Rally. Here Sherwood Johnston finished eighth overall in an Alpine, while he, Ian Garrad (Norman's oldest son, then working for Rootes in Canada) in a 90, and Sheila Van Damm with Ron Kessel in another Alpine, took the manufacturer's team award. Sherwood Johnston (1927-2000) was by profession a doctor; like Fitch, he was a multi-talented driver and member of the Cunningham team, and enjoyed a long racing career which

This photo taken before embarking on the Silver City plane is from Sheila Van Damm's personal album and annotated by her, "Anne and I at Lympne at the start of the great adventure." (Courtesy Chris Bryant)

SUNBEAM-TALBOT & ALPINE IN DETAIL

Three of the team cars at Cannes after the 1953 Alpine Rally; on the left the Murray-Frame/Pearman car, on the right the Fitch/Miller car; and we can't see whose car it is in the centre! (Courtesy CTM)

Desmond Scannell at the wheel, John Cooper in the navigator's seat and Moss in the back as they start the eventful 1954 Monte Carlo Rally from Athens as number 1. (Courtesy CTM)

continued into the early 1970s.

On the other side of the world, in the 1953 Victorian Alpine Rally in Australia, Harry Firth and Graham Hoinville came first overall in a Sunbeam Alpine. This was the first of no less than five wins for this pair in this event; their next victory was in a Hillman Minx in 1955, followed by wins in a Volkswagen, a Singer Gazelle and finally a Ford Anglia in 1962. Firth (born 1918) went on to great success with the Ford and Holden teams in both racing and rallying.

1954: A gold cup and a championship

It was the mixture as before for the 1954 Monte Carlo, with three works cars driven by the established partnerships of Moss/Scannell/Cooper, Johnson/Garrad/Cutts, and *Mesdames* Van Damm/Hall/Clarke; they finished fourteenth, 48th and 75th respectively, and took the Charles Faroux team award for a second time. Proos Hoogendijk and Seitz repeated their success in the *Concours* by taking the award for *confort* (there was now a separate award for *sécurité routière*).

For a third time, Cooper wrote up their experiences in *The Autocar*. This year he, Moss and Scannell elected to start from Athens, the first time that this had been a starting point in the post-war period. Their rally car was shipped directly to Greece while they drove down through Yugoslavia in another Sunbeam-Talbot; this was fortunate for due to snow and ice they were unable to make much progress south of Belgrade, and had to complete the outbound journey on the Orient Express. I wonder if their abandoned car might still be found in Belgrade? Conditions were only slightly better on the rally itself, and among other incidents, at one stage the roof rack broke loose and bounced off the bonnet. From then on two spare wheels occupied most of the rear seat while other gear was ditched. Various wildlife including "large foxes" was sighted in Yugoslavia, but no wolves... Matters improved in Italy and France. They hoped to do the Col des Leques run in 11min 15sec: Moss was six seconds slower, which was still the fastest run of all, but it upset their regularity and dropped them several places. That their fourteenth place was still a remarkable result is demonstrated by the fact that the next Athens starter to finish was in 189th place.[31]

The 1954 Monte was marred for the team when Leslie Johnson collapsed with a heart attack while at the wheel, at the end of the Col des Leques regularity section. He was rushed into hospital and Norman Garrad took over as the driver for the five-lap race over the Grand Prix circuit at the end of the rally. After a long convalescence Johnson recovered, but did not drive in competitions again; he died at the age of 47 in 1959.

Perhaps to replace Johnson, Norman Garrad brought Peter Harper into the works team. Harper (1921-2003) was a Rootes dealer from Letchworth who had started rallying at club level in 1947. He first appeared with a Sunbeam-Talbot 2-litre in the 1947 Blackpool rally and in the 1948 JCC Eastbourne Rally, and had run a Hillman Minx or a Sunbeam-Talbot in a number of owners' club events and rallies, including several Monte Carlo rallies – he was fifteenth in a Minx in 1950 – and the 1953 Tulip Rally where he was one of the three disqualified Sunbeam-Talbot drivers. His first drive in a works car was in the 1954 RAC Rally. Together with David Humphrey he finished fourth overall, while Hartwell and Scott were ninth and Van Damm/Clarke 23rd, as well as second for the Ladies' Cup.[32]

Sheila, with Anne Hall, took the Ladies' Cup in the Tulip and also finished tenth overall, just losing a class win to Denis Scott's Ford Zephyr Six by one-fifth of a second in the final test at the Zandvoort race circuit. The other works cars in the Tulip retired: Baxter/Imhof broke a half shaft and Harper/Cutts also had rear axle trouble.[33] Sheila drove the only works Sunbeam-Talbot in the Austrian Alpine Trial in June with the aim of securing the ladies' award, which she

After Leslie Johnson's collapse in the 1954 Monte Carlo Rally, Garrad drove the car in the round-the-harbour race at Monte Carlo. (Courtesy CTM)

The works cars in the 1954 RAC Rally were driven by Sheila Van Damm, Françoise Clarke, Garrad, Cutts, new recruit Peter Harper, and David Humphrey; the latter pair finished fourth overall. (Courtesy CTM)

Raymond Baxter and Godfrey Imhof with their 1954 Tulip Rally car; Baxter seems to have met a local fan. (Courtesy CTM)

Sadly a broken half-shaft prevented Baxter and Imhof from finishing the 1954 Tulip Rally.

did. Two US Serviceman stationed in Austria took part in this event with their Sunbeam Alpine. In the same month, Joe Lowrey of *The Motor* borrowed the works car ODU 746 for his "summer holiday" which involved taking part in the Adriatic Rally in Yugoslavia, where he won his class.[34]

The six Alpines which had run in the 1953 Alpine Rally were entered again for the 1954 event, together with a private car, Orr and Lewis in OAD 333. After the high number of cups awarded in 1953, the organisers had deliberately toughened up the event, including a new section over the treacherously loose-surfaced and narrow Vivione pass. Furthermore, their efforts were complemented by unusually poor weather for July, with ice and snow in the higher reaches; the Gavia and the Stelvio were both impassable and the itinerary had to be re-routed during the rally. There were many retirements, including Peter Collins, whose rear axle seized up – his co-driver was Norman Garrad's younger son Lewis, at the tender age of

Sheila Van Damm and Anne Hall took to the mountains in the 1954 Austrian Alpine Rally and duly won the ladies' award. (Courtesy CTM)

Not surprisingly everybody looks a little tired and dishevelled after the 1954 Alpine Rally: Pearman, Anne Hall, Murray-Frame, Sheila Van Damm, Moss and Cutts, with the car of the last-mentioned pair. (Courtesy CTM)

17 – and Peter Harper who lost a front wheel at 95mph (153km/h) when the stub axle sheared. A post-rally check revealed similar fractures on four out of the other five team cars, and a modification was soon introduced on production cars.[35]

The rest of the Alpines got through with the impressive result of third to seventh in class. Moss and Cutts in MKV 21 were ahead of the rest, with the only clean sheet of the team, but the car had lost second gear. To get through post-rally scrutineering, Stirling had to do some creative fiddling with the overdrive switch to convince the official that all his forward gears still worked. It passed, so they won a *Coupe des Alpes*, and since this was their third Alpine cup in a row they were awarded one of the rare Alpine gold cups, only the second such award to be made, the first having been won by Ian Appleyard in his Jaguar XK 120 (NUB 120).

Murray-Frame very narrowly missed out on a similar hat-trick by being one-fifth of a second too slow in a time trial, held in appalling conditions of torrential rain over a stretch of *Autobahn* near Munich. The only Sunbeam driver to beat the set time, and that only by another one-fifth of a second, was Moss, who had blanked off his radiator and ran with tyre pressures at 50lb, as well as extra-thin oil in the engine and gearbox; he even disconnected the fan.[36] Van Damm/Hall won the Ladies' Cup; the battered state of their car at the end of the rally tells its own story. Incidentally, rally photos often show the Alpines with their bonnets agape, only held by the leather strap: the bonnet locks were deliberately released to improve engine bay cooling.[37]

Sheila had entered for the 1954 Ladies' European Rally Championship, and went on to take the Ladies' Awards in the Viking and Geneva rallies, which secured the championship for her. Throughout the year, in fact since the 1953 Lisbon Rally, with the exception of the Alpine Rally she had driven the same car, ODU 700, clocking up some 8500 rally miles. In November 1954, the MCC Rally to Hastings, now sponsored by Redex, attracted what was probably a record 44 Sunbeam-Talbot privateers of a total of 334 entrants, including George Hartwell, but best results were second and third in class for Davis and Whatmough. At the end of the season, three Alpines were entered in the second Great American Mountain Rally, where they took the team award for a second time. The drivers were Van Damm/Hall, the Americans Krag and Giltzow, and Moss in his final appearance for the Rootes team, with Kessel.

Of Moss's two erstwhile Monte Carlo co-drivers, John Arthur Cooper (born 1916), who had been the sports editor of *The Autocar* since 1949, was tragically killed in a road accident on 19 March 1955. He had trained as an engineer with Alvis before the war. Later he was a designer with Roy Fedden Ltd, which unsuccessfully tried to produce a revolutionary new post-war car, and had been involved with the design of the Kieft 500cc racing car, which is how he came to know the young Moss.[38] Desmond Scannell (born 1910) served nineteen years as secretary of the BRDC but left at the end of 1955 and later became sales director of Borg Warner[39]; he was replaced at the BRDC by John Eason Gibson, journalist and occasional Sunbeam-Talbot rally driver.

1955: Finally, the Monte

For the 1955 Monte Carlo, the works team had the new Mark III saloon, and so did most other Sunbeam entrants, including the Norwegian pair of Malling (1914-79) and Fadum (born 1918). This was to be Sunbeam's finest result in this classic rally, as the Norwegian car won outright. Malling was a policeman, the head of the technical department of the Oslo police with the rank of Captain, while Fadum ran a crisp-bread

A happy crowd after the 1954 Great American Mountain Rally, William Giltzow, Ron Kessel, Sheila, Anne, Stirling and Kasimir Krag. This was Stirling's last rally in a Sunbeam. (Courtesy CTM)

No jokes about women reading maps but Anne Hall looks a little worried by Sheila's expostulations before the 1955 Monte Carlo Rally; Françoise Clarke stands behind. Well, clearly they read the map all right, since they went on to win the ladies' prize. (Courtesy CTM)

Norman and his winning ladies and their trophies after the 1955 Monte Carlo Rally, flanked by Jim Ashworth (left) and Gerry Spencer (right) of the competitions department workshop.

factory and was the leader of the national Norwegian rally team. Their Sunbeam was in third place after the road section but had broken its fan belt near the end of the rally (something which had already happened to Sheila Van Damm on the Viking), and no repairs or replacements were permitted before the deciding round-the-houses five-lap race at Monaco.

The story as first told in *The Autocar* is that Malling decided to start the race – where only the best lap counted – he did one lap at the stipulated speed, stopped, and calmly changed the fan belt which took him all of 40 seconds, after much practice the previous night on a non-competing Sunbeam! However, some later Norwegian sources claim it was *Fadum* who pulled this stunt off.[40] Of the works cars, Harper and Humphrey were ninth, and Van Damm/Hall/Clarke eleventh; the three highest-placed Sunbeams also won the *L'Equipe* team award for any three cars of the same make finishing highest, and Van Damm and her co-drivers won the *Coupe des Dames*. The two other works cars, of Fairman/Smith and Garrad/Cutts, also finished but were well down the list.

After the winning car came back to the UK for display, John Bolster of *Autosport* borrowed it for a weekend. He commented on the absence of specialised rally equipment, except for fog and spot lamps, and a harness for the passenger. There was also a "cyclometer" which lived in the glove box and recorded tenths and hundredths of kilometres. The car was unmarked and every aspect of its performance was fully up to standard, leaving Bolster "confident that it would do the trip to Monte Carlo all over again… As I once said before, this is a *tough* car." In recent times, Gunnar Fadum's son Harald has taken part in historic events with a Sunbeam Mark III bearing the old Oslo number plate A 68909, but this is a replica since it is a RHD car and the original 1955 winner was LHD.[41]

Sheila Van Damm's rally car PWK 604 was tried by Charles Haywood for *The Autocar*. This car, too, had stood up well to the ordeal; the most offensive noise came from the Pallas snow tyres, but the engine "would have easily repeated the journey without attention" even if it had a tendency to run on. He suggested "If I were to return to the Alps immediately it might be a good idea to inspect the brake linings…" The column change was described as one of the nicer one of its kind: "its action is like the car, taut and businesslike." Summing up, he felt "they are entitled to do a little trumpet blowing at that factory in Coventry."[42]

Three of the works cars were entered in the RAC Rally, where Van Damm/Hall won the Ladies' Award and Harper/Humphrey were second in the touring car class over 2000cc.

The winning car during the race at the end of the 1955 Monte Carlo Rally – whether this is before or after the "pit stop" to change the fan belt is not known. (Courtesy Derek Cook)

After the 1955 Monte Carlo Rally, winners Malling and Fadum and their car were flown to Britain by Silver City. They happily waved their trophies for the photographer as they got off the plane. (Courtesy CTM)

Peter Harper and John Cutts give their rally car a final check before the 1955 Tulip Rally. (Courtesy CTM)

Having gone off the road once or twice with only superficial damage to the car, Harper later fondly remembered that "The old 90 may have lacked a little steam, but she was certainly a strong baby."[43] In the Tulip, Peter Harper now with Cutts was seventh overall, while Van Damm and Hall were fifteenth overall and second to Greta Molander among the ladies. Garrad was having a team of six new Alpines prepared for the Alpine Rally but this was one of many motor sports events which were cancelled in the wake of the disaster at the 1955 Le Mans.

Unusually, a left-hand drive Mark III was prepared as a works car, registered RDU 253. The purpose of this was that it could be lent out to European drivers to use in Continental events, and a trio of Belgian Police officers duly

The Harper/Cutts car is at the front of this field lined up at the Zandvoort race track before the start for the deciding race at the end of the 1955 Tulip Rally, with Sheila and Anne just behind; they made it to seventh and 15th overall respectively. Count the Sunbeam-Talbots on this grid; I reckon there are eight, including all the works or works-supported cars. (Courtesy CTM)

Three of the new RHP-registered Alpines being prepared; alas, in vain, as the 1955 Alpine Rally was cancelled. (Courtesy CTM)

Three smartly-uniformed Belgian Police drivers and the equally well-turned out Mark III RDU 253 with which they won the 1955 Police Rally. (Courtesy CTM)

Anne Hall seems to be torn between amusement and disapproval as Sheila Van Damm strikes a pose at the 1955 Viking Rally. (Courtesy CTM)

won the International Police Rally to Hamburg in the summer of 1955.[44] In the Norwegian Viking Rally in September, none other than Per Malling borrowed RDU 253. This rally was also contested by Hartwell and by Sheila Van Damm who lost her way and consequently was only third of the ladies in this rally. However, for the second year running she took the title of Ladies' European Rally Champion, now jointly with Anne Hall. In October 1955 she decided to retire from rallying, but gave in to pleas from the Rootes brothers to do the next Monte as her final rally. In the MCC Rally in November, Whatmough's Mark III was second overall, to – unbelievably – a twenty-year-old MG.

1956: The Mark III bows out

Production of the Alpine ended in 1955, and the new Rapier was launched in the same year, so the end was in sight for the old-style Mark IIIs, but they were still being campaigned actively during the 1956 season. This got off to an excellent start with the Monte Carlo Rally, where Harper and Humphrey finished equal third overall, with team mates Ray and Cutts tenth overall, and Van Damm and Hall with Yvonne Jackson offering support in 122nd place. That all three cars finished clinched for Rootes the Charles Faroux team award for the third time, and they therefore won it outright – despite the reluctance of the rally organisers to part with the actual trophy at the prize-giving ceremony. They were consoled when Sir William Rootes promptly donated a replacement trophy. In this rally it was Gunnar Fadum's turn to borrow RDU 253, but he retired.

Peter Harper was second in his class in the RAC and still drove a Mark III in the Tulip, where the new Rapiers finished eleventh and nineteenth. Harper went on to become the most successful and longest-serving Rootes rally driver in the post-Sunbeam-Talbot era. In the Alpine rally, the Rootes team fielded four Rapiers and there were two privately-entered examples of the model; the best Rapier finished 23rd overall, but old hand George Hartwell in the single Mark III in this rally had the last laugh, as he finished 21st.

This event effectively marked the end of the Sunbeam-Talbot in rallying. There were sporadic private entries in 1957, including three cars in the Tulip, and even in the 1958 Monte Carlo and RAC rallies, but the baton now passed to the Rapier. Over a career spanning ten years there had been a win in the Monte Carlo and a number of other high places in this rally, together with four team awards, two *Grand Prix d'Honneur* in the *Concours de Confort*, and one *Coupe des Dames*. In the Alpine, there had been nine Alpine cups, together with one gold cup and one silver cup, as well as class wins. In the RAC, second and fourth places overall, and two Ladies' Awards. In the MCC National Rally, an overall win. In these and other rallies there were many other team awards, class wins, or Ladies' Cups. And then there was the award of the Dewar trophy in 1952 which recognised the Sunbeam-Talbot achievement as equal of the previous winner, Jaguar, who were awarded the Dewar trophy after their 1951 Le Mans win.

The team about to set out for the start of the 1956 Monte Carlo Rally, with Peter Harper on the left, while Garrad, Anne, Sheila and Yvonne Jackson are also in this group.

Known works rally cars:[45]

Reg. mark	Chassis number	Date of first reg.	Model	Remarks
EWD 222	388-200	18/07/1946	2-litre tourer	1947 Alpine, Douglas Clease
FAC 963	389-200	14/11/1946	2-litre tourer	1947 Alpine, Garrad; exists
GWD 100	3800005HSO	20/05/1948	90	1948-51 works rally car
GWD 101	3800006HSO	15/06/1948	90	1948-51 works rally car
GWD 102	3800003HSO	15/06/1948	90	1948-51 works rally car
GWD 668	2800003HSO	08/06/1948	80	1949 Monte Carlo Rally
GWD 853	3800029HSO	24/06/1948	90	1948 Eastbourne rally, Tommy Wisdom
HNX 80	2800080HSO	01/10/1948	80	Road test car but not rally car?
HNX 81	2800082HSO	01/10/1948	80	1949 Monte Carlo Rally
HNX 82	2800084HSO	01/10/1948	80	1949 Monte Carlo Rally
HUE 509	3800429HSO	07/02/1949	90	1949 Alpine
JDU 289	3801013RCO	11/08/1949	90 convertible	1950 Alpine press car
KNX 606	A3000022HCO	04/10/1950	90 Mark II convertible	1951 Alpine press car for Douglas Clease, *The Autocar*
KNX 955 re-reg. as HUR 1	Probably A3000027HSO	07/11/1950	90 Mark II	1951 Alpine support car; 1952 Alpine; sold to Peter Harper in December 1952
KUE 90	A3000111HSO	17/11/1950	90 Mark II	1951-52 works rally car
KWK 397	A3001557HSO	09/03/1951	90 Mark II	1952 works rally car
KKV 780	A3001927HSO	06/06/1951	90 Mark II	1952 Monte Carlo Rally
LHP 820	A3004431HSO	12/09/1951	90 Mark II	1952 RAC Rally; LHP 820 also seen on Mark IIA convertible in 1952
LHP 821	A3004432HSO	12/09/1951	90 Mark II	1952 works rally car
LHP 822	A3004318HSO	12/09/1951	90 Mark II	Not rally car?
LHP 823	A3004317HSO	12/09/1951	90 Mark II	1952 works rally car
LHP 824	A3004381HSO	12/09/1951	90 Mark II	Not rally car?
MWK 11	A3010550HSO	12/11/1952	90 Mark IIA	1953 works rally car
MWK 12	A3010496HSO	12/11/1952	90 Mark IIA	1953 works rally car
MWK 13	A3010475HSO	12/11/1952	90 Mark IIA	1953 works rally car
MWK 14	A3010545HSO	12/11/1952	90 Mark IIA	1953 works rally car
MWK 15	A3010527HSO	12/11/1952	90 Mark IIA	1953 works rally car
MWK 16	A3010544HSO	12/11/1952	90 Mark IIA	1953 works rally car
MWK 17	A3010467HSO	12/11/1952	90 Mark IIA	1953 works rally car; exists
MWK 18	A3010464HSO	12/11/1952	90 Mark IIA	1953 works rally car
MWK 969	EXP.006/3 Eng. EXP.146	21/01/1953	Alpine	Jabbeke record car; exists in Switzerland
MKV 21	A3012359HRO	06/05/1953	Alpine	1953-54 works rally car; exists
MKV 22	A3012404HRO	06/05/1953	Alpine	1953-54 works rally car; exists
MKV 23	A3012464HRO	13/05/1953	Alpine	1953-54 works rally car; exists
MKV 24	A3012471HRO	13/05/1953	Alpine	1953-54 works rally car; exists in New Zealand
MKV 25	A3012564HRO	22/05/1953	Alpine	1953-54 works rally car; exists
MKV 26	A3012658HRO	27/05/1953	Alpine	1953-54 works rally car; exists
ODU 699	A3013288HSO	13/08/1953	90 Mark IIA	1954 works rally car
ODU 700	A3013304HSO	14/08/1953	90 Mark IIA	1953-54 works rally car, Sheila Van Damm
ODU 746	A3013291HSO	14/08/1953	90 Mark IIA	1954 works rally car
OHP 318	A3013780HSO	08/10/1953	90 Mark IIA	1954 works rally car; exists
OWK 861	A3014169HRO	18/02/1954	Alpine	1954 Alpine rally press car
PRW 319	A3500133HSO	05/10/1954	Mark III	1955 Monte cinema car
PWK 466	A3500892HSX		Mark III	1955 Monte cinema car
PWK 603	A3500607HSO	07/12/1954	Mark III	1955 works rally car; now in Coventry Transport Museum
PWK 604	A3500614HSO	07/12/1954	Mark III	1955 works rally car
PWK 605	A3500350HSO	07/12/1954	Mark III	1955 works rally car; exists
PWK 606	A3500505HSO	07/12/1954	Mark III	1955 works rally car
RDU 253	A3500547LSO	04/04/1955	Mark III	Lent out for various rallies during 1955-56
RHP 700	A3501883HRO	25/05/1955	Alpine Mark III	Intended 1955 Alpine car
RHP 701	A3501886HRO	25/05/1955	Alpine Mark III	Intended 1955 Alpine car
RHP 702	A3501889HRO	25/05/1955	Alpine Mark III	Intended 1955 Alpine car; exists in Australia
RHP 703	A3501909HRO	25/05/1955	Alpine Mark III	Intended 1955 Alpine car; exists
RHP 704	A3501912HRO	25/05/1955	Alpine Mark III	Intended 1955 Alpine car; exists in Ireland
RHP 705	A3501915HRO	25/05/1955	Alpine Mark III	Intended 1955 Alpine car

A successful conclusion to a distinguished career, the three team winning cars and their drivers after the 1956 Monte Carlo Rally. That confectioner's nightmare on the bonnet on the car in the centre must be the actual Faroux trophy. (Courtesy CTM)

---

1. This chapter builds on the following main sources: Van Damm *No Excuses*; Frostick *Works Team*; Harper *Destination Monte*; Robson *Rootes Maestros*, apart from contemporary magazine articles, and Chris Derbyshire's research
2. *Motor Sport* Jul 1955; Montagu *Lost Causes of Motoring* p.25; Frostick p.77; Robson p.3; Cowbourne *British Trial Drivers 1919-1928* p.562
3. Robson pp.3-5; Cowbourne *British Rally Drivers* pp.85, 102 et passim; Louche *Le Rallye Monte-Carlo au XXe siècle* p.379; Symons *Monte Carlo Rally* p.39 et seq.; Blight *Georges Roesch and the Invincible Talbot* chapter 19 pp.327-42 passim
4. Van Damm p.39; Robson p.11; Davis *Rallies and Trials* p.75 et seq.
5. Pressnell quoting Peter Proctor in "Norman Garrad – rallying's first professional" *Classic and Sportscar* April 1992
6. Bullock "Please can we have our wheels back?" on www.nacho.org.uk; Van Damm pp.170-71 et passim
7. Bullock *Rootes Brothers* pp.147-49
8. Garrad interviewed by Pressnell for "Fruits of the Rootes" *Classic and Sportscar* July 1988; the author queries the quoted figure if it applies to the early 1950s
9. Described as such in *The Autocar* 18 Apr 1947
10. *The Autocar* 13 Jun and 4 Jul 1947; Harper p.18
11. May *Wheelspin Abroad* pp.153-54, citing Ian Appleyard's account; Hiskins's car was chassis number 443-200 according to the *Chassis Register*
12. Some sources credit Murray-Frame not only with taking part in this Alpine, but with winning his class in an 80; in fact the 1500cc class fell to Betty Haig in an MG TC
13. Robson *Monte Carlo Rally – The Golden Years* pp.82-84; *Rootes Maestros* pp.185-88
14. *Motor Sport* Dec 1950
15. Reminiscences of Joan Laurie's son in Collis *The Life and Times of Nancy Spain* cited by Peter Parker in review, *The Independent*, 7 Jun 1997
16. Harper p.124; Sutton in Robson *Rootes Maestros* p.99; on Van Damm see also obituary in *The Scotsman* on their web site not dated and the *Oxford Dictionary of National Biography*
17. Frostick pp.24-25
18. Cooper in *The Autocar* 15 Feb 1952. A very similar article appeared over Moss's name and is reproduced in Robson *Rootes Maestros* pp.69-74; Graham Robson and I conclude that Cooper ghost-wrote this.
19. Van Damm p.78
20. Bullock *Rootes Brothers* cover
21. Van Damm p.82
22. Hawthorn *Challenge Me the Race* p.39; Bailey and Skilleter *Mike Hawthorn Golden Boy* p.219
23. www.kujawja.org/kolaczkowski.html
24. Dugdale *Jaguar in America* p.28
25. Cooper in *The Autocar* 13 Feb 1953; Louche p.130; Robson *Monte Carlo* pp.97-101
26. *Autosport* 12 Apr 1957; Bullock *Rootes Brothers* p.188; obituary in *The Daily Telegraph* 24 Jan 2003; obituary in *XK Gazette* Mar 2003
27. Baxter with Dron *Tales of My Time* chapter 14 pp.192-210 passim (he mixes up the 1953 and 1954 rallies)
28. Harper pp.84-85
29. Adams *From Craigantlet to Monte Carlo* pp.37-40 et passim
30. *Ibid.* pp.40-43
31. Cooper in *The Autocar* 12 Feb 1954
32. Harper pp.92-93; obituary in *The Times* 19 Sep 2003
33. Harper pp.85-87
34. *The Motor* 30 Jun 1954
35. Harper pp.20-22
36. *Ibid.* pp.80-81
37. Information courtesy of Malcolm Champion
38. *The Autocar* 25 Mar 1955
39. *Who's Who in the Motor and Commercial Vehicle Industries* (1965 ed.) p.515
40. *The Autocar* 4 Feb 1955; www.bilhistorie.no; www.bilnorge.no
41. *Autosport* 4 Mar 1955; www.motorsportavisen.no; www.bilnorge.no
42. *The Autocar* 4 Feb 1955
43. Harper pp.93-94
44. *The Autocar* 12 Aug 1955
45. Mostly compiled from Warwickshire registration records, Warwickshire County Record Office, and Coventry registration records, Coventry Transport Museum archive

Chapter Eight

Sunbeam-Talbot rivals

Michael Sedgwick called it "Betjeman-Land": "...the world of tennis and bridge [where] one spent between £250 and £800 on a car..."[1] The pre-war Sunbeam-Talbot was a natural for this market sector, for which it might have been – probably was – deliberately intended. It was a car for the individualist who was prepared to spend a little more money than average to get an unusual, rather exclusive car; smart but never flash, sporty but not really sporting. And the smallest model, at least, was quite likely designed with the woman motorist in mind.

When discussing market conditions in Britain of the 1930s, it is necessary to explain that ever-present bugbear, the horsepower tax. The Royal

S.S.II saloon 1934-35 model. (courtesy Allan Crouch)

Automobile Club had originally devised its formula for calculating horsepower in 1906. It was based simply on the bore of the cylinder and the number of cylinders: the bore squared, multiplied by the number of cylinders, was divided by a constant of 2.5 if the bore was measured in inches, or 1612.9 if the bore was measured in millimetres. The formula was thus an expression of piston area but took no account of the stroke or of engine size as such. In 1909, Lloyd George first introduced a graduated system of annual vehicle tax based on RAC horsepower rating but with few and wide steps. In 1920 the fiscal screw was tightened so that the vehicle excise duty was increased to £1 per year for each RAC horsepower, the amount raised supposedly going into the road fund. A 12hp car now cost £12 annually to tax. The figure of £1 per hp was reduced to 15s. in 1935 but was increased to 25s. in the 1939 budget, and this was the rate still levied after the Second World War.[2]

The horsepower tax came completely to dominate the thinking of the motor industry, and of car buyers; quite understandably as in the 1930s, the annual tax could be 5 per cent or more of the list price of a new car, the equivalent of paying £500 per year for a car costing £10,000 in 2009. Another side effect was that British cars inevitably had under-square engines with small bores and long strokes, which in some cases persisted right through the 1950s and beyond, despite the replacement of the horsepower tax with the flat-rate tax in 1948 (originally £10 per annum for all new cars). An 8hp car was typically of 800-1000cc, a Ten of 1100-1300cc, a Twelve of around 1500cc, and so on. The motor manufacturers tried to cover every market niche with a plethora of models of different sizes, often with little regard for rationalisation, and especially in the depression years the market came to demand prestige, sports and luxury cars of low horsepower ratings, even when such models cost quite a bit more than the most popular models of similar size. This was the niche that Rootes entered with the Talbot Ten.

It could be argued that when Rootes introduced that car in 1935, the Talbot Ten had an almost unique presence in the British market. In the low-hp class, the nearest equivalent had been the S.S.II which was going out of production just as the Talbot was coming in. Both were attractive-looking but had no particular sporting pretensions. Both had two-door bodies, when the majority of British motorists preferred four doors. So, while there was a varied choice of "premium brands" even in the 9-11hp class, most of these were four-door saloons. The table below refers to 1936 models, except for the S.S., while the Wolseley only appeared partway through the model year.

The Rover Ten, here a 1939 model, was the leader in the low-hp prestige class.

Model	Body styles	Engine	Price	Top speed
Crossley Regis	Four-door saloon	1122cc, 9.8hp	£335	59-65mph
Lanchester Ten	Four-door saloon	1444cc, 11hp	£298-£375	61-66mph
Riley Nine	Four-door saloon	1089cc, 9.02hp	£269-£295	61-68mph
Rover Ten	Four-door saloon	1389cc, 10.8hp	£248	65mph
S.S.II 10hp	Two-door saloon, tourer	1343cc, 10hp	£235	61-63mph
Singer Eleven	Four-door saloon	1459cc, 10.95hp	£215-£245	
Talbot Ten	Two-door saloon, tourer, drophead coupé	1185cc, 9.8hp	£260-£295	64-68mph
Triumph Gloria four, Gloria Vitesse four	Four-door saloon, tourer, drophead coupé, sports	1087cc, 9.5hp or 1232cc, 10.8hp	£295-£365	65-72mph
Wolseley 10/48	Four-door saloon, two-door coupé	1292cc, 10hp	£220-£253	60-62mph

Of these cars, the most sporting was the Triumph Gloria, often touted as "the smartest car in the land" and the four-light saloon was indeed pretty, while there was also the open sports Southern Cross model in the range. However, a 10.8hp saloon cost £315 and the higher-performance Vitesse version another £30. The Riley Nine was a time-honoured favourite but was becoming overshadowed by the same maker's 1½-litre model, and although the Kestrel saloon was still available at £295, it was accompanied by a much less elegant if cheaper all-steel Merlin saloon. With twin-carburettor Special Series engine, the Kestrel would have had a performance comparable to the Triumph Vitesse with a top speed of around 70mph (113km/h); otherwise the class norm was around 65mph (105km/h).

The Rileys enjoyed the advantage of the easy-to-operate preselector gearbox, which was also found on the Crossley and Lanchester among the staider models. The drawbacks of this gearbox were its cost and its weight. The best buy for the family motorist with aspirations was undoubtedly the Rover Ten; the Wolseley was cheaper but suffered for its Morris-like styling and the fact that only another £5 would buy the same car with a 12hp engine, which always outsold its smaller sibling. The Wolseley, Triumph and Singer had hydraulic brakes, the latter also a single ohc engine and the option of Gordon Armstrong independent front suspension, otherwise all conformed to the contemporary norm, but once the S.S.II had gone the little Talbot had the only side-valve engine of the prestige tens, so it did quite well to achieve a top speed of 64-68mph (103-109km/h).

After the horsepower tax was reduced in 1935, some of the specialised car makers moved their smallest offerings up into the 12hp or 1½-litre class. By 1939, the choice of specialist cars in the below-12hp class had been reduced to the following:

Singer had now effectively moved itself down-market in an attempt to recoup lost market share, yet the company was unable to compete head-on with the big battalions on price. In the last pre-war season, most family "Tens" cost between £145 and £175, and most popular "Fourteens" – full-sized family cars, often with six-cylinder engines – were around £250 or less. The Sunbeam-Talbot was now the closest you got to a sports saloon in this horsepower bracket, yet it also had the only side-valve engine. The total of 3604 cars made in the 1939 and 1940 seasons came close to beating the Rover Ten with an estimated production of 3763 cars in the same period but both were some way behind the new Wolseley Ten with over 5000 cars. Compared to the average family Ten, what you got for your extra £50-100 was a famous brand name, better finish and equipment – and above all, style and exclusivity. The mass-market Tens, such as the Hillman Minx, now typically had top speeds of around 63mph (101km/h), so here most of the prestige brands also enjoyed a slight advantage.

There was little incentive for a British motorist in search of a prestigious small car to look at imports in the 1930s. There were no real European equivalents to a Rover, Sunbeam-Talbot or Wolseley. Despite the import duty of one-third of value, small European cars were often competitive on price, thanks to the advantageous exchange rates against the French Franc and Italian Lira, or in case of German cars, the alleged export subsidies. However, imported cars often suffered from attracting higher annual horsepower tax because of their more modern engines with bigger bores and shorter strokes. Compared to British cars, European cars were considered Spartan, with interiors of painted metal and cloth rather than wood and leather, while their engine characteristics and gearing made them less flexible on top gear, and sometimes noisier. That most of the imports scored

Model	Body styles	Engine	Price	Top speed
Lanchester Eleven	Four-door saloon	1444cc, 11hp	£295-£298	63mph
Rover Ten	Four-door saloon, two-door coupé	1389cc, 10.8hp	£275	67mph
Singer Super Ten	Four-door saloon	1185cc, 9.8hp	£195	62-64mph
Sunbeam-Talbot Ten	Four-door saloon, tourer, drophead coupé	1185cc, 9.8hp	£265-£285	68-70mph
Wolseley 10	Four-door saloon, drophead coupé	1140cc, 10hp	£215 (saloon)	68-70mph

highly in terms of road holding, handling and performance was irrelevant to all but a small minority of British motorists.

Because of their home market requirements, French manufacturers were not greatly interested in small cars in the 1930s; the smallest French car regularly available in the UK was the Citroën Super Modern Twelve, alias the 7CV *Traction Avant*, of 1628cc and taxed on 13hp, built at Slough and therefore available from only £198 by 1939. None of the German small cars made a lasting impression, and nothing smaller than a 2-litre BMW, helped by the Frazer-Nash moniker, would have any impact in Betjemanland. Italian cars however had an established following in Britain, notwithstanding the antics latterly displayed by Signor Mussolini in Abyssinia and Spain.

By 1937-39, there were two admirable modern small Italian cars on the British market. The new Fiat 508C 1100 was almost a bargain at £198 although its 1089cc engine was taxed on 12hp. The 1352cc Lancia Aprilia was taxed on 13hp, and was pricier at £298 upwards. The Fiat had independent suspension at the front, while on the Lancia this amenity was extended to the rear, and this car also featured unitary body construction. Both had aerodynamic styling, hydraulic brakes and modern short-stroke overhead-valve engines, a V4 on the Lancia. The Fiat did over 70mph (113km/h) with ease, the Lancia over 78mph (126km/h). Despite glowing reports in the magazines, their impact in Britain was minimal, and they were the choice only of the better-informed *cognoscenti*.

It is equally difficult to justify the bigger Sunbeam-Talbots on purely rational grounds, especially as Rootes themselves offered large Humbers at lower prices but with nearly the same performance. There was obviously a far greater choice in the 3- to 4-litre bracket, at between £300 and £500. In this sector of the market, the tax horsepower rating was not quite such an important factor as it was for smaller cars, and the only imports competitive on price came from North America. The table below is a selection of those 1939 cars which might have been considered by potential Sunbeam-Talbot buyers.

The big Ford V8 was British-built from 1935 onwards and therefore escaped the import duty. Clearly it appeared to have an unbeatable lead by virtue of its combination of price and performance – the high top speed was coupled with remarkable acceleration – yet it was often shunned as it was considered very non-U. Chassis design was simple and unsophisticated, whereas styling was blowsy Detroit and changed annually. With transverse springs and until 1938 mechanical brakes, it did not shine in terms of road holding, handling or braking, but as well as being quick, it was sturdy, reliable and blessed with excellent ground clearance. I suspect it was

Rootes's own in-house competitor, the Humber Super Snipe, which outsold the big Sunbeam-Talbots.

Model	Body styles	Engine	Price	Top speed
Buick Special	Saloon	4065cc, 30.6hp	£495	82-83mph
Chrysler Royal	Saloon	3970cc, 27.3hp	£450	82mph
Ford V8 30	Saloon, drophead coupé	3622cc, 30hp	£280 (saloon)	85mph
Humber Snipe	Saloon	3181cc, 20.9hp	£355	76-79mph
Humber Super Snipe	Saloon (and others)	4086cc, 26.9hp	£385-£430	82-86mph
MG WA	Saloon, tourer, drophead coupé	2561cc, 19.8hp	£442-£468	91mph
Rover Speed Twenty	Saloon, drophead coupé	2512cc, 19.8hp	£425 (saloon)	80mph
SS Jaguar 3½-litre	Saloon, drophead coupé	3485cc, 25hp	£445-£465	92mph
Sunbeam-Talbot 3-litre	Saloon, tourer, drophead coupé	3181cc, 20.9hp	£415-£525	81-85mph
Sunbeam-Talbot 4-litre	Saloon, tourer, drophead coupé, limousine	4086cc, 26.9hp	£455-£630	82-87mph
Vauxhall 25	Saloon	3215cc, 25hp	£345	75-77mph
Wolseley 25	Saloon, drophead coupé	3485cc, 25hp	£395-£498	82-85mph

a great favourite in rural communities, and shooting brake bodywork was a regular option.

Less of a stigma attached to other American cars, often imported from Canada at the preferential Empire rate of duty. Buick and Chrysler were only two of many such models in a class which included even the lesser species of Packard and the Lincoln Zephyr V12. Cars of a similar type and size from Alvis, Armstrong-Siddeley or Daimler were more expensive, in the £500-£800 bracket. For the buyer who looked for a sporting image and performance at an affordable price, the most serious contender was undoubtedly the biggest SS Jaguar, equally as smart as any of the various Sunbeam-Talbot body styles, and with a top speed of 92mph (148km/h) which put even the MG WA in the shade. Crucially, the big Sunbeam-Talbots were outsold by the Humber Super Snipe which had a performance not far behind them.

After 1945, Betjeman-Land still survived, in spite of inflation and the falling value of fixed incomes, higher income tax and the difficulties of getting domestic servants. Well into the 1950s, sectors of the middle class continued to buy British specialist rather than mass-production motorcars. However, that market niche was under attack from several fronts. Jaguar and Rover undercut and out-competed every other independent specialist producer. While the mass-produced offerings became increasingly sophisticated, many later "badge-engineered" deluxe variants from the great combines were not sufficiently different from base models to continue to attract their traditional clientele. Finally, the tide of imports rose inexorably. Even in the 1960s, these factors would overwhelm many a proud old British brand name, which by then was on its uppers, if it survived at all. Sixty-plus years on, the grandchildren or great-grandchildren of the original denizens of Betjeman-Land drive BMW or Mercedes-Benz estate cars, SUVs, or if they have gone green, Japanese hybrids.

For a while, the Sunbeam-Talbot continued to occupy that particular, traditional niche in the British car market, of the mid-range semi-specialist quality saloon with sporting overtones. In the post-war period, this was almost exclusively a British preserve. Very few other European car makers offered cars of similar types, but Mercedes-Benz and Lancia were obvious comparisons, joined a little later by Alfa Romeo and BMW. None of these would be available in Britain until 1953 at the earliest.

By the late 1940s, cars of this type usually sold in Britain at basic prices anywhere between £500 and £1000, and once the horsepower tax had been replaced by the flat-rate tax in 1948, most had engine sizes between 1.5 and 2.5 litres. Of the "Big Six", Nuffield, Rootes and Standard-Triumph all had one or more models in this bracket. Jaguar and Rover were naturally represented, as were other of the smaller independent specialists.

Below this mid-range quality bracket came the "ordinary" large family saloons, of which the Austin A70, Morris Six, Standard Vanguard and Vauxhall Velox were of similar size to the 90 and some times not far behind on performance, but which in 1949 cost only between £430 and £525 basic. At the top end of the group came the AC 2-litre, the Alvis TA14, Armstrong-Siddeley and Lea-Francis, from manufacturers who by this

3½ litre SS Jaguar: fastest British car of its class and a commercial success.

Apart from the Sunbeam-Talbot 80, the MG Y-type was the most important of the dwindling number of small-capacity British prestige cars.

time were all struggling to keep the basic price below £1000 to avoid the two-thirds Purchase Tax which was then levied on cars of a basic price of £1000 or more. The Daimler Consort had already crossed this Rubicon.

The following table, with prices quoted as at July 1949, represents the most relevant competitors for the two new Sunbeam-Talbots around this time:

It is difficult to avoid drawing the conclusion that the 80 was somewhat overpriced for what it offered. The 1100-1300cc bracket, which used to be the "10hp" class, was rapidly going out of favour after the tax change in 1948, with most manufacturers introducing new models of at least 1500cc but often bigger. Singer, Rover and Wolseley had all offered their pre-war 10hp models as part of their initial post-war

Model	Body styles	Price	Engine	Top speed
MG Y-type	Saloon, tourer	£525/£672	4/1250/46	71mph
Wolseley 4/50	Saloon	£550/£704	4/1476/51	74mph
Wolseley 6/80	Saloon	£600/£767	6/2214/72	77mph
Singer SM 1500	Saloon	£625/£799	4/1506/48	71mph
Humber Hawk	Saloon	£625/£799	4/1944/56	71mph
Sunbeam-Talbot 80	Saloon, drophead coupé	£695/£889	4/1185/47	71mph
Riley 1½-litre	Saloon	£714/£913	4/1496/55	78mph
Lanchester Ten	Saloon	£725/£927	4/1287/40	68mph
Jowett Javelin	Saloon	£738/£944	4/1486/50	78mph
Triumph 2000	Saloon, roadster	£775/£991	4/2088/68	75mph
Sunbeam-Talbot 90	Saloon, drophead coupé	£775/£991	4/1944/64	77mph
Rover P3 60	Saloon	£845/£1080	4/1595/50	72mph
Rover P3 75	Saloon	£865/£1106	6/2103/72	75mph
Jaguar Mark V 2½-litre	Saloon, drophead coupé	£930/£1189	6/2663/102	85mph (est.)
Riley 2½-litre	Saloon, drophead coupé	£958/£1225	4/2443/100	95mph
AC 2-litre	Two-door saloon, tourer	£982/£1277	6/1991/74	84mph
Armstrong-Siddeley 16	Saloon, drophead coupé	£995/£1272	6/1991/70	75mph (est.)
Alvis TA14	Saloon, drophead coupé	£998/£1276	4/1892/65	80mph
Lea-Francis 14	Saloon	£998/£1276	4/1767/56	70mph (est.)

programmes but had dropped them in 1948. The MG Y-type and the Lanchester Ten had both originally been conceived in 1939-40 but their introduction had been delayed until 1946.

The 90 was better placed in the market as regards price and performance. In terms of styling, the Sunbeam-Talbots were at this time among the best-looking and most modern of the cars selected. Separate wings, running boards and separate headlamps were still found on many of the cars listed. On the other hand, Sunbeam-Talbot was in one respect distinctly behind the times, as one of few cars on this list with semi-elliptic leaf springs on a beam front axle. Among the few other hold-outs from independent front suspension by now were AC and Alvis. One advantage of the Sunbeam-Talbot range was that both models were available with the alternative drophead coupé or convertible body style, by now fast becoming a rarity.

The most obvious rivals for the 90 were the Rileys, more old-fashioned in looks but in some respects more modern mechanically, with independent front suspension and rack-and-pinion steering. The performance of the 1½-litre was comparable with the 90, and the 2½-litre was the outstanding British sports saloon of its day, its main drawback being heavy steering. Much to their credit, the Riley saloons retained a floor gear change; column change was confined to the US-orientated Roadster model. Otherwise the sporting family motorist might take a chance on a Javelin, a distinctive and advanced design which had (and has) a devoted following, regardless of the mechanical problems that it suffered from. Its performance was complemented by excellent road holding and handling, while it was also roomy and comfortable. If you had no sporting inclinations, a Triumph or Rover would do just as well. The smaller-engined Jaguar Mark V was always in the shadow of its big 3½-litre brother but was an adequate performer in its own right. However, already then the image of the big Jaguar saloon was moving firmly in the direction of prestige car rather than sports saloon.

What then upset the applecart was that in 1950 Ford launched the Zephyr Six. By 1951, when Purchase Tax of two-thirds was levied on all cars irrespective of basic price, the Zephyr Six cost a mere £817 and, with the exception of the £803 Vauxhall Velox, undersold all other family cars in the 2 to 2.5-litre bracket. The Zephyr and its smaller four-cylinder Consul sibling were by far the most modern British family cars, with up-to-the minute styling, unitary construction, over-square short-stroke engines, and independent McPherson strut suspension at the front. With 68bhp to propel its relatively lightweight structure (2604lb, 1182kg), the Zephyr would do an honest 80mph (129km/h) and more if breathed upon. Its combination of performance and six-cylinder refinement meant that sooner or later all competitors would have to fall in line. It might only have had three forward gears, which at least made its column change easier to master than some. Its handling and road holding may not have been perfect, but they were good enough for a Zephyr to win the 1953 Monte Carlo Rally. Laurence Pomeroy junior, the eminent technical editor of *The Motor*, was a convert; so was Raymond Mays of ERA and BRM fame.

Towards the end of the production run of the original 90, now called the Sunbeam Mark III, the choice of mid-range quality or sports saloons was shrinking. Many of the manufacturers who had offered such cars in 1949 had either disappeared, or had wisely moved into a higher bracket where they did not face competition from the mass-producers, if still from Jaguar. In 1955, a formidable new competitor appeared: the Jaguar 2.4 litre. There was now also a trend towards sporting 1.5-litre saloons, in part created by Sunbeam's own Rapier, while mass-market six-cylinder family cars in the 2.5-litre class by late 1955 cost between £532 and £620 basic, or between £799 and £931 including Purchase Tax which was now of 60 per cent. Most expensive in this bracket were the "aspirational" deluxe versions from Ford and Vauxhall, the Zodiac and the Cresta.

The Rileys, here a 1954 1½-litre, were among the most important Sunbeam-Talbot 90 rivals.

Model	Body styles	Price	Engine	Top speed
MG Magnette ZA	Saloon	£645/£969	4/1489/60	80mph
Singer Hunter	Saloon	£687/£1033	4/1496/50	74-76mph
Sunbeam Rapier	Two-door saloon	£695/£1044	4/1390/62	85mph
Humber Hawk	Saloon	£715/£1074	4/2267/75	83mph (est.)
Wolseley 6/90	Saloon	£750/£1126	6/2639/95	94mph
Sunbeam Mark III	Saloon, drophead coupé	£835/£1254	4/2267/80	91-95mph
Rover P4 60	Saloon	£840/£1261	4/1997/60	77mph
Riley Pathfinder	Saloon	£875/£1314	4/2443/102	98mph
Rover P4 75	Saloon	£915/£1375	6/2230/80	86mph
Jaguar 2.4 litre SE	Saloon	£916/£1375	6/2483/112	102mph
Rover P4 90	Saloon	£945/£1419	6/2638/93	91mph
Armstrong-Siddeley 234	Saloon	£1065/£1599	4/2290/120	97mph
Daimler Conquest	Saloon, drophead coupé	£1066/£1600	6/2433/75	82mph
Armstrong-Siddeley 236	Saloon	£1104/£1657	6/2309/85	80mph (est.)
Daimler Conquest Century	Saloon, drophead coupé	£1172/£1759	6/2433/100	87mph

The Mark III was no sluggard, but on the one hand much cheaper 1.5-litre cars were knocking on the door, with almost comparable performance due to their more compact and lighter unitary construction bodies, and on the other hand Rover and Jaguar were consolidating their positions in the six-cylinder prestige market, even to the detriment of BMC. Furthermore, the unreconstructed 1948 styling with its limitations on passenger as well as boot space was beginning to tell against the Sunbeam, as was its "big four" engine. Above all, the 2.4-litre "Jag" with its handsome styling and promise of 100mph (161km/h) performance, at only £121 more (tax paid) than the Sunbeam, was the final nail in the coffin of the still excellent but ageing Rootes product. The deficiencies of the Jaguar design in terms of road holding and braking would only manifest themselves when the larger 3.4-litre engine was installed in 1957. Meanwhile, in September 1956 when the Mark III was clearly on the way out, its factory price was slashed to a lowest-ever £765, or £1149 including P.T.

Only when it was almost too late did Rootes introduce a fine modern medium-sized six-cylinder engine, in the new Humber Super Snipe of 1958, initially of 2651cc and 105bhp, soon enlarged to 2965cc and 121bhp. The design of this engine was actually based on that of the Armstrong-Siddeley Sapphire. The Super Snipe had the new Humber unitary bodyshell, shared with the latest Hawk and of distinctly American styling. It sat a little uneasily in the market, above Austin, Ford and Vauxhall, below the Jaguars and six-cylinder Rovers. The potential of its engine in a more sporting saloon was never realised. In any case, Rootes by then had every reason to be happy about the success of the swiftly-improving Rapier in the sports saloon market.

Over the lifetime of the Sunbeam-Talbot 90 from 1948 to 1956, in round figures a total of 24,000 cars were made (excluding the 80 and the Alpine). Looked at over their entire production periods, this compared well with the most obvious competitors of Jowett and Riley and was ahead of Triumph, but as will be seen from the figures in the table below, the clear winner in the prestige class was Rover. When the P4 range was extended with the 60 and 90 models for 1954, Solihull's annual production effortlessly shot up to over 13,000 cars.

Britain's most modern family car, the Ford Zephyr Six, also became a rally contender.

Make, model	Body styles	Period	Total production (rounded off)	Annual average
Humber Hawk side-valve	Saloon	1948-1954	31,000	5150
Jowett Javelin	Saloon	1947-1953	23,000	3800
Riley RM 1½ and 2½ litre	Saloon, drophead, roadster	1946-1955	23,000	2550
Rover P4 75	Saloon	1949-1953	30,000	7500
Singer SM1500 and Hunter	Saloon	1948-1956	22,000	2750
Sunbeam-Talbot 90	Saloon, drophead	1948-1956	24,000	3000
Triumph 1800, 2000 and Renown	Saloon, roadster	1946-1954	20,000	2500
Wolseley 4/50 and 6/80	Saloon	1948-1954	34,000	5700

Another advanced design, the Jowett Javelin.

In the UK, for the lifetime of the post-war Sunbeam-Talbot, imports of foreign cars were banned, or they were subject to duty of one-third by value, effectively rendering them uncompetitive. The picture was little different in most export markets where typically, British cars of a certain type competed amongst themselves. Only in some European market did the Sunbeam-Talbot – or plain Sunbeam, as it was often known to avoid confusion with the French Talbot – meet foreign competitors. Its most consistent European markets were Switzerland, Belgium and Sweden, where it was adopted by much the same type of sporting motorist who would have bought it in the UK.

To demonstrate how the Sunbeam 90 compared with competitors in Europe, let us look at the best European market, "neutral" Switzerland, first in March 1952:[3]

Model	Country	Price	Equivalent in £ at £1 = Sfr 12.25	Engine, cyl/cc/PS	Top speed
Humber Hawk	Britain	Sfr 12,450	£1016	4/2267/59	115km/h
Jowett Javelin	Britain	Sfr 12,500	£1020	4/1486/53	120km/h
Wolseley 6/80	Britain	Sfr 13,520	£1104	6/2215/73	130km/h
Triumph Renown	Britain	Sfr 14,400	£1176	4/2088/69	118km/h
Riley 1½-litre	Britain	Sfr 14,450	£1180	4/1496/56	125-130km/h
Rover P4 75	Britain	Sfr 14,500	£1184	6/2103/76	129km/h
Sunbeam 90 Mark II	Britain	Sfr 15,000	£1224	4/2267/71	137km/h
Riley 2½-litre	Britain	Sfr 16,900	£1380	4/2443/101	150km/h
Lancia Aurelia B10	Italy	Sfr 18,150	£1482	6/1754/56	135km/h
Mercedes-Benz 220	Germany	Sfr 18,300	£1494	6/2195/80	142km/h
Hotchkiss Anjou 13CV	France	Sfr 19,100	£1559	4/2312/75	130-135km/h
Talbot Lago Baby	France	Sfr 20,150	£1645	4/2690/110	140km/h
Alfa Romeo 1900	Italy	Sfr 21,300	£1739	4/1884/80	150km/h

The happy union of two famous brand names, the Austin-Healey 100 was an instant success.

This list is not surprisingly dominated by British cars. The only two French contenders, apart from being expensive, were woefully out of date and were in stark contrast to the two modern Italian cars. The only other French car of similar type was the Salmson but this does not appear to have been available in Switzerland.

By March 1956, British cars still dominated the selection of mid-range prestige cars, but French cars of the old school had disappeared. At this time, Sfr 10-12,000 would buy a European 2-litre-plus six-seater family saloon, and the cheapest American cars were in the Sfr 15,000 bracket.

Model	Country	Price	Equivalent in £ at £1 = Sfr 12.25	Engine, cyl/cc/PS	Top speed
Borgward Isabella TS	Germany	Sfr 11,450	£935	4/1493/75	150km/h
Alfa Romeo Giulietta	Italy	Sfr 11,800	£963	4/1290/50	135km/h
MG Magnette	Britain	Sfr 11,800	£963	4/1489/60	130-135km/h
Humber Hawk	Britain	Sfr 12,535	£1023	4/2267/75	130km/h
Rover P4 60	Britain	Sfr 12,800	£1045	4/1997/61	120km/h
Sunbeam Rapier	Britain	Sfr 12,890	£1052	4/1390/62	145km/h
Citroën DS19	France	Sfr 13,400	£1094	4/1911/75	140km/h
Wolseley 6/90	Britain	Sfr 13,800	£1127	6/2639/96	150-155km/h
Sunbeam Mark III	Britain	Sfr 14,480	£1182	4/2267/81	140km/h
Rover P4 75	Britain	Sfr 15,950	£1302	6/2230/81	129km/h
Riley Pathfinder	Britain	Sfr 16,800	£1371	4/2443/110	155-160km/h
Mercedes-Benz 220a	Germany	Sfr 16,900	£1380	6/2195/92	152km/h
Rover P4 90	Britain	Sfr 16,950	£1384	6/2638/93	140-145km/h
Jaguar 2.4-litre SE	Britain	Sfr 17,600	£1437	6/2483/114	160km/h
BMW 501-6	Germany	Sfr 17,700	£1445	6/2077/72	145km/h
Alfa Romeo 1900 Super	Italy	Sfr 18,000	£1469	4/1975/90	160km/h
Lancia Aurelia B12	Italy	Sfr 18,800	£1535	6/2267/87	151km/h
Daimler Conquest	Britain	Sfr 19,500	£1592	6/2433/76	130km/h
Daimler Century	Britain	Sfr 20,800	£1698	6/2433/101	145km/h

These comparisons suggest that if judged on price alone, most British cars were competitive with European counterparts in Continental markets, and that the 90 occupied a very similar position to that which obtained in the UK. However, price was not the only factor, and the single most important European car in this bracket was and remained the Mercedes-Benz 220. The 1951-54 model had been a half-way house with a separate chassis and body styling still clearly inspired by pre-war models, while the 220a introduced in 1954 had an up-to-date full-width unitary body in the so-called "ponton" style. Both versions shared similar mechanicals, with a modern and excellent single ohc six-cylinder engine, and all-independent suspension. Neither was overtly sporting but performance was above average, and the German car always had that built-in feeling of solidity, reliability and quality which so endeared it to successive generations of solid European citizens. Not even Rover or Jaguar could make much headway against the Stuttgart car in European markets.

The more sporting European driver had the difficult choice between two equally tempting Italian offerings, from Alfa Romeo and Lancia. On paper, the 1900 had the edge in terms of performance but the Aurelia had superior road holding and was just as quick from point to point. Then the Citroën DS19 appeared and immediately made every other car look old-fashioned. Despite a modest power output, its aerodynamic shape, combined with outstanding road holding and handling, made it quick for its size, and it soon appeared in road rallies. It was a roomy and comfortable family car, but its appearance and quirky features made it a "love-it-or-hate-it" car, except of course in the French home market where it was quickly adopted and dearly loved as the most prestigious of the few indigenous large saloons, even if the complexities of its design were nearly beyond understanding.

The Sunbeam Alpine was aimed at a very different sector of the market, and was above all intended to sell in the USA, competing against other British sports cars. For a number of reasons, it did not turn out to be the commercial success that Rootes had hoped. Firstly, it was too closely related to the saloon, both in terms of performance and of features such as its dashboard and column gear change. It was therefore arguably more of a "sporting tourer", in the same category as the by-then defunct Triumph and Riley roadsters. Secondly, it had the misfortune to be launched at more or less the same time as the Austin-Healey 100 and the Triumph TR2. Thirdly, it was always rather expensive for what it offered.

This is how the Alpine compared with the established British competition, in terms of performance, price and production figures:

	Austin-Healey 100	**Jaguar XK 120, 140 (OTS only)**	**MG TD, TF**	**Sunbeam Alpine**	**Triumph TR2, TR3**
Cyl/cc	4/2660	6/3442	4/1250 or 1466	4/2267	4/1991
Bhp	100: 90 100M: 100-110	XK 120: 160-180 XK 140: 190-210	TD: 54 or 57 TF: 57 or 63	77-80 Special 97.5	TR2: 90 TR3: 95
Weight	2150 lb	2856 lb	1930 lb	2900 lb	TR2: 1848 lb TR3: 1988 lb
Top speed	106mph	120-125mph	TD, TF: 80mph TF 1500: 85mph	95mph Special 104mph	103mph
UK price, incl. PT, Oct 1954	£1064	£1598 (XK 140)	£780 (TF)	£1212 Special £1375	£887
Swiss price, Feb 1955	Sfr 14,500	Sfr 20,500	Sfr 9500 (TF)	Sfr 14,750	Sfr 11,850
US price	$2985 (Jul 1954)	$3450 (XK 140)	$1995 (TF 1500)	$3000	$2499 (TR2)
Production:					
1953	1274	1310	7145	1130	305
1954	5940	2496	6516	235	4897
1955	4510	1424	1449	217	4463
Total	11,724	5230	15,110	1582	9665

The Triumph TR2 was the cheapest British sports car to offer a genuine 100mph top speed.

This covers only the most important competitors, since all other British sports models of the early 1950s were made in much smaller numbers and were typically more expensive – these included the AC Ace, Allard Palm Beach, Daimler Conquest roadster, Jowett Jupiter, Frazer Nash, Morgan Plus-Four and Swallow Doretti. There were very few European sports cars on the market, but in Switzerland in 1955, you could buy an Alfa Romeo Giulietta Sprint coupé for Sfr 16,000, a Mercedes-Benz 190SL for Sfr 19,500, and a variety of Porsches from Sfr 14,600 upwards.

Still, the strongest competition undoubtedly came from the Austin-Healey 100 and the Triumph TR2. This pair had many similarities with the Alpine. Like the Sunbeam, they were made by large mass-producers with a strong presence in the USA, and used mechanical components adapted from family saloons, including rugged "big four" engines. Unfortunately for the Alpine, both were much lighter, yet had more powerful engines – and both looked like, and were, purpose-designed open two-seaters. The Alpine always struggled to overcome its built-in handicap as a saloon derivative, and its steering column gear change was a disadvantage in this market sector, even in the USA! The Healey and the Triumph were cheaper than the Sunbeam, and although the Jaguar was dearer still, it was arguably better value for money than an Alpine. The production figures tell their own story. Sadly, the Alpine did not hit the mark, especially not in the USA. Rootes were to do much better with their second attempt at a sports car, also called the Sunbeam Alpine, from 1959 onwards.

---

1. Sedgwick *Cars of the 1930s* p.300
2. Plowden *The Motor Car and Politics in Britain* esp. chapters 3, 8 and 14
3. Figures from the Swiss *Automobil Revue*, annual catalogue issue; top speeds either factory figures or estimated by editor

Chapter Nine

The Legacy

The original 1955 Sunbeam Rapier had very up-to-date styling.

There was to be no direct replacement for the Sunbeam Mark III. By the time it went out of production, an altogether new type of Sunbeam had been put on the market: the first of the Rapiers – or, if you prefer, with the Sunbeam Rapier the Rootes Group returned to their original concept for the first Talbot Ten that had been launched exactly twenty years before. Both cars were developed from a contemporary Hillman Minx, and both cars replaced upmarket versions of the Minx, the Talbot Ten the Aero Minx, the Rapier the Minx Californian hard top coupé. The Talbot Ten and the Rapier even had a similar type of body, a pillarless two-door saloon or hard top.

When I say that the Rapier was based on the Hillman Minx, I need to add the qualification that the Rapier appeared at the 1955 Motor Show but the new Minx only followed in mid-1956. Clearly, however, the new design was developed primarily for the important new mass-production four-door family saloon, and the upmarket sporting version was conveniently added on to this programme. When Rootes bought the Singer company, in short order a third variant was added in the shape of the Singer Gazelle, replacing the unlovable Hunter.

All three cars – the Rapier, the new Minx and the Gazelle – shared the same basic unitary bodyshell, with styling which undoubtedly owed a great deal to the influence of the Loewy studio, more precisely the 1953 Studebaker – in fact one may think of the Rapier as being the British equivalent of the Studebaker Hawk coupé range. Under the bonnet of both Minx and Rapier was a new "square" overhead-valve four-cylinder engine, of 76.2mm by 76.2mm and 1390cc: a little on the small side at a time when competing British family saloons were all of 1.5 litres, the new 1956 Ford Consul even of 1.7 litres. This engine had been introduced in the final model of the previous generation Minx in October 1954. In the Hillman, power output was 47.5bhp, but in the Sunbeam it was boosted to 62.5bhp, thanks to a different carburettor and other changes. The Gazelle at first retained the

Singer ohc 1.5-litre engine but received the Minx/Rapier engine in 1958.

The four-speed gearbox still had a column change but on the Rapier an overdrive was standard. The rear axle had spiral-bevel final drive which seemed a retrograde step. The chassis specification in general was strictly conventional, with coil-and-wishbone independent front suspension, semi-elliptic leaf springs on a live rear axle, hydraulic brakes and worm-and-nut steering. The Rapier's top speed of 85mph (137km/h) – *The Autocar* even suggested it might do 90mph (145km/h)[1] – was a useful improvement over the 77mph (124km/h) offered by the 1956 Minx, but the price was naturally correspondingly higher. In October 1956 the Rapier was listed at £695 basic or £1044 including Purchase Tax, while the Minx was £515/£774 in deluxe form, and the Singer Gazelle £598/£898.

The Rapier's styling was rather snazzy. The pillarless effect was achieved when the side windows were lowered, taking their slim chrome-plated channel frames with them. The rear side window had the classic Rootes reverse-angle shape, now matched by a wrap-around rear window. Even on the original Rapier the rear wings nearly had fins, and the 1958 model certainly did. A chrome trim strip along the flanks served as the dividing line for two-tone colour schemes, with the bottom colour then also applied to the roof. The simple full-width grille had plain horizontal bars, which was at least an improvement over the "bone-in-teeth" effect of the Minx. The full-diameter turbo-style wheel trims were pure period, as were the hooded headlamps. The interior often as not had a two-tone trim scheme too, and there was a full set of round instruments, including a rev. counter.

One authority describes the original Rapier as an "ill-handling little beast"[2] which must have been rather a let-down compared to the paeans of praise bestowed on the Mark III. Now I do not think that the Rapier would strictly speaking have appealed to the majority of Mark III buyers – it was simply a too-different type of car – but inevitably there were those Sunbeam aficionados who did buy it, and in some respects the Rapier had a lot going for it compared to the Mark III. For a start it was probably roomier, the boot was positively enormous, it was an easier car to drive and thanks to its lower weight it was much more economical at 34mpg without giving too much away on performance. I cannot but wonder that the Rapier – like the Talbot Ten – must also have held greater appeal to woman drivers, whereas the Mark III and the earlier Sunbeam-Talbot 90 always came across very much as a man's car, notwithstanding the notable achievements of a certain Miss Van Damm.

However, with the demise of the Mark III, the Rapier was the obvious – some say only – choice for Norman Garrad and the Rootes Competitions Department, even if according to Lewis Garrad, Norman's son, they felt like packing up when first confronted by their new charge.[3] Somewhat atypically, it was decided to have a go at the Mille Miglia, which saw the debut in competition for the model. The two cars entered both finished and a class win fell to the car of Peter Harper and Sheila Van Damm – this was in the Category for Touring Cars up to 1600cc which must have been rather narrowly defined, but the Rapiers did beat the MG Magnettes on this occasion.[4] In 1956 there were also class wins in the Tulip and the Alpine Rallies, although in the latter the Rapiers were beaten by a Mark III, as previously related.

Again, one speculates that Garrad had some influence on the development of the Rapier. Twelve months after the debut of the model, production cars received a more powerful engine with two Zenith carburettors and 67bhp, and the finest result for the revised model came

After a shaky start, the Rapier became an efficient rally car, here seen competing in the 1959 Alpine Rally.

The Venezia was actually officially unveiled in the Piazza San Marco in the city from which it took its name, having been precariously ferried there by gondola. (Courtesy David Yeomans)

in the 1958 Monte Carlo Rally where Peter Harper finished fifth overall. For the next few years the Rapier was steadily improved, with changes occurring regularly and rapidly. A Series II version was launched in early 1958. This had the engine bored out to 79mm with a capacity of 1494cc and 68bhp. The gear lever finally migrated to the floor, but the overdrive was relegated to the options list. The slightly anodyne Hillman-shape grille was replaced by a central vertical grille more in traditional Sunbeam style, with flanking horizontal side grilles, and there were now proper tail fins. A convertible version was added. The Series II made its competitive debut in the 1958 RAC Rally, which Peter Harper and Bill Deane won outright – the best result so far for a Rapier.

With the Series III of 1959, improvements included an aluminium cylinder head which helped to boost power to 73bhp, a close-ratio gearbox and front disc brakes, all shared with the new recently-introduced Sunbeam sports car which again was called the Alpine (see below). In 1960, a hypoid-bevel rear axle was finally introduced, while a more powerful engine of 1592cc and 75bhp followed in the Series IIIA of 1961. The Series IV appeared in 1963, with a 78.5bhp engine and 13in instead of 15in wheels, and this car received a new all-synchromesh gearbox in the following year, but the convertible version had been discontinued with the Series IIIA. The last version of this generation of Rapier was the Series V of 1965 to 1967, with a 1725cc 85bhp engine. By then the car was somewhat out-of-date and the intention to produce a new four-door Rapier based on the Hillman Super Minx had been abandoned when that car was launched as the 1963 Humber Sceptre instead; its Sunbeam-like front end rather gave the game away. An odd, short-lived cross-breed between Sceptre and Rapier was the Sunbeam Venezia, put together in small numbers in Italy between 1963 and 1965, with a pretty two-door body by Touring.

As already indicated, where the Rapier carried on the tradition of the Sunbeam-Talbot was in rallying. After its hesitant start, from 1958 to 1963 the Rapier was a formidable contender in rallies, and together with the Austin-Healey 3000 the most consistently successful British rally cars of this period when the Mini Cooper had not quite yet got into its stride, while the Jaguar Mark II was always denied full factory support. It was rarely in the running for overall honours but there were many class wins and team awards. Then in 1961 and again in 1962 a Rapier won the Circuit of Ireland Rally; the driver on both occasions was a certain Paddy Hopkirk. In every year from 1958 to 1962, Rapiers were the highest-placed British cars in the Monte Carlo Rally, with third and fourth overall in 1962 as the best result. Amazingly, Rapiers were raced by the young Rodriguez brothers in Mexico in 1961, although I suspect mainly as a publicity stunt, since both were already well beyond this level in their racing careers. Ricardo won his class in two races, and Pedro was second in one of them.[5]

Garrad retired – or was removed – at the end of 1963. He was replaced as Rootes's Competition Manager by Marcus Chambers (born 1908)

The Sunbeam Alpine was the most modern and stylish British sports car in 1959, but always lagged a little on performance.

who had previously been in charge of BMC's Competitions Department. By this time, the Rapier was out-of-date as a competition car, and Chambers delivered a scathing verdict: "The power was there, but the suspension might not have existed; they could have bolted the axles to the chassis and I would not have noticed the difference." One is reminded of Garrad's 1947 report on the Sunbeam-Talbot 2-litre! When Chambers took over, he found the department demoralized, perhaps because it was increasingly becoming a political football within Rootes, with various departments jostling for control, and factions extending upwards in the hierarchy as far as board level.[6]

Alpine – again

In the meantime, Rootes had another go at the sports car market. The new car launched in 1959 was called the Alpine like its forebear, but the name and the two-seater body style were the only similarities between the two cars. The second-generation Alpine had a unitary construction body shell which was based on the floorpan of the short-wheelbase Hillman Husky estate car, with up-to-the-minute styling by in-house designer Kenneth Howes. With prominent tail fins the result was certainly bold but rather attractive, and a generation ahead of most other popular British sports cars, also for its use of wind-down windows. A hard top version was available. The Alpine featured an aluminium cylinder head, a hypoid-bevel final drive, front disc brakes and 13in road wheels, which would all in due course find their way on to the Rapier, as detailed above. With the original 1494cc 78bhp engine, top speed was around 98mph (158km/h), comparable with the contemporary MGA 1600 which had a top speed of 96-98mph (155-158km/h) but which on a good day would hit the ton. The 1959 price was £685/£971, slotting neatly between the MG at £663/£940 and the Triumph TR3A at £699/£991, and actually cheaper than the Rapier which by then was £695/£985.[7]

The usual Rootes process of continuous upgrading kicked in with the Alpine Series II of 1960 with a 1592cc, 80bhp engine, although with little effect on performance. In 1963, the Alpine Series III became available in two versions, the soft-top Tourer and the GT with a redesigned hard top fitted as standard – detachable, but with no soft top alternative. They had slightly differently tuned engines, with 77bhp for the GT but 82bhp for the Tourer. This practice was abandoned with the Series IV which appeared just a year later, featuring the only major change to the Alpine's styling, as the tail fins were cut back to vertical with new lamp clusters, and there was a new single-bar grille. With the Series IV, Rootes again became a pioneer in the sports car field by offering the option of an automatic gearbox, with the usual penalties of impaired performance – top speed was down to 93mph (150km/h) – and poorer economy. This was a short-lived experiment, and was dropped on the last Alpine, the Series V of 1965-68. Like the Rapier, this featured the new 1725cc engine and had 92.5bhp, but top speed still refused to reach the magic 100mph (161km/h) figure.

The Harrington Alpine was an interesting idea but eventually MG took over this market niche with the MGB GT.

There was also an attempt at turning the Alpine into a proper mini-GT car, some years before MG cornered this market. The Harrington Alpine was a fastback coupé conceived by an outside coachbuilder. Thomas Harrington of Hove in Sussex was long-established but since the early 1930s had been mainly engaged on building coaches and buses; they were also Rootes dealers. Their first modified Alpine of 1961 had a fibreglass hardtop with a fastback extending halfway back along the original boot lid. They succeeded so far in selling the idea to Rootes that the Harrington business was soon taken over by the Robins and Day Group, a dealership owned by the Rootes family, and George Hartwell took charge.[8] The original styling was modified to look more cohesive, and the car went on the market with a choice of three different stages of tune for the engine, partly developed by Hartwell.

After a Harrington Alpine had performed so well in the 1961 Le Mans (see below), a revised model was introduced called, naturally enough, the "Le Mans", with a re-style which deviated further from the standard Alpine, since the rear fins were completely removed, and there was a rear hatch rather than a boot lid. It is estimated that altogether around 450 Harrington Alpines were made, and despite being at least indirectly owned by Rootes, Harrington also made the Dove conversion of the Triumph TR4, similar in principle to their Alpine, and some special Minis, but the company was abruptly closed down in 1966.[9]

Rootes then made a bid for the upper echelons of the sports car market, with a car which would rival at least the Austin-Healey 3000, if not the Jaguar E-type. Inspired by the AC Cobra and actively assisted by Carroll Shelby who had conceived the Cobra, they adopted an American Ford V8 engine which they fitted into the Alpine body shell to create the Sunbeam Tiger. The original 4261cc engine of 1964 had 164bhp (gross) and gave the car a top speed of 117mph (188km/h) while the short-lived Series II of 1967 had a 4727cc, 200bhp engine and even better performance with a top speed of 122mph (196km/h). The Tiger was always handicapped by looking more or less just like the Alpine, although the Series II at least had an egg-crate grille and contrast-colour side stripes which had not yet become such a cliché as they later did. However, when Chrysler finalised their takeover of Rootes in 1967, the Ford-engined Tiger was an early casualty.[10]

Neither the Alpine nor the Tiger quite lived up to the earlier models in terms of competitive successes. A number of Alpines were entered in the 1960 Monte Carlo Rally, and the private Swedish entry of Bäcklund and Falk in 31st place overall won the GT Category. In 1961, three Alpines finished the 12-hour race at Sebring in the USA. There was a rare overall win in the Scottish Rally, and then Norman Garrad was convinced (or persuaded, possibly by Peter Harper) to enter the Le Mans 24-hour race with two cars, one of which was a modified Harrington coupé. This was unexpectedly rewarded with a narrow victory over a Porsche in the Index of Thermal Efficiency contest, by Harper and Procter in the Harrington car, and they were sixteenth overall. They improved this to a fifteenth overall in 1962 but were by then well adrift in the Index competition. In the 1963 Tour de France rally, Rosemary Smith – who had now taken over from Sheila Van Damm as Rootes's "leading lady" – won the *Coupe des Dames*.

In 1964, Marcus Chambers inherited a commitment to running the Sunbeam Tiger at Le Mans and in rallies. The Le Mans entry was a failure with both cars blowing their engines. In the 1965 Monte Carlo Rally Peter Harper and Ian Hall surprised everybody – perhaps not least themselves – by coming fourth overall in atrocious weather conditions, and later that year Harper would have won the Alpine Rally but for the fact that post-rally scrutineering discovered that the engine valves were *smaller* than homologated, leading to instant disqualification. As a consolation prize, there were class wins in other major rallies.[11]

Chrysler and after

With the Rapier, Alpine and Tiger all reaching the end of their lives in 1967-68, what next for the Sunbeam brand? The new Chrysler UK company had an answer, of sorts, in the shape of a new car, again called Rapier, which was a two-door fastback coupé version of the new corporate "Arrow" design, better known as the Hillman Hunter. The Rapier was styled by Roy Axe and had the classic feature of a pillarless, reverse-angle rear quarter light, but might otherwise be considered as a British equivalent of the Plymouth Barracuda; Axe later claimed that styling similarities were coincidental. With an 88bhp 1725cc engine, this became the first Rapier with a top speed of over 100mph, reaching 103mph (166km/h), but it was not really a sporting car in its original guise. Two years later, in 1969, the Alpine name was revived for a simplified and cheaper sister car with a single-carburettor 74bhp engine and the top speed reduced to 91mph (146km/h). There was also the more interesting Rapier H120 with

A Sunbeam Tiger prototype undergoing high-speed testing on the MIRA banking.

Frankly, the fastback Rapier was rather a compromise, getting the most out of the body tooling for the "Arrow" range – but it did offer 100mph motoring.

The Sunbeam Stiletto: pretty, but that was about as far as it went.

This time, it really was only the name which was the same: this Alpine was no sports car.

a Holbay-tuned 105bhp engine, but top speed was improved only slightly to 105mph (169km/h). This range of three cars survived until 1976.

The Rootes Group had embarked on the final stage of their journey with the launch of the Hillman Imp in 1963. In an effort to create publicity to enhance the reputation of the car compared with the Mini and other rivals, the Imp was recruited to the competition programme. As best he could, Marcus Chambers had to make it competitive against the Mini Coopers. The engine was the biggest handicap, as the die-cast aluminium cylinder block made it difficult to increase either bore or stroke, and only by some hocus-pocus with cylinder liners did it become possible to increase the 875cc engine to 998cc. It is greatly to the credit of Chambers, and to driver Rosemary Smith, that she and Val Domleo won the 1965 Tulip Rally outright in one of these Rallye Imps – helped by the class improvement marking system of the special stages. She would have added the *Coupe des Dames* in the 1966 Monte Carlo to Rootes's dwindling list of successes, but like the works Minis, fell victim to the lighting disqualification scandal.[12]

Inevitably there were Sunbeam-badged versions of the Hillman Imp, as a Sunbeam Imp Sport appeared in 1966 with a mildly-tuned 51bhp version of the 875cc Imp engine, and where deemed appropriate, the 998cc 60bhp Hillman Rallye Imp was sometimes badged as a Sunbeam. A year later there was the Sunbeam Stiletto, which was basically a badge-engineered version of the Hillman Imp Californian fastback coupé. Since 1964 there had been a parallel range of upmarket Imp derivatives under the Singer Chamois name, until the Singer brand was discontinued in 1970. These are cars which I am frankly tempted to call the "Sunbeam *Impostor*" and the "Singer *Charade*" respectively. They were about as "genuine" as the Riley and Wolseley versions of the Mini offered by BMC, and the more potent Rallye Imp model, although it had its moments in competition, always suffered in comparison with the much more successful Mini Cooper.

With Sunbeams largely out of the picture, a last hurrah for the Rootes Competitions Department came with the completely unexpected victory for one of the new Hillman Hunters, driven by Andrew Cowan, Bryan Coyle and Colin Malkin, in the 1968 *Daily Express* London to Sydney Marathon Rally. As in the heyday of the Sunbeam-Talbot, stamina and strength were major contributors to this result, since the cars in front of the Hunter were all eliminated by accidents or various mechanical maladies during the final Australian leg of the rally. It was to no avail; within a few months Chrysler had closed the competitions department and Marcus Chambers was made redundant. His assistant Des O'Dell (1927-99) stayed with the company and lived to fight another day.[13]

Even the later completely badge-engineered Sunbeams were laid to rest in 1976, as part of a process which gradually saw all the cars made by the former Rootes Group companies re-badged as Chryslers. Only the model name Alpine survived, on an excellent five-door front-wheel drive family hatchback which was a joint Anglo-French design: mechanically based on the French Simca 1100 but with an attractive body styled by Roy Axe, it was a worthy winner of the European "Car of the Year" award. Then in 1978, in a surprise move Peugeot took over the European interests of Chrysler. It was found that the corporate heritage in both France and Britain included the rights to the Talbot name, as the French Talbot company had been taken over by Simca in 1957, so in 1979 Talbot was re-introduced on both side of the Channel for all the former Rootes, Simca and Chrysler products.

With the Imp range being discontinued in 1976, a crash programme was instituted to make a new small car which turned out to be a truncated three-door version of the Hillman/Chrysler Avenger which had been introduced in 1970 as a competitor for the Ford Escort. The smaller version was launched in 1977 as the Chrysler *Sunbeam*, which inevitably two years later became the *Talbot* Sunbeam… Like the Imp, it was made in the Linwood factory in Scotland. Originally there was a choice of a "stretched" Imp engine of 928cc, or the 1.3 and 1.6-litre engines from the Avenger, with a 1600TI version showing some sporting promise. Mainly I suspect because there was nothing else in the corporate range which was remotely suitable, the Talbot Sunbeam was chosen as the basis for a "homologation special" fitted with a Lotus 2174cc engine. With twin overhead camshafts and sixteen valves, this developed a prodigious 150bhp, and was combined with a ZF five-speed gearbox. The Talbot Sunbeam Lotus was sold as a road car, although at a resounding £7000 it was more expensive than similar models from Ford or Vauxhall, so only around 2300 cars were made.

More important was the rally programme started by Des O'Dell with a prototype in 1978. After a slow build-up during 1978-79, an assault on the World Championship was launched in 1980, with Henri Toivonen and Guy Frequelin as the principal drivers. In six rallies the best result was Toivonen's victory in the British Lombard-RAC Rally. In the following year the only win was by Frequelin in Argentina, but with five second places in other championship events the Talbot won the championship for makes, although Ari Vatanen in a Ford Escort narrowly won the drivers' championship from Frequelin. Incidentally, this was the last time that these rally championships were won by or in British cars. In 1979, rallying regulations had been changed and for the first time allowed four-wheel drive cars to take part. This according to rally historian Graham Robson was where the rot set in: since the 1980s rally cars have become completely specialised machines run at vast expense by works teams, and the amateur with a near-standard production car does not stand a chance.[14]

Talbot's final fling in rallying came to an end when the Linwood factory was closed in 1981 and the Sunbeam range was discontinued; future rally participation was to be confined to French cars bearing the Peugeot name. In 1986, the Talbot name and range were dropped altogether, and the old Rootes factory at Ryton outside Coventry simply became the British Peugeot assembly plant. This phase lasted another twenty years but production came to an end in 2006 and the factory was demolished in 2007, ironically in Hillman's centenary year.

The real legacy?

It was Norman Garrad's great achievement to establish the Rootes Competitions Department as the first modern-day works team in the British motor industry. Broadly speaking, this was the example which inspired the other large-scale manufacturers to follow suit. Standard-Triumph

Surprisingly, with the Lotus engine the Talbot Sunbeam became an effective rally car, despite its modest origins.

began in 1953-54 under the direction of Ken Richardson, with Graham Robson taking over in 1962. BMC set up a competitions department in 1955, headed first by Marcus Chambers, and then from 1961 to 1967 by Stuart Turner. During Turner's tenure at BMC, the Mini Cooper S became the most formidable rally car anywhere, with among others three Monte Carlo wins to the credit of the team – and it really should have been four, except for the infamous 1966 disqualification.

The BMC and Standard-Triumph competitions departments were to become some times uneasy bedfellows after the Leyland-BMC merger in 1968, and the new BL Motorsport Department never enjoyed quite the same success as had Standard-Triumph or BMC before the merger. Efforts were sporadic and often seemed half-hearted, and finally petered out after the disaster with the MG 6R4 in the 1980s. Even that cloud had a silver lining, as the 6R4's engine went on to become the basis for the TWR-Jaguar sports-racing car engines, and helped to win three World Sports Car Championships.

The biggest long-term success story was Ford. This company had supported private drivers in rallying on and off since the late 1940s, with Ken Wharton scoring notable successes, winning three Tulip Rallies, a feat that escaped Rootes at the time. In 1952 Ford set up a proper works team at Brentford to run the Zephyr Six, and was immediately rewarded by Maurice Gatsonides winning the 1953 Monte Carlo Rally. From 1959 onwards more promising material came along in the shape of the new Anglia and the Cortina, and the Ford team moved to Boreham in Essex. Apart from rallying and touring car racing, in the 1960s there was an interesting and highly successful diversion known as the GT40, which notched up three wins at Le Mans (plus one for the Mark IV).

Then there was Formula Ford, and the Ford-Cosworth engine which went on to dominate Formula One. In rallying the real glory days began in 1968 when Ford won the first World Rally Championship with the Escort Twin-Cam, and Escort derivatives of one sort or another stayed competitive right through the 1970s. In 1969, Walter Hayes of Ford's PR Department hired ex-BMC competition manager Stuart Turner as Director of Motor Sport, and he stayed in charge until 1990. Ford as a company is still involved in motor sport, although now on a European rather than a strictly British level.

Of the major British companies in the 1950s and 1960s, only Vauxhall stayed out of motor sport. Jowett had a go before the company folded in 1954, while Jaguar had a works team from 1951 to 1956, mainly for racing, but also lending cars to and supporting private rally entrants. Some unlikely contenders flirted with the idea of works rally cars, such as Armstrong-Siddeley, Aston Martin, Daimler and Rover. The successes accumulated by the Rootes and other British works rally teams may even have inspired European car manufacturers to follow their example, including SAAB, Citroën, Renault, Volvo, Mercedes-Benz, Fiat, Peugeot and Audi; even Lancia, although they had both rallied and raced in the early to mid-1950s. Later on the Japanese manufacturers followed suit.

As I stated in my introduction, while rallying is still a thriving branch of motor sport, in recent years it has become overshadowed by Formula One, and somehow I do not think that a leading Formula One driver – such as Lewis Hamilton – would take part in the Monte Carlo in the way that the young Stirling Moss did over fifty years ago. Surely the development of modern rallying in the post-Second World War period owes very much to the continued involvement of the works teams, and I remain convinced that the pioneer was a certain Norman Garrad, with his Rootes team, and with the Sunbeam-Talbots in particular.

---

1. Road test *The Autocar* 20 Apr 1956
2. Langworth *Tiger, Alpine, Rapier* p.51
3. Langworth p.62
4. Van Damm *No Excuses* pp.222-28
5. Sutton in Robson *Rootes Maestros* pp.93-160 for details of Rapier competition successes
6. Chambers *Works Wonders* pp.217-18
7. McGovern *Alpine the Classic Sunbeam*; passim
8. Langworth p.104
9. Walker in *The Beaulieu Encyclopaedia – Coachbuilding* p.182
10. Taylor *Tiger the Making of a Sports Car*, passim
11. Robson pp.161-84 and 213-50 for details of Alpine and Tiger competition careers
12. Chambers pp.244-47, Robson pp.263-67
13. Chambers pp.270-71, Robson pp.325-27
14. Robson *Monte Carlo Rally – The Golden Years* pp.6, 234

Chapter Ten

Ownership today

by Paul Walby

The restored MWK 969 as it appeared on the STAR stand at the NEC Classic Car Show in 1994. (Courtesy Derek Cook)

Why a Sunbeam-Talbot?

When you're looking for an "old" car, what's the special attraction of these cars, which are, at best, over 50 years old and at worst 75 years old? Is it their sporting lines, the variety of body styles, their ruggedness, their proven track record in Continental and UK rallies of the 1950s? Perhaps it is merely a case of "my dad/uncle/neighbour had one and I've always liked them." Any of these will do, but sometimes it is just a spur of the moment decision (not often regretted!).

As has been described in this book, the Sunbeam-Talbot range is quite diverse; new prospective owners have to decide whether their preference is for the pre-war cars (which effectively include the side-valve cars until

1948), or the post-war ohv cars. Then to the body style: open or closed?

In the pre-war range, there is a choice of two open cars, tourer or drophead coupé. The tourer is a more sporty-looking car; hood down, open sides, wind through your hair stuff. The coupé, however, is more refined; whilst it still has a hood, it also has wind-up windows which offer more protection from the wind. Both are two-door, four-seater cars.

Then there is a choice of engines: 10hp, 2, 3, or 4 litres. The Ten is the most widely available. Of the others, some 2-litre cars survive, and are sometimes available, but there are currently only six 3-litre tourers known, and no 4-litres – and no dropheads of either of these two types. Obviously the 3-litre tourer offers more pace, and being built on a larger chassis, more space, and could therefore be deemed more desirable. But size isn't everything; the 10hp cars can be quite desirable in their own, quirky way. The 2-litre shares the same bodies as the Ten, and isn't that much quicker.

If you prefer "closed in" motoring, your pre-war choice would be saloon or sports saloon. Up to 1938 only a two-door saloon (known as the Airline) was available on the Ten chassis. Then a new four-door sports saloon replaced the Airline, but on the larger 3- and 4-litre cars there was a choice between a six-light saloon or the more "streamlined" four-light Sports Saloon. Personally, I much prefer the bigger sports saloons, but there aren't many about.

Post-war from 1948 to 1950, the choice is between the Sunbeam-Talbot 80 – which is underpowered – or the 90 range with its much better motive power, which is more common. Both offer the choice of saloon or coupé bodywork. From 1950 the 90s were fitted with independent front suspension, and were later joined by the Alpine roadster. Most people would like an Alpine in their Christmas stocking, with its superb, sporting lines, but a coupé is a good compromise between the open top motoring of the Alpine and the enclosed saloon.

In today's market an Alpine is at the top end of the desirability stakes, with the Rootes works-prepared rally cars at the top of the list, followed by the rare Alpine Special. For less money a two-door four-seater coupé could be up there, too, with its flexibility of fully open top, three-quarter open, or fully closed. If open-top motoring isn't your style, probably the later Sunbeam Mark III Saloon fitted with overdrive would be the most desirable, with the convenience of four doors and its ability to cope better with modern traffic.

It is fair to say that Sunbeam-Talbots in general have been undervalued, but in recent years prices have begun to reflect their true worth as a quality sporting car. For obvious reasons Alpines, followed by Mark III coupés, attract higher values than saloons. Market values may go out of date quickly, and always vary widely depending on the condition of the car, but in 2009 the best Alpines could be worth around £20,000 while even the best of saloons would struggle to reach half that, unless with a particular provenance. Of the pre-war models, the open cars again attract higher values.

On the road

What's your style of driving? Are you quite happy to take your time and enjoy the scenery, or do you prefer to get from A to B reasonably quickly?

If it is the former, then a Ten would suit you. With a top speed effectively limited today to around 50mph (80km/h), its sometimes quirky brakes and erratic steering, the quieter back roads are its natural habitat. Motorways? Best not! The 2-litres fare a bit better, but with a 3 or 4-litre, motorways can be used with care – they

Patrick Vanson's first Alpine was featured in a 1956 photo earlier in this book. Here, 50 years later, is Patrick with his second Alpine, undergoing restoration! (Courtesy Patrick Vanson)

can achieve higher speeds but do try to maintain space around you, as the brakes, whilst quite effective, do need more pressure and are not anywhere near as good as modern ones. In towns, stop-start driving can cause overheating problems, and the relatively heavy steering on the larger cars can make parking an effort.

The Sunbeam-Talbot 90s are better equipped for modern roads, with the ability to maintain a reasonable speed on motorways – and with better brakes they can stop better than the pre-war cars, although still needing more pressure and more distance than modern cars. They are still prone, however, to overheat in heavy stop-start traffic; an electric fan is a sensible addition.

Modifications

As with many cars of the period, modern driving conditions dictate that certain modifications are, bluntly, essential. Not many owners of pre-war Sunbeam-Talbots drive them at night from choice, due to the lights and signalling systems which are poor by today's standards.

Pre-war cars, and post-war until 1954 or so, were fitted with trafficators – an arm fitted with a bulb behind an amber plastic lens – which popped out of the side of the car to indicate a right or left turn. Sensibly, most owners fit an independent flashing indicator kit to the car, which complies with modern expectations but which can be partially removed when authenticity demands. Some owners uprate the stop and tail lights to aid rear visibility, in the eventuality that they are still on the road when darkness falls! – again, sympathetic kits are widely available. Better reversing lights have been fitted, too – the original wasn't very effective.

In the last few years a conversion kit has become available for the 90s, to enable owners to fit power steering, which makes driving and parking so much easier, and it is even possible to change the brakes of these cars to discs, giving better braking.

The column gear change, so much a USA/fifties feature, is something you either love or hate. Some owners will put up with it for the sake of authenticity, but this gear change is complicated and is obviously subject to wear in the many parts. When this gets to the point where further adjustment or repair is impossible, alternatives have to be found. A 1950s alternative was the Castle change – a floor-mounted gear change made by Castles of Leicester. The original gearboxes were not too strong anyway, and many owners have opted for a fitting a later Rootes gearbox, for instance from a Humber Sceptre, with floor change, better synchromesh and the option of overdrive. It works well and enables quicker gear changes… no more waving the column change around trying to find a gear!

There was a period when radial tyres were the thing to fit – better road holding, easier steering, etc (but not so easy getting the spare wheel in or out!), but modern cross-plies have got better over the years so now it is really only a matter of choice.

Engines generally were robust, but if an engine needs replacing, Humber Hawk and Commer engines through the 1960s will fit the 90, but even these later engines are hardly common any more. Some owners faced with poor original engines have fitted more modern engines – and gearboxes – from Hillman Hunters and even Toyotas in their cars, which give more power with better economy, and access to more readily available spare parts. Is it a good modification? If it keeps the car, which externally still looks original, on the road, yes. However, I always advocate keeping the original unit – at some later stage it might be possible to rebuild it.

This was how MWK 969 looked in 1970 when Graham Wilson first found the car. (Courtesy Derek Cook)

This is the stunning result of the restoration of Stirling Moss's 1953 Monte Carlo car by Peter Lancaster, after it was found in a barn in a parlous condition and nearly scrapped. (Author)

Maintenance

Keeping a Sunbeam-Talbot on the road is relatively easy; the engine bay is readily accessible and the engine is simple to work on. The Sunbeam Talbot Alpine Register has, for the later cars, a useful "Technical Tips" manual which illustrates the most helpful way to make repairs, and there are original Workshop Manuals available for the ohv cars. The earlier cars often come with an original "Owner's Handbook" which comprehensively illustrates various aspects of maintenance. Most owners of classic cars such as these will have a degree of maintenance knowledge; however, within the Sunbeam Talbot Alpine Register there are many members only too happy to help with more detailed work.

The cars were robust and well built, and are not any more prone to rust than other cars of the period, although side-valve models with coachbuilt bodies may need attention to the ash frame. However, cars of this age still in preservation are likely to have seen some remedial or restoration work undertaken already, to bodywork as well as mechanicals.

Depending on basic skills, restoring a Sunbeam-Talbot is not an unduly difficult task; many cars now on the road have been restored in small garages with limited room and facilities! Again, help is available where needed, but there are also many commercial establishments able to complete work that the D.I.Y. "amateur" restorer can't do.

Spares availability

You can't buy new spares off the shelf for cars of this age. There are specialist suppliers who will probably have "new/old stock" and reconditioned parts for most of your mechanical needs, but the supply is predictably gradually diminishing. STAR, like many clubs, are investing in remanufactured parts but obviously tooling costs must be incorporated, which then makes parts costs higher. Some owners have found compatible parts, or something which can be modified to suit, from contemporary cars of the period, or even from later cars.

Cars are, sadly, still left to deteriorate due to various factors, often to the point where they are considered unrestorable. The truth is that as with so many saloon cars of the period, restoration costs for a poor example will usually exceed the value of the car when finally restored. However, wrecks could still yield very useful spares – items such as interior trim, etc – and such cars are better advertised for sale in the club's magazine or the classic car press rather than sent for scrap!

It goes without saying that body panels and exterior chromed parts are no longer available new. Damaged or rusted panels can be repaired, and there are skilled craftsmen out there who can make new panels – at a price! Chrome trim can often be difficult to source; it will only be acquired from a scrapped car, and will probably need work to get it up to standard. The same goes for interior trim and seats. Only a scrapped car will yield suitable seats, and these will most likely need to be rebuilt.

Supporting you and your car

Reference has already been made to the Sunbeam Talbot Alpine Register (STAR). The club was founded in 1969, as a successor to a Rootes supported club known as The Sunbeam-Talbot Owners Club: Rootes wouldn't allow this name to be subsequently used by a collective of enthusiasts! Today the club's membership is in excess of 600 worldwide, and some members have more than one car. But there are still many more cars out there – "new" cars still turn up, such as two successful rally saloons which have both been restored in recent years. STAR has an extensive archive and a register of cars, and within its membership there are many who are willing to pass on their knowledge and experience gained over years of ownership of Sunbeam-Talbots. The club has a spares provider run by members, a father and sons team known as *Sunbeam-Talbot Spares*, with years of experience repairing and restoring these cars. However, they are probably more experienced with the post-war ohv rather than pre-war side-valve cars.

One of the club's officers is the Sidevalve Secretary who will gladly offer his experience to owners of these cars; however, because there aren't that many, the 3- and 4-litre cars are dealt with by the club's 3- and 4-litre registrar. Because a lot of the pre-war spares are Humber or Hillman based, it is generally worthwhile contacting Rootes specialists such as Speedy Spares of Shoreham, Sussex; the relevant marque clubs may also be able to help.

Australia, Europe and the USA all have STAR representatives offering help and advice, with a link to STAR in the UK. Australia has a number of Sunbeam Car Clubs which cater for Sunbeam-Talbots, kept on the road by various means (sometimes with ingenious modifications!) and there is a growing remanufacturing system of small parts there.

STAR has its own website, www.stardust.uk.com with useful links to other relevant websites, one run by a STAR member in Canada which offers much useful information and a forum. Other useful websites exist, and can be accessed by searching for Sunbeam or Sunbeam-Talbot.

A final tribute to a lost cause: the classic Sunbeam-Talbot radiator.

The Supreme

SUNBEAM TALBOT

Appendix 1

Specifications, prices and colours

Technical specifications

	Talbot Ten, 1935-38	**Sunbeam Thirty, 1936**	**Talbot and Sunbeam-Talbot 3-litre, 1937-39**
Number of cylinders	4	8	6
Valves	Side valves	Overhead valves, pushrods	Side valves
Bore and stroke	63x95mm	80x112mm	75x120mm
Capacity	1185cc	4503cc	3181cc
RAC rating	9.84hp	31.8hp	20.9hp
Bhp/rpm	40/4200-4500	150/4500	1937-38 78/3300; 1938-39 82/3800
Torque, lb ft/rpm	n/a	n/a	n/a
Compression	6.8:1-7.0:1		6.5:1
Carburettor	Zenith V1.M.36	Two Zenith	Stromberg DBV 36
Clutch	Single dry plate		Single dry plate 9in
Gearbox	4-speed all synchromesh, remote control; 1937-38 centre change	4-speed, sychromesh on 2/3/4, centre change	4-sped, sychromesh on 3/4, centre change
Final drive, ratio	Spiral bevel; 5.44:1 on saloon, 5.0:1 on open cars	Spiral bevel	Spiral bevel, 4.3:1
Front suspension	Semi-elliptic springs, Luvax shock absorbers	Independent, transverse leaf, with radius arms, Luvax adjustable shock absorbers	Independent, transverse leaf, Luvax adjustable shock absorbers
Rear suspension	Live axle with semi-elliptic springs, Luvax shock absorbers	Live axle with semi-elliptic springs, Luvax adjustable shock absorbers	Live axle with semi-elliptic springs, Luvax adjustable shock absorbers
Brakes	Bendix duo-servo cable, handbrake on all four wheels, 8in drums	Bendix cable, Dewandre servo	1937-38 Bendix-Cowdrey cable, handbrake on all four wheels; 1938-39 Lockheed hydraulic, handbrake on rear wheels
Steering gear	Burman Douglas worm and nut	Burman Douglas worm and nut	Burman Douglas worm and nut
Wheels, tyres	1935-37 centre-lock wire wheels, 1937-38 disc wheels, 5.25-16 tyres	Wire wheels with wheel discs, 7.00-17 tyres	Disc wheels, 6.25-16 tyres
Wheelbase	7ft 9in (2362mm)	10ft 4in or 11ft 4.5in (3150mm or 3467mm)	9ft 10in (2997mm)
Front track	4ft (1219mm)	4ft 10.6in (1488mm)	4ft 7.5in (1410mm)
Rear track	4ft (1219mm)	5ft 0.25in (1530mm)	4ft 8in (1422mm)
Overall length	12ft 3in (3734mm)	16ft 4in or 17ft 4.5in (4978mm or 5296mm)	15ft 8in (4775mm)
Overall width	4ft 10in (1473mm)	6ft 2in (1880mm)	5ft 9.5in (1765mm)
Overall height	4ft 9.5in (saloon) (1461mm)		5ft 6.5in (saloon) (1689mm)
Unladen weight	19.5cwt (992kg)		31.5cwt (1602kg)
Body types	Two-door saloon, Tourer, Drophead coupé	On short chassis: Saloon Touring saloon, Phaeton On long chassis: Limousine Sedanca de ville	Saloon, Sports Saloon, Tourer Drophead coupé. 1939 also: Touring saloon, Limousine, Phaeton
Top speed	64-68mph (103-109km/h)	Estimated 100mph (161km/h)	82-85mph (132-137km/h)
0-50mph (0-80km/h)	18-23sec		11.6-13.7sec
Standing quarter-mile	24.8-25.4sec		20.6sec
Fuel consumption	27-32mpg		17-20mpg

APPENDIX

	Sunbeam-Talbot Ten, 1938-40; 1945-48	**Sunbeam-Talbot 4-litre, 1938-39**	**Sunbeam-Talbot 2-litre, 1939; 1946-48**
Number of cylinders	4	6	4
Valves	Side valves	Side valves	Side valves
Bore and stroke	63x93mm	85x120mm	75x110mm
Capacity	1185cc	4086cc	1944cc
RAC rating	9.84hp	26.88hp	13.95hp
Bhp/rpm	Pre-war 38-40/4500; post-war 41/4500	100/3400	Pre-war 52/3800; post-war 56/3800
Torque, lb ft/rpm	58/2700	n/a	97/2000
Compression	6.8:1	6.5:1	6.4:1-6.5:1
Carburettor	Pre-war Zenith; post-war Stromberg	Stromberg	Stromberg
Clutch	Single dry plate 7.125in	Single dry plate	Single dry plate 8.875in
Gearbox	4-speed, synchromesh on 2/3/4, centre change	4-speed, synchromesh on 3/4, centre change	4-speed, synchromesh on 2/3/4, centre change
Final drive, ratio	Spiral bevel; pre-war 5.44 or 5.37:1, post-war 5.22:1	Spiral bevel, 4.09:1	Spiral bevel, 4.44:1
Front suspension	Semi-elliptic springs, Luvax shock absorbers	Independent, transverse leaf, Luvax adjustable shock absorbers	Semi-elliptic springs, anti-roll bar, Luvax shock absorbers
Rear suspension	Live axle with semi-elliptic springs, Luvax shock absorbers	Live axle with semi-elliptic springs, Luvax adjustable shock absorbers	Live axle with semi-elliptic springs, Luvax shock absorbers
Brakes	Bendix duo-servo cable, 8in drums	Lockheed hydraulic	Lockheed hydraulic, 10in drums
Steering gear	Burman Douglas worm and nut	Burman Douglas worm and nut	Burman Douglas worm and nut
Wheels, tyres	Disc wheels, 5.25-16 tyres	Disc wheels, 6.25-16 tyres	Disc wheels, 5.25-16 tyres
Wheelbase	7ft 9in (2362mm); post-war 7ft 10in (2388mm)	9ft 10in (2997mm)	8ft 0.5in (2451mm); post-war 8ft 1.75in (2483mm)
Front track	3ft 11.5in (1207mm)	4ft 7.5in (1410mm)	3ft 11.5in (1207mm)
Rear track	4ft 0.5in (1232mm)	4ft 8in (1422mm)	4ft 0.5in (1232mm)
Overall length	12ft 5.75in to 13ft 1in (3804mm to 3988mm)	15ft 8in (4775mm)	13ft 2.5in to 13ft 4.5in (4026mm to 4077mm)
Overall width	4ft 11in (1499mm)	5ft 9.5in (1765mm)	5ft (1524mm)
Overall height	4ft 10in (1473mm)	5ft 6.5in (1689mm)	4ft 10.5in to 4ft 11.75in (1486mm to 1518mm)
Unladen weight	19.5cwt-20.75cwt (992kg-1055kg)	32.4cwt (1647kg)	22.25cwt-23cwt (1131kg-1170kg)
Body types	Four-door saloon, Tourer Drophead coupé 1939-40 also: Open two-seater	Saloon, Sports Saloon, Tourer, Drophead coupé, Touring Saloon, Limousine. 1939 also: Phaeton	Four-door saloon, Tourer Drophead coupé 1939 also: Open two-seater
Top speed	68-70mph (109-113km/h); post-war 67mph (108km/h)	82-87mph (132-140km/h)	76-80mph (122-129km/h); post-war 69.5mph (112km/h)
0-50mph (0-80km/h)	19.8-21.9sec; post-war 22.4-23.4sec	12.2sec	14.3sec; post-war 18.8-19sec
Standing quarter-mile	24.2sec; post-war 25.2sec		Post-war 23.9sec
Fuel consumption	30-34mpg; post-war 26.1-30mpg	17-19mpg	28-31mpg; post-war 24.8-27mpg

	Sunbeam-Talbot 80, 1948-50	Sunbeam-Talbot 90 (Mark I), 1948-50	Sunbeam-Talbot 90 Mark II, 1950-52
Number of cylinders	4	4	4
Valves	Overhead valves, pushrods	Overhead valves, pushrods	Overhead valves, pushrods
Bore and stroke	63x95mm	75x110mm	81x110mm
Capacity	1185cc	1944cc	2267cc
RAC rating	9.84hp	13.95hp	16.25hp
Bhp/rpm	47/4800	64/4100	70/4000
Torque, lb ft/rpm			113/2400
Compression	6.88:1	6.57:1 (or 6.59:1)	6.45:1
Carburettor	Stromberg	Stromberg	Stromberg
Clutch	Single dry plate 9in	Single dry plate 9in	Single dry plate 9in
Gearbox	4-speed, synchromesh on 2/3/4, column change	4-speed, synchromesh on 2/3/4, column change	4-speed, synchromesh on 2/3/4, column change
Final drive, ratio	Spiral bevel, 5.22:1	Spiral bevel, 4.3:1	Hypoid bevel, 3.9:1
Front suspension	Semi-elliptic springs, Girling piston-type shock absorbers	Semi-elliptic springs, Girling piston-type shock absorbers	Independent, coil springs and wishbones, anti-roll bar, Armstrong shock absorbers
Rear suspension	Live axle with semi-elliptic springs, Girling piston-type shock absorbers	Live axle with semi-elliptic springs, Girling piston-type shock absorbers	Live axle with semi-elliptic springs, located by Panhard rod, Armstrong shock absorbers
Brakes	Lockheed hydraulic, twin leading shoes at front, 9in drums	Lockheed hydraulic, twin leading shoes at front, 10in drums	Lockheed hydraulic, twin leading shoes at front, 1.75x10in drums
Steering gear	Burman Douglas worm and nut	Burman Douglas worm and nut	Burman re-circulating ball
Wheels, tyres	Steel disc wheels, 5.50-16 tyres	Steel disc wheels, 5.50-16 tyres	Steel disc wheels, 5.50-16 tyres
Wheelbase	8ft 1.5in (2477mm)	8ft 1.5in (2477mm)	8ft 1.5in (2477mm)
Front track	3ft 11.5in (1207mm)	3ft 11.5in (1207mm)	3ft 11.5in (1207mm)
Rear track	4ft 2.5in (1283mm)	4ft 2.5in (1283mm)	4ft 2.5in (1283mm)
Overall length	13ft 11.5in (4255mm)	13ft 11.5in (4255mm)	13ft 11.5in (4255mm)
Overall width	5ft 2.5in (1588mm)	5ft 2.5in (1588mm)	5ft 2.5in (1588mm)
Overall height	5ft 0.75in (saloon) (1543mm)	5ft 0.75in (saloon) (1543mm)	5ft 0.75in (saloon) (1543mm)
Unladen weight	23.25cwt (1182kg)	25.25cwt (1284kg)	2905lb (25cwt 3qtr 21lb) (1319kg)
Body types	Saloon, Convertible coupé	Saloon, Convertible coupé	Saloon, Convertible coupé
Top speed	71-74mph (114-119km/h)	76.6-80mph (123-129km/h)	84.5-86mph (136-138km/h)
0-50mph (0-80km/h)	19.4-22.2sec	15.9-17.6sec	13.9-16.3sec
Standing quarter-mile	24.4sec	23.1sec	22.2-22.4sec
Fuel consumption	26-31mpg	21-23mpg	21-24mpg

APPENDIX

	Sunbeam-Talbot 90 Mark IIA, 1952-54	**Sunbeam Alpine and Alpine Special, 1953-55**	**Sunbeam Mark III, 1954-56**
Number of cylinders	4	4	4
Valves	Overhead valves, pushrods	Overhead valves, pushrods	Overhead valves, pushrods
Bore and stroke	81x110mm	81x110mm	81x110mm
Capacity	2267cc	2267cc	2267cc
RAC rating	16.25hp	16.25hp	16.25hp
Bhp/rpm	70/4000; later 77/4100	80/4200; Special 97.5/4500	80/4400; Mark IIIS 92bhp
Torque, lb ft/rpm	113/2400	124/1800; Special 142/2600	122/2400
Compression	6.45:1	7.42:1, later 7.5:1; Special 8:1	7.5:1; Mark IIIS 8:1
Carburettor	Stromberg DBA 36	Stromberg DAA 36, later D1 36; Special Solex 40 PII twin-choke	Stromberg D1 36; Mark IIIS Stromberg D1 42
Clutch	Single dry plate 9in	Single dry plate 9in	Single dry plate 9in
Gearbox	4-speed, synchromesh on 2/3/4, column change	4-speed, synchromesh on 2/3/4, column change; overdrive standard 1954-55 and on Special	4-speed, synchromesh on 2/3/4, column change; overdrive optional; Mark IIIS, centre change
Final drive, ratio	Hypoid bevel, 3.9:1	Hypoid bevel, 3.9:1; 4.22:1 on overdrive cars	Hypoid bevel, 3.9:1; 4.22:1 on overdrive cars
Front suspension	Independent, coil springs and wishbones, anti-roll bar, Armstrong shock absorbers	Independent, coil springs and wishbones, anti-roll bar, Armstrong shock absorbers	Independent, coil springs and wishbones, anti-roll bar, Armstrong shock absorbers
Rear suspension	Live axle with semi-elliptic springs, located by Panhard rod, Armstrong shock absorbers	Live axle with semi-elliptic springs, located by Panhard rod, Armstrong shock absorbers	Live axle with semi-elliptic springs, located by Panhard rod, Armstrong shock absorbers
Brakes	Lockheed hydraulic, twin leading shoe at front, 2.25x10in drums	Lockheed hydraulic, twin leading shoe at front, 2.25x10in drums	Lockheed hydraulic, twin leading shoe at front, 2.25x10in drums
Steering gear	Burman re-circulating ball	Burman re-circulating ball	Burman re-circulating ball
Wheels, tyres	Perforated steel disc wheels, 5.50-16 tyres	Perforated steel disc wheels, 5.50-16 tyres	Perforated steel disc wheels 5.50-16 tyres
Wheelbase	8ft 1.5in (2477mm)	8ft 1.5in (2477mm)	8ft 1.5in (2477mm)
Front track	3ft 11.5in (1207mm)	3ft 11.5in (1207mm)	3ft 11.5in (1207mm)
Rear track	4ft 2.5in (1283mm)	4ft 2.5in (1283mm)	4ft 2.5in (1283mm)
Overall length	13ft 11.5in (4255mm)	14ft 0.25in (4274mm)	14ft (4267mm)
Overall width	5ft 2.5in (1588mm)	5ft 2.5in (1588mm)	5ft 2.5in (1588mm)
Overall height	5ft 0.5in (saloon) (1537mm), 4ft 11in (convertible) (1499mm)	4ft 8in (hood up) (1422mm)	5ft 0.75in (1543mm)
Unladen weight	2954lb (1341kg)	2968lb (26.5cwt) (1347kg)	2950lb (1339kg)
Body types	Saloon, Convertible coupé	Open two-seater	Saloon, Convertible coupé
Top speed	81-83mph (130-134km/h)	95mph (152km/h); Special 104mph (in overdrive) (167km/h)	91-95mph (in overdrive) (146-152km/h)
0-50mph (0-80km/h)	14.4sec	12.9sec	12.4-12.6sec
Standing quarter-mile	22.2sec	21.1sec	21.2-21.4sec
Fuel consumption	24-32mpg	24-32mpg	19-31mpg

Prices

1935-40

Ten

	Chassis	Two-door saloon	Four-door saloon	Tourer	Drophead coupé	Two-seater
1935-36	£165	£265		£260	£295	
1936-37	£155	£248		£248	£278	
1937-38	£160	£255		£248	£285	
1938-39	£165		£265	£250	£285	
1939-40	£165		£265	£248	£285	£248

Sunbeam Thirty 1936:

Short chassis £750, Saloon £1195, Touring saloon £1240, Phaeton £1295
Long chassis £800, Limousine £1325, Sedanca de ville £1475

3-litre

	Chassis	Saloon	Sports saloon	Tourer	Drophead coupé	Touring saloon	Touring limousine	Phaeton
1937-38	£295	£398	£475	£435	£525			
1938-39	£310	£415	£485	£445	£525			
1939-40	£310	£415	£485	£445	£525	£598	£625	£645

4-litre

	Chassis	Saloon	Sports saloon	Tourer	Drophead coupé	Touring saloon	Touring limousine	Phaeton
1938-39	£350	£455	£525	£485	£565	£598	£630	
1939-40	£350	£455	£525	£485	£565	£638	£665	£685

2-litre

	Chassis	Saloon	Tourer	Drophead coupé	Two-seater
1939-40	£215	£315	£298	£335	£298

1945 onwards

From *The Autocar* and *The Motor*; the dates are the publication dates of these magazines; prices quoted both basic (ex factory) and including Purchase Tax.

From	Ten tourer	Ten saloon	Ten dhc	2-litre tourer	2-litre saloon	2-litre dhc
November 1945	£455	£485	£520			
	£582.2.10	£620.9.6	£665.3.11			
17/05/1946	As above	As above	As above	£575		
				£735.9.5		
06/09/1946	£505	£535	£570	£595	£625	£660
	£646.0.7	£684.7.1	£729.1.8	£761.0.7	£799.7.2	£844.1.8
09/05/1947	£545	£575	£610	£635	£665	£700
	£697.2.9	£735.9.5	£780.3.11	£812.2.9	£850.9.5	£895.3.11
15/10/1947	£585	£625	£645	£685	£725	£745
	£748.5.0	£799.7.3	£824.18.4	£876.0.7	£927.2.9	£952.13.11
23/06/1948	Range discontinued					

APPENDIX

From	80 saloon	80 convertible	90 saloon	90 convertible	Alpine	Rapier
30/06/1948	£695 £888.16.1	£745 £952.13.11	£775 £991.0.7	£825 £1054.18.4		
18/10/1950 90 Mark II	Discontinued	Discontinued	£775 £991.0.7	£825 £1054.18.4		
07/02/1951			£820 £1048.10.7	£875 £1118.16.1		
18/04/1951 PT increase			£820 £1277.1.2	£875 £1362.12.2		
26/09/1951			£845 £1315.18.11	£895 £1393.14.5		
20/02/1952			£865 £1347.1.1	£895 £1393.14.5		
22/04/1953 PT reduction			£865 £1226.10.10	£895 £1269.0.10		
05/08/1953			As above	As above	£895 £1269.0.10	
07/10/1953			£825 £1169.17.6	£855 £1212.7.6	As above	
08/10/1954 Mark III (1)			£795 £1127.7.6	£845 £1198.4.2	£855 £1212.7.6 (3)	
14/10/1955 (1)			£835 £1184.0.10	Discontinued	Discontinued	£695 £985.14.2
04/11/1955 PT increase (2)			£835 £1253.17.0			£695 £1043.17.0
21/09/1956 (2)			£765 £1148.17.0			As above

(1) Overdrive extra on Mark III £45/£63.15.0, standard on Alpine
(2) Overdrive extra on Mark III £45/£67.10.0
(3) Alpine Special £970/£1375

Notes on Purchase Tax rates, which were calculated on wholesale factory price:
1940, introduced at 33.3 per cent
1947, increased to 66.6 per cent on cars costing £1000 or more basic retail
April 1951, increased to 66.6 per cent on cars costing less than £1000 basic retail
April 1953, reduced to 50 per cent on all cars
October 1955, increased to 60 per cent on all cars

Colour schemes

The colour listings for the side-valve cars 1935-48 are based on the article by John Wallingford in Lem *Register* pp.85-87, and contemporary sources.

1935-36: Talbot Ten

Body style	Paint	Trim	Hood
Saloon	Black	Brown	
Saloon	Platinum Grey	Blue	
Saloon	Talbot Blue	Blue	
Saloon	Talbot Green	Green	
Saloon	Talbot Grey	Grey	
Tourer	Black	Brown	Black
Tourer	Green	Green	Black
Tourer	Platinum Grey	Blue	Light Grey
Tourer	Red	Red	Light Grey
Tourer	Talbot Grey	Blue	Grey
Drophead coupé	Black	Green	Green
Drophead coupé	Two-tone Blue	Blue	Grey
Drophead coupé	Two-tone Green	Green	Green
Drophead coupé	Two-tone Grey	Red	Grey

1936-37: Talbot Ten

Body style	Paint	Trim	Hood
Saloon	Black	Brown	
Saloon	Talbot Blue	Blue	
Saloon	Talbot Green	Green	
Saloon	Talbot Grey	Red	
Saloon	Talbot Gun	Green	
Saloon	Talbot Ruby	Maroon	
Tourer	Black	Brown	Black
Tourer	Green	Green	Black
Tourer	Red	Red	Light Grey
Tourer	Platinum Grey	Blue	Light Grey
Tourer	Talbot Grey	Blue	Grey
Drophead coupé	Black	Green	not quoted
Drophead coupé	Steel-dust	Grey or Maroon	not quoted
Drophead coupé	Two-tone Blue	Blue	not quoted
Drophead coupé	Two-tone Green	Green	not quoted
Drophead coupé	Two-tone Grey	Red	not quoted

1937-38: Talbot Ten and 3-litre

(see also *The Motor* 10 Aug 1937)

Body style	Paint	Trim
Saloon and tourer	Black	Brown
Drophead coupé	Black	Blue, Grey or Maroon
All models	Gun jewelessence	Grey
Saloon and drophead coupé	Lapis Blue jewelessence	Blue
Saloon and drophead coupé	Ruby (or Maroon) jewelessence	Maroon
Tourer	Green	Green
Tourer	Red	Red

1938-40: All models
(taken from brochures; cp. *The Autocar* 19 Aug and 23 Sep 1938; *The Motor* 20 Sep 1938)

Body style	Paint	Trim
All models	Black	Brown
All models	Copper Bronze jewelessence	Brown
All models	Gun jewelessence	Grey
Saloon and drophead coupé	Carborundum Blue jewelessence	Blue
Saloon and drophead coupé	Ruby jewelessence	Maroon
Tourer	Green	Green
Tourer	Red	Red
All models, 1939-40	Granite jewelessence	Grey
Saloon and two-seater, 1939-40	Silver Green jewelessence	Green

Post-war Ten and 2-litre

Body style	Paint	Trim
All models	Black	Fawn
All models	Gun jewelessence	Grey
All models	Granite jewelessence	Grey
Saloon and drophead coupé	Ruby jewelessence	Maroon
Tourer	Carnadine (crimson) jewelessence	Red

80 and 90, all models, from sales brochures

Paint	Trim	Notes
80, 90 Mark I 1948-50		
Black	Red or Buff	
Gun jewelessence	Grey	
Ruby	Not known	Found on 90s in sales ledger
Satin Bronze metallic	Red	
Silver-Green metallic	Buff	Possibly grey trim on a 1949 Motor Show car
90 Mark II 1950-52		
Black	Red or Light Fawn	
Gun jewelessence	Grey	
Satin Bronze jewelessence	Red	
Beech Green metallic	Red	
Light Metallic Blue	Light Fawn	
Silver-Green metallic	Red	
Steel Grey	Grey	
Ivory	Red	On a 1951 Motor Show car
90 Mark IIA 1952-53		
Black	Bright Red or Light Fawn	
Gun jewelessence	Grey	
Satin Bronze jewelessence	Bright Red	
Beech Green metallic	Light Fawn	
Alpine Mist metallic	Bright Red	
Sapphire Blue	Light Fawn	
90 Mark IIA 1953-54		
Black	Red	
Gun jewelessence	Bright Red	
Alpine Mist metallic	Bright Red	
Sapphire Blue	Light Fawn or French Grey	
Crystal Green	Light Green	
Light Stone	Bright Red	Red wheels
Mark III 1954-55		
Black	Bright Red or French Grey	
Light Gun metallic	Bright Red	
Alpine Mist metallic	Bright Red	

Sapphire Blue	French Grey	
Crystal Green	Light Green	
Dark Green	Not known	Found in sales ledger
Island Mist	Not known	Found in sales ledger
Rose Beige	Not known	Found in sales ledger
Severn Blue	Not known	Found in sales ledger
Mark III 1955-56		
Embassy Black (was Black)	Bright Red or Light Fawn	
Claret	Light Fawn or Ascot Grey	
Thistle Grey (was Island Mist)	Bright Red or Blue-Grey	
Cactus Green over Pine Green (Pine Green was Dark Green)	Light Green	Two-tone; also Dark Green over Crystal Green
Dawn Mist over Corinth Blue (Corinth Blue was Severn Blue)	Blue-Grey	Two-tone
Dove Grey over Claret (Dove Grey was Pebble Grey)	Ascot Grey	Two-tone
Alpine		
Alpine Mist metallic	Bright Red	Body colour wheels
Black	Not known	Used on a few cars only
Coronation Red	Light Fawn	Body colour wheels
Crystal Green	Not known	Found in sales ledger
Ivory	Bright Red	Bright Red wheels
Sapphire Blue	Light Fawn	Body colour wheels
Severn Blue (Corinth Blue)	Not known	Found in sales ledger

ICI paint codes from 90 Mark II/IIA/III and Alpine parts list, and ICI list ca. 1958

Paint colour	Model application	ICI ref. no.
Alpine Mist metallichrome	Mark IIA, Mark III, Alpine	2261
Beech Green metallichrome	Late Mark II, early Mark IIA	2226
Coronation Red	Alpine	224 (?)
Cactus Green	Mark III two-tone	2834
Claret	Mark III 1956 model	Not quoted
Corinth Blue was Severn Blue	Mark III two-tone	2847
Crystal Green	Late Mark IIA, Mark III	1762
Dawn Mist	Mark III two-tone	2948 or 2949 (?)
Dove Grey was Pebble Grey	Mark III two-tone	2952
Embassy Black was Black	Mark II, Mark IIA, Mark III	122
Gun metallic	Early Mark II	2180
Gun metallichrome	Late Mark II, early Mark IIA	2189
Ivory	Mark IIA, Mark III, Alpine	2688
Light Gun metallichrome	Late Mark IIA, Mark III	2260
Light Stone	Late Mark IIA, Mark III	2786 or 16472 (?)
Mayfair Grey was Seal Grey	Mark III – use uncertain	2749
Pine Green was Dark Green	Mark III two-tone	2844
Rose Beige	Mark III	2733
Sapphire Blue	Mark II, Mark IIA, Alpine	1672
Satin Bronze metallic	Early Mark II	1466
Satin Bronze metallichrome	Late Mark II, early Mark IIA	2064
Silver Green metallic	Early Mark II	1464
Steel Grey	Early Mark II	1394
Thistle Grey was Island Mist	Mark III 1956 model	2837

According to a Rootes Service Newsletter, some colour names were changed in 1955 for unspecified marketing reasons.

APPENDIX

The cover of the MkIIA brochure shows a drophead coupé in Satin Bronze jewelessence with a red interior in the foreground. The saloon is finished in Alpine Mist.

The MkIII brochure cover artwork shows two saloons in in two-tone finishes: Dove Grey over Claret and Dawn Mist over Corinth Blue.

199

Appendix 2

Production and identification

Production figures 1935-40, by model year

Model year	Ten	3-litre	4-litre	2-litre	Annual totals
1935-36	850				850
1936-37	1000				1000
1937-38	1800	639			2439
1938-39	2752	430	100		3282
1939-40	852	197	129	181	1359
Total	7254	1266	229	181	8930

Individual models by body style

Talbot Ten by chassis numbers	Period	2-door saloon	DHC	Tourer	Other	Chassis	Destroyed in fire at Abbotts	Total
1001-2500	1935-37	1017	228	216	8	9	22	1500
3001-3350	1937	252	35	58		5		350
5001-6800	1937-38	1181	318	280	1	20		1800
Total		2450	581	554	9	34	22	3650

The following are included in the "other" category:
Chassis numbers 1784, 1962, 1969, 1993, 1994, 2088, 2089 and 5859 were Abbott two-seater drophead coupés with a dickey seat. Chassis number 2149 was an "experimental pillarless four-door saloon" probably by Thrupp & Maberly.
Of the 34 chassis, it is known that 2259, 3300, 5912 and 6657 were also fitted with Abbott two-seater DHC bodies. Chassis 6451 was badged "Sunbeam" and had LHD for export to an unknown European destination; it now exists in Denmark with a two-seater DHC body which is probably not by Abbott.

Sunbeam-Talbot Ten by chassis numbers	Period	4-door saloon	DHC	Tourer	OTS	Other	Chassis	Total
40001-42752	1938-39	2049	386	286		2	29	2752
101010-952010	1939-40	508	182	136	11		15	852
1001010-4719010	Post-war	3098	199	400			21	3718*
Total		5655	767	822	11	2	65	7322

*post-war chassis number 3825-010 appears not to have been built

The following are included in the "other" category:
Chassis number 40002, effectively a prototype, had a Talbot Ten-type two-door saloon body. Chassis number 42703 had a DHC body by Thrupp & Maberly.
Of the chassis, 40301 and 40302 were unassembled for export. 40442 was returned to stock by the original agent and was later fitted with a standard Abbott DHC body. 288-010 went to Abbott and was presumably bodied by them. Seven chassis were destroyed by bombing at Whittingham & Mitchel in 1940. 948-010 was allocated to Humber in Coventry for experimental work. 950-010 and 951-010 were retained and were fitted, respectively, with "experimental coupé" and "experimental saloon" bodywork.
Of the 1938-39 saloons, there were 10 "SKD" (semi knock-down) cars for export, and 6 "CKD" (completely knock-down) for export to Ireland. There were a further 6 CKD saloons in the 1939-40 model year.
The following were the eleven open two-seater cars: 256-010, 304-010, 350-010, 391-010, 504-010, 514-010, 524-010, 534-010, 554-010, 558-010 and 947-010.

Other models all years	Saloon	Sports saloon	DHC	Tourer	OTS saloon	Touring limousine	Touring	CKD	Chassis	Total	
3-litre	1019	173	38	21				1	6	8	1266
4-litre	121	44	7	2		28	22			5	229
2-litre, 1939-40		152	17	9	3						181*
2-litre, post-war		977	50	96							1123**

*including two prototypes built on Ten chassis, numbers 42001 and 42002
**post-war chassis numbers 965-200 and 970-200 appear not to have been built

The following were the chassis deliveries of 3-litre and 4-litre cars:
3-litre: chassis 8575 (unknown bodywork), 8649 (Offord fixed-head coupé), 8701 (Burlingham, Blackpool), 8702 (Maltby Redfern saloon tourer), 8703 (possibly Maltby), 9058 (exported to The Netherlands), 9070 (unknown bodywork) and 9072 (Offord fixed-head coupé).
4-litre: 152-400 and 153-400 for export; 154-400 and 155-400 for export in CKD form; 159-400 (Cox of Watford, two-seater with dickey for Captain Schreiber).
The following were the three 2-litre two-seaters: 161-200, 184-200 and 202-200.

Production figures 1945 onwards, by calendar year (annual figures are approximate)

Year	Ten	2-litre	80	90	90 Mk II	90 Mk IIA	Mk III	Alpine Mk IIA	Alpine Mk III	Annual total
1945	125									125
1946	1125	225								1350
1947	1799	498								2297
1948	669	400	185	315						1569
1949			1420	1692						3112
1950			1895	1993	573					4461
1951					5946					5946
1952					3189	1673				4862
1953						2220		1130		3350
1954						1504	943*	152	83	2682
1955							2271		217	2488
1956							1738			1738
Total	**3718**	**1123**	**3500**	**4000**	**9708**	**5397**	**4952**	**1282**	**300**	**33,980**

*including three pre-production cars with chassis numbers starting A34...

Detailed Alpine figures

	HRO	HROS	RRO	LRO	LROS	LRX	LRXS	Total
1953	311	3	77	65	0	666	8	1130
1954, Mk IIA	3	40	0	2	5	68	34	152
1954, Mk III	37	0	7	1	0	38	0	83
1955	51	0	18	1	0	147	0	217
Total	**402**	**43**	**102**	**69**	**5**	**919**	**42**	**1582**

Notes to Alpine figures:
HRO, RHD home market; RRO, RHD export; LRO, LHD general export; LRX, LHD believed North American export; S suffix, Special

Exports to leading markets 1947-54, from Nuffield Exports statistics (BMIHT archive)

	1947	1948	1949	1950	1951	1952	1953	1954	Total	Rank
Argentina	21	7	22	1	1	0	0	0	52	22
Australia	114	232	434	164	333	76	57	97	1507	2
Austria	0	0	0	0	7	12	10	7	36	27
Belgium inc. Luxembourg	20	4	33	38	58	56	56	106	371	5
Bermuda	21	2	0	0	9	34	7	17	90	16
Brazil	1	1	5	2	34	6	2	0	51	23
Canada inc. Newfoundland	2	25	34	1	43	32	124	48	309	7
Denmark	1	1	4	2	2	5	12	7	34	29
Egypt	29	6	42	4	6	3	0	2	92	Equal 14
Eire	6	6	5	8	1	7	3	4	40	25
France	7	3	14	6	19	22	43	63	177	10
Germany	0	0	3	0	16	5	33	22	79	17

Gibraltar	7	1	8	1	5	5	3	3	33	30
Hong Kong	41	22	25	3	8	9	11	13	132	12
India and Pakistan	250	27	48	14	12	7	2	1	361	6
Japan	0	0	0	3	6	8	16	2	35	28
Malaya inc. Singapore	29	7	25	23	82	19	15	5	205	9
Malta	24	7	7	1	1	1	4	2	47	24
Netherlands	3	0	2	2	10	37	34	38	126	13
New Zealand	30	9	1	12	358	25	5	38	478	4
Portugal	28	18	53	14	6	14	12	8	153	11
Rhodesia, South & North	2	0	7	0	52	6	18	7	92	Equal 14
South Africa	27	11	14	0	2	1	1	1	57	21
Sri Lanka (Ceylon)	32	7	10	3	9	7	6	1	75	19
Sweden	36	6	21	130	50	13	15	20	291	8
Switzerland	67	15	134	146	94	12	31	31	530	3
Thailand (Siam)	18	1	9	5	8	22	14	0	77	18
Trinidad	13	2	8	0	5	4	2	4	38	26
Uruguay	1	0	16	6	5	0	0	4	32	31
USA	1	49	34	175	339	379	1304	179	2460	1
Venezuela	7	6	12	1	2	4	10	17	59	20
Total of above	838	475	1030	765	1583	831	1850	747	8119	
Total of all exports	**919**	**500**	**1108**	**808**	**1654**	**918**	**1917**	**829**	**8653**	

First chassis numbers by year

Year	Notes	Ten	3-litre	4-litre	2-litre
1935 Sep	First	1001			
1936 Jan	First in year	Approx. 1265			
1936 Jul	Last 36 model	Approx. 1850			
1936 Jul	1937 models	Approx. 1851			
1937 Jan	First in year	Approx. 2301			
1937 Feb		2500			
1937 Feb		3001			
1937 Jul	Last 37 model	3350			
1937 Jul	1938 models	5001	8001 (Sep 37)		
1938 Jan	First in year	Approx. 5951	Approx. 8050		
1938 Jul	Last 38 model	6800	8639		
1938 Jul	1939 models	40001	8640	101-400	
1939 Jan	First in year	Approx. 41151	Approx. 8701	Approx. 110-400	
1939 Jun	Last 39 model	42752	9069		
1939 Jun	1940 models	101-010	9070 to 9097 (Jul 1939 on) 9128 on (Apr 1939 on)	201-400 (?)	101-200 (Jun 1939)
1939/40	Last pre-war models	952-010 (Aug 1940)	9296 (Nov 1939)	328-400 (Nov 1939) Also 100-400	279-200 (Oct 1939)
1945 Aug	First	1001-010			
1946 Jan	First in year	Approx. 1126-010			301-200 (Feb 46)
1947 Jan	First in year	Approx. 2251-010			Approx. 526-200
1948 Jan	First in year	Approx. 4051-010			Approx. 1026-200
1948	Last	4719-010 (Apr 1948)			1425-200 (May 48)

Year	Notes	80	90	90 Mk II	90 Mk IIA and Alpine	Mk III and Alpine
1948 Jun	First	28-00001	38-00001			
1949 Jan	First in year	28-00186	38-00316			
1950 Jan	First in year	28-01606	38-02008			
1950 Oct	Last		38-04000			
1950 Nov	Last	28-03500				
1950 May	First			A30-00001		
1951 Jan	First in year			A30-00574		
1952 Jan	First in year			A30-06520		
1952 Sep	Last			A30-09708*		
1952 Sep	First				A30-09709*	

Year	Notes	80	90	90 Mk II	90 Mk IIA and Alpine	Mk III and Alpine
1953 Jan	First in year				A30-11382	
1953 Jan	First Alpine				A30-11393	
1954 Jan	First in year				A30-14732	
1954 Aug	Last				A30-16387	
1954 Oct	First					A35-00001**
1955 Jan	First in year					A35-01024
1955 Jun	Last conv.					A35-02233
1955 Jul	Last Alpine					A35-02429
1956 Jan	First in year					A35-03512
1956 Dec	Last					A35-05249

* Approximate numbers; it seems likely that there were some Mark II models with numbers higher than A30-09708 at least up to around A30-09804
** Plus three pre-production cars with numbers starting A34...

Notes on chassis numbers

Until 1938/39 the chassis numbers were allocated in batches from 1001 upwards, also for the last Roesch Talbot models, as follows:
    1001-2500: Ten type BE 1936 and 1937 models
    2501-3000: 75 type BD
    3001-3350: Ten type BE 1937 models
    4001-4097: 105 Speed type BI
    4101-4300: 105 type BD
    4501-4589: 110 (and 3½ litre) type BG
    4701-4750: 100 (3½ litre) limousine type AZ
    5001-6800: Ten type BE 1938 models
    8001-9097 and 9128-9296: 3-litre types BP and BX
    40001-42752: Sunbeam-Talbot Ten type BT 1939 models

From 1938/39 to 1948, chassis numbers were *suffixed* with a model identification code (except on the 3-litre):
    010 for Ten type BU
    200 for 2-litre type BV
    400 for 4-litre types BY and BZ
The series of numbers for each model began with 101, but there was also a 4-litre with chassis number 100-400.

In 1948, a common Rootes system for seven-digit chassis numbers was adopted:
    No prefix letter: Model manufactured prior to 1950
    Prefix letter A: Model manufactured during the period from 1950 to 1959
    First digit 2: Sunbeam-Talbot 80
    First digit 3: Sunbeam-Talbot 90 etc
    Second digit 8: Model introduced in 1948
    Second digit 0: Model introduced in 1950
    Second digit 5: Model introduced for 1955 model year
The two first digits were followed by a five-digit serial number, commencing with 00001.

Suffixes:
First letter, class:
    H: Home market
    R: Right-hand drive export
    L: Left-hand drive export
    E, W or X were used on CKD (Completely Knocked Down) export cars; E probably for Eire, W with right-hand drive and X with left-hand drive. I have not found any Sunbeam-Talbot 80s or 90s in CKD form in the sales ledgers, but I believe that such cars would have had separate chassis number series.
Second letter, body type:
    S: Saloon
    C: Convertible coupé
    R: Roadster
    X: Chassis only
    (Other body type letters were found on other Rootes cars)
Third letter (or number), variation:
    M: Ministry of Supply
    O: Standard specification

P: Police
X or Y: Non-standard, e.g. for the USA
3: Small-bore engine fitted for Bermuda

Additional letters are found on some Sunbeam (-Talbot) models, e.g.:
OD: Car equipped with overdrive
S: Alpine Special

Notes on engine numbers

Ten engines:
1935-37, four-digit numbers, no prefix.
1937-38 models, four-digit numbers, prefix T1, T2 or T3.
1938-39 models, four-digit numbers, prefix N1 (or NI).
1939-40 models, six-digit numbers starting with 221.
1945-48 models, seven-digit numbers starting with 178.

3-litre engines:
1937-39, five-digit numbers from 41001 upwards.
1939-40, six-digit numbers starting with 201.

4-litre engines:
1938-39, six-digit numbers starting with 131.
1939-40, six-digit numbers starting with 211.

2-litre engines:
1939-40, six-digit numbers starting with 121.
1945-48, seven-digit numbers starting with 272.

From the start of the 80/90 series in 1948, the chassis number was stamped on the engine when this was installed in the chassis, so the two numbers were the same, and this system was followed until the end of production.

80 (Mark I) VMF 16: This is the type of plate fitted to the 1948-50 generation of 80 and 90 models. Confusingly it claims that 5696 is the chassis number, when in fact 5696 is the body number. This number is also stamped on the small plate below which was fitted by BLSP, British Light Steel Pressings, who made the body.

Alpine MKV 21: On this later type of plate, the "chassis and engine number" and "body number" are correctly designated. Interestingly this Alpine still has a BLSP body plate, while the body number 1008 may indicate that MKV 21 had the eighth Alpine body.

Sunbeam-Talbot Motor Show cars, 1948-56

Year	Stand, number	Model	Paint	Trim
1948	Sunbeam-Talbot, no. 154	80 saloon	Gun	Grey
		80 saloon	Silver Green	Buff
		80 convertible	Satin Bronze	Red
		90 saloon	Black	Buff
		90 saloon	Satin Bronze	Red
		90 convertible	Gun	Grey
		90 sectioned saloon	n/a	n/a
	Thrupp & Maberly, no. 113	80 convertible	Silver Green	Buff
		90 convertible	Gun	Grey
1949	Sunbeam-Talbot, no. 159	80 saloon	Gun	Grey
		80 saloon	Silver Green	Buff
		80 convertible	Satin Bronze	Red
		90 saloon	Black	Red
		90 saloon	Satin Bronze	Red
		90 convertible	Silver Green	Buff
		Sectioned unit	n/a	n/a
	Thrupp & Maberly, no. 120	90 convertible	Satin Bronze	Red
		90 convertible	Silver Green	Buff or Grey
1950	Sunbeam-Talbot, no. 163	90 Mark II saloon	Black	Red
		90 Mark II saloon	Steel Grey	Grey
		90 Mark II saloon	Light Metallic Blue	Light Fawn
		90 Mark II saloon	Silver Green	Red
		90 Mark II convertible	Satin Bronze	Red
		90 Mark II convertible	Light Metallic Blue	Fawn
		Sectioned unit	n/a	n/a
	Thrupp & Maberly, no. 116	90 Mark II convertible	Silver Green	Red
		90 Mark II convertible	Gun	Grey
1951	Sunbeam-Talbot, no. 127	90 Mark II saloon	Gunmetal	Grey
		90 Mark II saloon	Green	Red
		90 Mark II saloon	Light Metallic Blue	Light Fawn
		90 Mark II convertible	Ivory	Red
		90 Mark II convertible	Satin Bronze	Red
		90 Mark II convertible	Light Metallic Blue	Fawn
		Sectioned unit	n/a	n/a
	Thrupp & Maberly, no. 98	90 Mark II convertible	Satin Bronze	Red
1952	Sunbeam-Talbot, no. 147	90 Mark IIA saloon	Sapphire Blue	Light Fawn
		90 Mark II saloon	Blue (Murray-Frame's ex-Alpine Rally car no. 320)	
		90 Mark IIA convertible	Beech Green	Light Fawn
		90 Mark IIA convertible	Satin Bronze	Red
	Thrupp & Maberly, no. 103	90 Mark IIA convertible	Beech Green	Light Fawn
1953	Sunbeam-Talbot, no. 134	90 Mark IIA saloon	Sapphire Blue	French Grey
		90 Mark IIA convertible	Crystal Green	Light Green
		Alpine	Alpine Mist*	Red*
		Alpine	Coronation Red*	Light Fawn*
	Thrupp & Maberly, no. 99	90 Mark IIA convertible	Sapphire Blue	French Grey
	Mulliners, no. 111	Alpine	Ivory	Red
1954	Sunbeam, no. 161	Mark III saloon	Sapphire Blue	French Grey
		Mark III convertible	Crystal Green	Light Green
		Alpine	Alpine Mist	Bright Red
		Alpine	Cream	Bright Red
	Mulliners, no. 110	Alpine	Sapphire Blue	Blue-Grey
1955	Sunbeam, no. 159	Mark III saloon	Dawn Mist & Corinth Blue	Blue-Grey
	BLSP, no. 113	Mark III saloon	Dove Grey & Claret	Ascot Grey
1956	Sunbeam, no. 144	Mark III saloon w. overdrive	Cactus Green & Pine Green	Light Green
	BLSP, no. 115	Mark III saloon w. overdrive	Dawn Mist & Corinth Blue	Blue

*The Autocar in 1953 has these two cars in Ivory with Red trim, and Blue, trim not quoted

Information researched from *The Autocar* and Motor Show catalogues.

Coventry registration marks found on works registered cars

Until 1946, Sunbeam-Talbot works cars were typically registered in London, and from 1946 to 1950, it appears that works cars were mainly registered in Warwickshire, in the AC, NX, UE and WD series.

Letters	From	To	Notes
KRW	December 1950	February 1951	First in 1951: KRW 140
KWK	February 1951	April 1951	
KVC	April 1951	May 1951	
KKV	May 1951	June 1951	
LDU	June 1951	July 1951	
LHP	July 1951	September 1951	
LRW	September 1951	November 1951	
LWK	November 1951	January 1952	First in 1952: LWK 540
LVC	January 1952	March 1952	
LKV	March 1952	May 1952	
MDU	May 1952	July 1952	
MHP	July 1952	September 1952	
MRW	September 1952	November 1952	
MWK	November 1952	January 1953	First in 1953: MWK 791
MVC	January 1953	April 1953	
MKV	April 1953	June 1953	
ODU	June 1953	August 1953	
OHP	August 1953	October 1953	
ORW	October 1953	December 1953	
OWK	December 1953	February 1954	First in 1954: OWK 50
OVC	February 1954	April 1954	
OKV	April 1954	May 1954	
PDU	May 1954	July 1954	
PHP	July 1954	September 1954	
PRW	September 1954	November 1954	
PWK	November 1954	December 1954	
PVC	December 1954	February 1955	First in 1955: PVC 228
PKV	February 1955	March 1955	
RDU	March 1955	April 1955	
RHP	April 1955	June 1955	
RRW	June 1955	July 1955	
RWK	July 1955	August 1955	
RVC	August 1955	October 1955	
RKV	October 1955	November 1955	
SDU	November 1955	January 1956	First in 1956: SDU 756
SHP	January 1956	March 1956	
SRW	March 1956	April 1956	
SWK	April 1956	June 1956	
SVC	June 1956	July 1956	
SKV	July 1956	October 1956	
TDU	October 1956	December 1956	
THP	December 1956	February 1957	First in 1957: THP 206

This table omits those registration marks (NDU to NKV series, 1953-57) which were reserved for the Home Delivery Export Scheme, i.e. cars sold tax-free for Personal Export Delivery, since Sunbeam-Talbot PED cars were handled by Rootes at Devonshire House in Piccadilly and were therefore registered in London.

Based on *Glass's Index of Registration Numbers 1929-1965*.

Alpine MKV 21: The cars also had the number stamped into the chassis, on the nearside (i.e. left-hand) front dumb iron under the front wing. The front socket for the jack is to the left.

APPENDIX

Chassis frame of 80, 90 and MkIII models

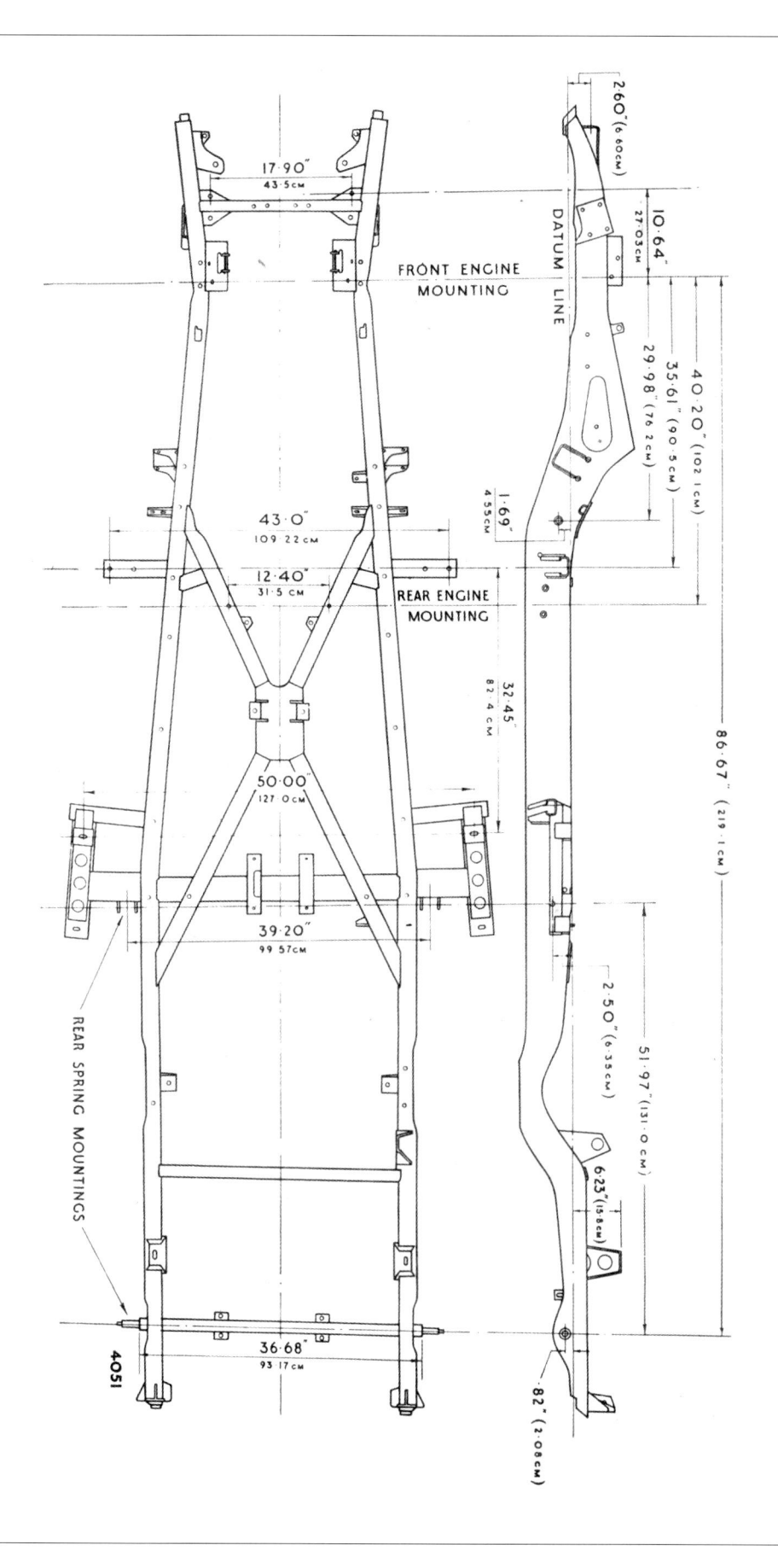

Appendix 3

Sunbeam-Talbots in competition, post-1945

I am greatly indebted to Chris Derbyshire of the Sunbeam Talbot Alpine Register for his generous assistance with the following compilation. It is by no means a complete list, as this would run to well over 1000 entries… but I have selected what I hope are the most important rallies, and rally entries. Many British national rallies have been omitted, as they did not attract participation of the works cars, and in any case full details can be very difficult to find. For the major international rallies, including the Alpine, Monte Carlo, and Tulip, the list is hopefully complete, and in all other cases, should include most entries of works or ex-works cars. Much of this information is based on reports in the contemporary magazines, notably *The Autocar*, *The Motor*, *Autosport* (from 1950 onwards) and *Motor Sport*, as well as the Rootes Group's own magazine, *Modern Motoring and Travel*. For a list of later sources, please refer to the bibliography elsewhere in this book.

1947

Circuit of Ireland, April 1947: Norman Garrad took part with a works Sunbeam-Talbot Ten (no.10) and finished third in class.

Lancashire Automobile Club's Blackpool Rally, June 1947: Peter Harper took part with his own 2-litre but broke his gearbox and HH Birrell won his class in another 2-litre.

Junior Car Club's Eastbourne Rally and Concours, June 1947: Garrad took part with a 2-litre and won a first class award.

Alpine Rally, July 1947

No.	Entrant	Model	Reg.	Result
42	AG Douglas Clease, Mrs Clease	2-litre tourer	EWD 222	6th in 2-litre class, concours class win
n/a	N Garrad, D Horton	2-litre tourer	FAC 963	Press car; given special award

1948

Junior Car Club's Eastbourne Rally and Concours, July 1948: Tommy Wisdom took part with a works Sunbeam-Talbot 90, registered GWD 853, and Garrad with an 80, while Peter Harper was in his own 2-litre.

Alpine Rally, July 1948

No.	Entrant	Model	Notes	Reg.	Result
51	Hiskins, Marsden	2-litre tourer		AHL 740	Retired after accident
52	T Wisdom, Mrs Wisdom	90	Works	GWD 100	Retired, gearbox
53	N Garrad, D Horton	90	Works	GWD 101	4th in 2-litre class, 14th o/a
54	G Murray-Frame, LJ Onslow-Bartlett	90	Works	GWD 102	1st in 2-litre class, Alpine cup

1949

Monte Carlo Rally, January 1949

No.	Entrant	Model	Notes	Reg.	Start point	Result
59	WB Black	Ten tourer		SY 6852	Glasgow	165th o/a
123	G Hartwell, LJ Onslow-Bartlett	80	Works	HNX 81	Glasgow	49th o/a; concours team plaque
124	N Haines, L Johnson, J Eason Gibson	80	Works	HNX 82	Glasgow	41st o/a; concours team plaque
125	P Monkhouse, J Brown	80	Works	GWD 668	Glasgow	34th o/a, 4th in 1500 cc class; concours team plaque

Circuit of Ireland, April 1949

No.	Entrant	Model	Notes	Reg.	Result
32	J Cutts, J Pearman	90	Works	GWD 101	8th o/a, 1st in class
33	R Adams	90		MZ 2496	11th o/a, 2nd in class

Lisbon Rally, May 1949: Edward Oakley took part with a 90, registered FAW 636, rally no.25, and won class 2 in the concours.

Junior Car Club's Eastbourne Rally and Concours, July 1949

No.	Entrant	Model	Notes	Reg.	Result
8	Freed	Ten or 80			Standard award
26	Blackmore	Ten or 80			
70	G Hartwell	90	Works	GWD (?)	First class award
77	J Cutts	90	Works	GWD (?)	

Alpine Rally, July 1949 (all works cars)

No.	Entrant	Model	Reg.	Result
74	AG Douglas Clease, J Cutts	90	GWD 102	20th o/a; foreign team challenge trophy
75	P Monkhouse, G Hartwell	90	GWD 100	5th o/a, 3rd in 2-litre class; foreign team challenge trophy
76	N Haines	90	HUE 509	Retired
77	N Garrad, D Horton	90	GWD 101	25th o/a; foreign team challenge trophy

1950

Monte Carlo Rally, January 1950 (all works cars)

No.	Entrant	Model	Reg.	Start point	Result
94	G Hartwell, P Monkhouse	90	GWD 100	Glasgow	46th o/a
95	N Garrad, J Cutts	90	GWD 101	Glasgow	66th o/a
96	J Pearman, WR Chipperton	90	GWD 102	Glasgow	68th o/a

Circuit of Ireland, April 1950

No.	Entrant	Model	Notes	Reg.	Result
60	Wharton, WR Chipperton	90	Works	GWD 100	
61	N Garrad, J Cutts	90	Works	GWD 101	
62	J Pearman, Henson	90	Works	GWD 102	
86	R Adams	90		MZ 2496	3rd in class
108	Templeton	80			3rd in class

Tulip Rally (second), April 1950

No.	Entrant	Model	Reg.	Start point	Result
111	CF Weil, J Lasne-Sauvigny, Mme Lasne-Sauvigny		French	Paris	Retired
165	LH Burt, SM Park, F Fish	90		Bruxelles	102nd in cat. I

Alpine Rally, July 1950

No.	Entrant	Model	Notes	Reg.	Result
84	M Gatsonides	90		G 3440 (Dutch)	Retired, stripped crown wheel
85	G Turnbull, R Harper	90		FDR 278	33rd o/a, 7th in 2-litre class
86	G Hartwell, WR Chipperton	90	Works	GWD 100	28th o/a, 5th in 2-litre class; team award on performance index
87	N Garrad, J Cutts	90	Works	GWD 101	13th o/a, 2nd in 2-litre class; team award on performance index
88	G Murray-Frame, J Pearman	90	Works	GWD 102	6th o/a, 1st in 2-litre class; team award on performance index
90	DH Perring, G Griffiths	90 conv.		OPA 6	29th o/a, 6th in 2-litre class

JDU 289, a 90 convertible, was used as a press car.

MCC *Daily Express* National Rally to Torquay (first), November 1950

A total of 15 Sunbeam-Talbots took part, the most important are listed below:

No.	Entrant	Model	Notes	Reg.	Start point	Result
14	C Oldbury, O'Neil (or Wright)	Ten dhc		FRL 587	Plymouth	158th o/a; won concours class A
90	JE De Bont, Norman	90 conv.			Norwich	3rd in concours class F
215	Wheeler, Wheeler	1944cc			Glasgow	116th o/a
259	L Tanner, Merritt	80 conv.			Leamington Spa	131st o/a; 3rd in concours class E
269	DH Perring, G Griffiths	90 conv.		OPA 6	Leamington Spa	45th o/a
372	Dr JPS Slatter, Weinbren	90		OPF 300	London	12th o/a, 2nd in class
374	G Hartwell, WR Chipperton	90	Works	GWD (?)	London	95th o/a
375	Miss S Van Damm, Miss N Van Damm	90 (2267cc)	Works	GWD (?)	London	150th o/a; 3rd in ladies' awards
376	N Garrad, T Wisdom	90	Works	GWD (?)	London	

1951
Monte Carlo Rally, January 1951

No.	Entrant	Model	Notes	Reg.	Start point	Result
37	Trulson, Laveno	90 conv.		N 10419 (Swedish)	Stockholm	227th o/a
120	M Gatsonides, van Luyk	90 Mk II		G 3440 (Dutch)	Monte Carlo	215th o/a; Brevex cup in concours
125	G Hartwell, WR Chipperton, P Monkhouse	90 Mk I	Works	GWD 102	Monte Carlo	Equal 195th o/a
262	WB Black, Gillies (Clark?)	90 Mk I		HUE 509	Glasgow	Equal 88th o/a
268	N Garrad, B Cardew	90 Mk I	Works	GWD 101	Glasgow	51st o/a
305	T Wisdom, D Humphrey	90 Mk II	Works	KUE 90	Lisbon	27th o/a

Circuit of Ireland, April 1951: Ten Sunbeam-Talbots took part, no works cars. The best result was 16th overall and second in class for R Adams, in his 90 Mark II registered OZ 2222, rally no.86. Keatley and Scott (no.105) were 25th overall and third in class.

Tulip Rally (third), April 1951 (no works cars)

No.	Entrant	Model	Start point	Result
21	SJ Tucker, JF Rowbotham	90	Harrogate	Retired
43	EG Pipe, N Robinson, WA Grayson	90	Harrogate	53rd in cat. I
45	GWA Aitkenhead, LW Bird, Dr JH Noble	90	Harrogate	47th in cat. I

BRDC Production Car Race at Silverstone 5 May: George Hartwell ran a 90 Mark II, he finished last in the over-2-litre heat, 25th overall, and 10th in the 3000cc class.

RAC Rally (first post-war), June 1951
A total of eight Sunbeam-Talbots took part, the most important are listed below:

No.	Entrant	Model	Reg.	Start point	Result
122	G Hartwell	90 Mk II	KRU 172	Cheltenham	2nd closed cars over 1500cc (?)
123	Williams			Cheltenham	29th closed cars over 1500cc
125	Dr JPS Slatter	90 Mk I (?)	OPF 300 (?)	Brighton	36th closed cars over 1500cc
127	L Sherley-Price	90 Mk I	GWD 101	Harrogate	34th closed cars over 1500cc

Alpine Rally, July 1951

No.	Entrant	Model	Notes	Reg.	Result
51	DH Perring, G Griffiths	90 Mk I conv.		OPA 6	4th in 2000cc class
71	J Cutts, J Pearman	90 Mk II	Works	KUE 90	3rd in 3000cc class
72	G Hartwell, WR Chipperton	90 Mk II special		LEL 333	Best in Mont Ventoux test but retired
78	Dr AW Lilley, Mrs M Lilley	90 Mk II		NTC 400	Retired

In this event, Norman Garrad ran a 90 Mk II support car, registered KNX 955, with Sheila Van Damm and David Humphrey, while Douglas Clease of *The Autocar* used a 90 Mk II convertible KNX 606 to cover the rally.

MCC *Daily Express* National Rally to Hastings (second), November 1951
A total of 34 Sunbeam-Talbots took part, mostly private entrants; the most important are listed below:

No.	Entrant	Model	Notes	Reg.	Start point	Result
10	C Oldbury, GH Smith	Ten dhc		FRL 587	Plymouth	1st in concours class B
54	G Hartwell, JM Sparrowe	90 supercharged			Plymouth	1st in class Fc
102	CB Offley, WE Offley	90 Mk II			Manchester	2nd in class Dc
181	AD McKay, JH Knee	90 Mk II			Leamington Spa	1st in concours class Ho
277	E Burt, G Gould	90 Mk II			Cardiff	1st in concours class Hc
298	N Garrad, WR Chipperton		Works		Glasgow	4th in class
299	Miss S Van Damm, Miss CMP Hornby		Works		Glasgow	3rd in ladies' awards

1952
Monte Carlo Rally, January 1952

No.	Entrant	Model	Notes	Reg.	Start point	Result
51	DH Perring, G Griffiths (?)	Mk II conv.		OPA 6		Retired
65	Dr AW Lilley, Mrs M Lilley	Mk II			Lisbon	Non starter
75	ES Sneath, RS Sneath	Mk II		NWB 909	Glasgow	24th o/a
78	Mrs EM Wisdom, Miss S Van Damm, Mrs N Mitchell	Mk II	Works	KWK 397	Glasgow	Equal 129th o/a
87	GN Milton, DS Done, WS Leaman	Mk II		OFM 90	Glasgow	121st o/a
101	G Hartwell, WR Chipperton, J Pearman	Mk II	Works	LHP 821	Glasgow	Equal 28th o/a
111	TA Anderson, JR Skeggs	Mk II		MPX 340	Glasgow	83rd o/a

113	J Clegg, N Hill	Mk II			Glasgow	Retired
123	B McCaldin, G Houston, Porter	Mk II		KZ 6534	Glasgow	154th o/a
124	CB Offley, WE Offley	Mk II		OMA 400	Glasgow	Equal 87th o/a
137	RW Merrick, JD Sleeman	Mk II		LOV 4	Glasgow	30th o/a
140	N Garrad, J Cutts	Mk II	Works	KKV 780	Glasgow	Retired
144	A Pownall, JC Wallwork	Mk II		MNC 707	Glasgow	70th o/a
283	Dr JPS Slatter, L Sherley-Price	90 Mk I		OPF 300	Monte Carlo	Retired
341	S Moss, JA Cooper, DJ Scannell	Mk II	Works	LHP 823	Monte Carlo	2nd o/a
366	McKenzie				Monte Carlo	Retired

RAC Rally, April 1952
At least 25 Sunbeam-Talbots took part, the most important are listed below. Results are all in the closed car class except where indicated.

No.	Entrant	Model	Notes	Reg.	Start point	Result
8	TB Jennings				Hastings	Equal 39th
9	PSR Smith				Hastings	61st
41	JC Marshall	90 conv.			Hastings	63rd open class
71	G Hartwell	Special (?)		LEL 333 (?)	Hastings	–
120	AG Payne				Scarborough	35th
131	C Fothergill, J Bullock	Mk II	Works	LHP 820	Scarborough	73rd
146	RA Dando				Scarborough	17th
164	Miss S Van Damm, Viscountess Erleigh; then Mrs M Hardman	Mk II	Works	LHP 823	Scarborough	Disqualified for change of co-driver
165	N Garrad	Mk II	Works	KKV 780	Scarborough	30th
169	J Blumer	Mk II		PHN 482	Scarborough	43rd
182	CB Offley	Mk II		OMA 400	Scarborough	11th
204	GN Milton				Scarborough	51st
209	FJ Merritt				Scarborough	25th
219	ES Sneath, J Pearman	Mk II		NWB 909	Scarborough	10th

Circuit of Ireland, April 1952: Of the 15 Sunbeam-Talbots taking part, Jones (no.71) won his class, while Keatley and Scott (no.81) were third in class. Ronnie Adams took part in his 90 Mark II registered OZ 2222, rally no.70, with unknown result.

Tulip Rally (fourth), April 1952

No.	Entrant	Reg.	Start point	Result
6	EG Pipe, N Robinson, JW Gowland		London	91st o/a, 13th in class
12	MA Illston, HG Smith		London	183rd o/a, 24th in class
159	AA Kouwenberg, unknown	Dutch	Den Haag	124th o/a, 9th in class
224	RA Collier, R Collier		Den Haag	Retired

1952 Alpine Rally, July 1952

No.	Entrant	Model	Notes	Reg.	Result
204	Mrs N Mitchell, Dr Denise Kelleher	90 Mk I		GWD 102	Retired; front wheel collapsed
300	G Hartwell	Special		LEL 333	Retired, broken con rod
302	DH Perring, Marshall	Mk II conv.		OPA 6	
304	Dr JPS Slatter, Cramp	Mk II		LLJ 900	Retired
306	Fraser, Scott	Mk II		MEL 63	14th o/a
316	S Moss, J Cutts	Mk II	Works	LHP 823	10th o/a, Alpine cup; team prize
318	L Johnson, D Humphrey	Mk II	Works	KUE 90	Retired, accident
320	G Murray-Frame, J Pearman	Mk II	Works	LHP 821	8th o/a, Alpine cup; team prize
322	J Fitch (USA), Miller	Mk II	Works	KUE 90	Retired; hub bearing broke
324	Count Wojciech Kolaczkowski (USA)	Mk II	Works	KWK 397	21st o/a
326	M Hawthorn, WR Chipperton	Mk II	Works	KNX 955	9th o/a, Alpine cup; team prize
336	Henson, Collinson	Mk II	Ferodo	MVM 797	
342	Elliott	Mk II		FVY 520	Retired

MCC *Daily Express* National Rally to Brighton (third), November 1952: Full details are not available but at least five Sunbeam-Talbots took part, drivers including Murray-Frame and Sneath. Sheila Van Damm and Françoise Clarke (90 Mk II, KWK 397, rally no.317) took the Ladies' Prize and were third in class, 27th overall.

At the end of 1952, the Rootes Sunbeam-Talbot team was awarded the RAC Dewar Trophy for their achievements in the Alpine Rally.

SUNBEAM-TALBOT & ALPINE IN DETAIL

1953

Monte Carlo Rally, January 1953

No.	Entrant	Model	Notes	Reg.	Start point	Result
30	Mrs A Needham, Mrs L Renaud	Mk II		KWK 397	Lisbon	Retired
129	EW Quero, C Harrington	Mk IIA		GPN 11	Glasgow	Equal 314th o/a
130	JH Kemsley, P Fotheringham-Parker	Mk II		LHP 823 (?)	Glasgow	89th o/a
131	TS Christie, G Menzies, AS Buchanan	Mk II		KFG 333	Glasgow	Collison with lorry; Buchanan was killed
140	J Skeggs, AE Teer, T Cranfield	Mk IIA	Works; Met. Police	MWK 16	Glasgow	29th o/a
142	M Hawthorn, J Pearman		Works		Glasgow	Non-starter
147	ES Sneath, JW Fleetwood	Mk IIA			Glasgow	Equal 127th o/a
150	CB Offley, W Offley	Mk II		OMA 400	Glasgow	69th o/a
156	J Blumer, RH Harris (or White?)	Mk IIA		PKM 927	Glasgow	Equal 123rd o/a
161	A Pownall, Williamson	Mk II		MNC 707	Glasgow	80th o/a
164	G Hartwell, PG Cooper, FW Scott	Mk IIA	Works	MWK 13	Glasgow	51st o/a
170	PR Bolton, P Morrell	Mk IIA			Glasgow	27th o/a
172	RA Sinclair, FC Grant	Mk II		PKE 145	Glasgow	Equal 337th o/a
174	Miss LF Ashfield, Miss JM Slatter	Mk IIA		MLJ 492	Glasgow	321st o/a
189	P Harper, S Asbury	Mk IIA		HUR 1	Glasgow	17th o/a
195	RW Merrick, JD Sleeman	Mk II		LOV 4	Glasgow	88th o/a
196	AB Fraser, WR Chipperton	Mk II		MEL 63	Glasgow	75th o/a
202	DH Perring, JH Suter	Mk II (?)		OPA 6 (?)	Glasgow	Non-starter
204	L Johnson, D Humphrey, J Eason Gibson	Mk IIA	Works	MWK 12	Glasgow	58th o/a, CF team award
209	ER Evans, W Watkin	Mk IIA		JAW 704	Glasgow	163rd o/a
211	ED Maguire, Mrs Maguire (or Mackie?)	Mk II		OZ 5490	Glasgow	23rd o/a
219	C Edge, A Roberts	Mk IIA		PFM 808	Glasgow	44th o/a
227	AG Imhof, Raymond Baxter, Dr Ian Pearce	Mk IIA	Works	MWK 15	Glasgow	24th o/a, CF team award
229	C Cooper, J Fischel				Glasgow	82nd o/a
230	A Collinson, S Henson, B Balham	Mk II	Ferodo	MVM 797	Glasgow	Equal 292nd o/a
246	B Proos Hoogendijk, G Seitz	Mk IIA		GZ-27 (Dutch)	Stockholm	Equal 148th o/a; *Grand Prix d'Honneur, Concours de Confort*
318	S Moss, JA Cooper, DJ Scannell	Mk IIA	Works	MWK 17	Monte Carlo	6th o/a, CF team award
331	Miss S Van Damm, Mrs F Clarke, Mrs A Hall	Mk IIA	Works	MWK 18	Monte Carlo	90th o/a; second for ladies' cup
367	WH Waring, G Wilkins	Mk II		MDU 997	Monte Carlo	228th o/a
389	N Garrad, G Murray-Frame, J Pearman	Mk IIA	Works	MWK 11	Monte Carlo	26th o/a
390	J Fitch, J Cutts, P Collins	Mk IIA	Works	MWK 14	Monte Carlo	Equal 112th o/a

Scarborough Rally (Yorkshire Sports Car Club), February 1953: Peter Bolton borrowed the works car MWK 14 and won.

RAC Rally, March 1953

At least 21 or 22 Sunbeam-Talbots took part, the most important are listed below:

No.	Entrant	Model	Notes	Reg.	Start point	Result
45	IL Watkins, JE Crozier			PFN 68	Hastings	52nd o/a
47	Major L Sherley-Price	Special		LEL 333	Hastings	65th o/a
51	G Hartwell, FW Scott	Mk IIA	Works	MWK 15	Hastings	9th o/a, 3rd in class
52	N Garrad, J Cutts	Mk IIA	Works	MWK 11	Hastings	13th o/a
53	Dr D Barker, E Snuscher	Mk IIA		MWK 13	Hastings	92nd o/a
81	PSR Smith, A Riglin			CHJ 1	Hastings	63rd o/a
87	Miss S Van Damm, Mrs F Clarke		Works	MWK 16	Hastings	23rd o/a, 1st ladies' cup
88	DH Perring, G Griffiths			OPA 6	Hastings	80th o/a
122	V Cooper, GA Barker			OTU 866	Blackpool	95th o/a
128	Miss M Walker, Miss A McF Balfour			FTY 333	Blackpool	43rd o/a, 2nd ladies' cup
146	JD Marsh, AP Powner			YRE 850	Blackpool	83rd o/a
185	RJ Adams, J Pearman	Mk IIA	Works	MWK 17	Blackpool	2nd o/a, 1st in touring cat.

Circuit of Ireland, April 1953: Of 14 Sunbeam-Talbots taking part, Houston (no.103) and Glover (no.93) were first and second in class, both in Mark IIAs.

212

Tulip Rally (fifth), April-May 1953

No.	Entrant	Model	Reg.	Start point	Result
41	AA Kouwenberg, ATH van Luyk		Dutch	Den Haag	Retired
43	H Kattenburg, JJ Langelaan		Dutch	Den Haag	84th o/a
70	T Dik, Mrs L van Strien		Dutch	Den Haag	88th o/a
75	J van Nieuwenhuyzen, HA van der Laan		Dutch	Den Haag	98th o/a
77	WGD Verzijl, S Jansen		Dutch	Den Haag	Retired
101	AC Ruiter, P van Malsen, GJ Brugman		Dutch	Den Haag	103rd o/a
124	JH Kemsley, P Fotheringham Parker	Mk II	LHP 823 (?)	Den Haag	Disqualified
125	P Harper, E Brinkman	Mk IIA	HUR 1	Den Haag	Disqualified
167	LJLFM Martin, AAJ Pennings, Mrs AMH Martin-Janssen		Dutch	Bruxelles	117th o/a
172	HB van Gelderen, AJ van Veen		Dutch	Bruxelles	30th o/a, 2nd in class
211	JH Suter, DH Perring	Mk II	OPA 6 (?)	London	81st o/a
215	AG Payne, JD Lampit, JG Phillips	Mk IIA	RFM 100	London	32nd o/a, 3rd in class
216	E Elliott, Miss N Elliott, D Wright	Mk IIA	MWK 17 (?)	London	Disqualified (class win)
220	TA Boothroyd, A Parkes, J Bliss			London	Retired
245	AJ Tatham, AB Shelley			London	Retired

In May 1953, Elliott ran the works (or ex-works) car MWK 17 in the Morecambe and Scottish rallies, results not known. Sheila Van Damm and Françoise Clarke ran another works car in the Scottish Rally and won the ladies' prize in the closed car class.

Alpine Rally, July 1953

No.	Entrant	Model	Note	Reg.	Result
500	G Hartwell, FW Scott	Special		VRE 690	Retired
501	Dr JPS Slatter, P Massey	Mk IIA		LLJ 900	39th o/a, 11th in class
503	A Fraser, L Sherley-Price	Special		MRU 666	Retired, gearbox
504	W Bennett, P Galliford	Mk IIA		JAY 469	35th o/a, 8th in class
505	Dr D Barker, M Sleep	Mk IIA		MWK 13 (?)	Retired, accident
506	Mrs A Needham, Dr Denise Kelleher	Mk II		KWK 397 (?)	Retired, accident
507	S Moss, J Cutts	Alpine	Works	MKV 21	14th o/a, 4th in class, Alpine cup
508	G Murray-Frame, J Pearman	Alpine	Works	MKV 22	18th o/a, 5th in class, Alpine cup, silver cup
509	P Collins, RJ Adams (replaced by D Humphrey)	Alpine	Works	MKV 23	Retired, rear axle and gearbox
510	J Fitch (USA), P Miller	Alpine	Works	MKV 24	20th o/a, 6th in class, Alpine cup
511	Miss S Van Damm, Mrs A Hall	Alpine	Works	MKV 25	24th o/a, 7th in class, Alpine cup, ladies' cup
512	L Johnson, D Humphrey	Alpine	Works	MKV 26	Retired, engine
515	P Lee, R Dando	Mk IIA			37th o/a, 10th in class
522	E Elliott, D Wright (replaced by Dick Edmond)	Mk IIA		MWK 17	Retired, accident
n/r	Mrs Tozzi-Condivi				Retired, accident

The Sunbeam works cars also won the team award.

Lisbon Rally, October 1953 (both works cars)

No.	Entrant	Model	Reg.	Result
	A G Imhof, JH Suter	Mk IIA		4th o/a, 1st in class
	Miss S Van Damm, Mrs F Clarke	Mk IIA	ODU 700	7th o/a, second for ladies' cup

MCC *Daily Express* National Rally to Hastings (fourth), November 1953

A total of 13 Sunbeam-Talbots took part but no works cars; the most important are listed below:

No.	Entrant	Model	Reg.	Result
	F Downs, WH Bartley, D Heagren	Mk II	JOU 898	1st o/a, 1st in class mod. prod. cars 1501-2600cc
	AJM Milner, Mrs SM Milner	Mk IIA		7th o/a
	HAC McKenzie, C Tennyson	90		10th o/a
	Miss JML Slatter, Mrs GK Armitage	Mk IIA	MLJ 492	18th o/a
218	EA Lloyd-Davies, G Bond	Alpine		3rd in class, open standard cars 1501-2600cc
269	AC Whatmough, AH Cooke	90		2nd in class, closed standard cars 1501-2600cc
	DH Perring, G Griffiths	Mk II	OPA 6 (?)	1st in class, closed special cars 1501-2600cc
	PC Todd, RF Mackenden	90 Mk I		3rd in class, closed special cars 1501-2600cc
358	WG Edgerton	Mk IIA	GDY 66	Concours, closed cars to £850

Victorian Alpine Rally, Australia, November 1953: This was won by Harry Firth and Graham Hoinville in a Sunbeam Alpine, registered GBY 444.

First Great American Mountain Rally, November 1953

No.	Entrant	Model	Result
	Sherwood Johnston, Richmond-Crumm	Alpine	7th o/a, 1st in 3-litre sports car class
	Kasimir Krag, William Giltzow	90	8th o/a, 1st in touring category
	Ian Garrad, Carter (or Fedeski?)	90	13th o/a, 2nd in touring category
	Sheila Van Damm, Ron Kessel	Alpine	18th o/a, 2nd in 3-litre sports car class

Manufacturers' Team Award for Johnston, Garrad and Van Damm. See *Autosport* 18 Dec, for Sheila Van Damm's personal account.

1954

Monte Carlo Rally, January 1954

No.	Entrant	Model	Notes	Reg.	Start point	Result
1	S Moss, JA Cooper, DJ Scannell	Mk IIA	Works	ODU 699	Athens	14th o/a, CF team award
134	C Lesage, H Gery				Monte Carlo	61st o/a
147	Miss JML Slatter, Mrs LF Ashfield	Mk IIA		MLJ 492	Glasgow	253rd o/a
173	JH Kemsley, P Fotheringham-Parker	Mk II		LHP 823 (?)	Glasgow	76th o/a
183	Miss M Walker, Miss P Faichney, Miss M Dodd	Mk IIA		FTY 333	Glasgow	232nd o/a
184	ER Evans, G Duke	Mk IIA		JAW 704	Glasgow	Equal 135th o/a
202	M Kozubski, WC Ody, E Bickham				Glasgow	226th o/a
207	RJ Sanders				Glasgow	Non-starter
213	RW Merrick, AP Grant (or Bevan?)	Mk II		LOV 4	Glasgow	220th o/a
214	Duchess of Newcastle, Ms LD Snow, Ms R Whittelle (or Mrs Lawrence?)	Mk II		LXO 699	Glasgow	267th o/a
217	C Oldbury, D Pott (or Lee?)	Mk IIA		RRL 333	Glasgow	311th o/a
235	WE Humphries, J Biggin	Mk II		NTO 90 or NTU 90	Glasgow	326th o/a
272	B Proos-Hoogendijk, G Seitz	Mk IIA		GZ-27 (Dutch)	Stockholm	269th o/a; *Grand Prix d'Honneur, Concours de Confort*
360	NH Richards, M Austin	Mk IIA		RKT 550	Munich	259th o/a
361	Miss S Van Damm, Mrs A Hall, Mrs F Clarke	Mk IIA	Works	ODU 700	Munich	75th o/a, CF team award
379	L Johnson, N Garrad, J Cutts	Mk IIA	Works	ODU 746	Munich	48th o/a, CF team award
405	HL Brooke, I Fraser-Jones	Mk IIA		MWK 11	Lisbon	198th o/a
n/r?	Dr D Barker	Mk IIA		MWK 13 (?)	Munich	Retired, accident

RAC Rally, March 1954

A total of 29 or 30 Sunbeam-Talbots took part, the works cars are listed below:

No.	Entrant	Model	Notes	Reg.	Start point	Result
142	Miss S Van Damm, Mrs F Clarke	Mk IIA	Works	ODU 700	Hastings	23rd o/a; 2nd ladies
144	N Garrad, J Cutts	Mk IIA	Works	ODU 746	Hastings	Finished
146	P Harper, D Humphrey	Mk IIA	Works	ODU 699	Hastings	4th o/a; 2nd in class
206	G Hartwell, FW Scott			OLJ 87	Hastings	9th o/a; 3rd in class

Of the 25 or 26 private entries, 19 finished.

Lyon-Charbonnières Rally, March 1954: Lee and Easton ran (ex-)works car MWK 16 under rally number 130, result unknown.

Circuit of Ireland, April 1954: There were seven Sunbeam-Talbots entered, with a first and second in class for Keatley (no.141) and Houston (no.117) respectively, both in Mark IIAs.

Tulip Rally (sixth), May 1954

No.	Entrant	Model	Notes	Reg.	Start point	Result
103	JH Suter, DH Perring	Mk II		OPA 6 (?)	Den Haag	Retired
104	Miss S Van Damm, Mrs A Hall, Mrs F Clarke	Mk IIA	Works	ODU 700	Den Haag	10th o/a, 2nd in class, ladies' cup
105	P Harper, J Cutts	Mk IIA	Works	ODU (?)	Den Haag	Retired
106	JPH Orr, IDL Lewis	Mk II		OHW 867 (?)	Den Haag	40th o/a, 6th in class
107	RF Holland, JG Woodruff, FG Mortimore	Mk II		NPO 36 (?)	Den Haag	32nd o/a
108	G Moss, Mrs JB Moss				Bern	107th o/a
109	L Bird, J Henderson Noble				London	Retired
110	JM Rupert, Mrs N Rupert-van Roosmalen			Dutch	Den Haag	125th o/a

SUNBEAM-TALBOTS IN COMPETITION

111	KE Wits, J Pos				Dutch	Den Haag	122nd o/a
112	L Martin, BC Dresens, AMH Janssen				Dutch	Den Haag	90th o/a
113	J van Nieuwenhuijzen, JH Boekhout				Dutch	Den Haag	Retired
128	AG Imhof, R Baxter	Mk IIA	Works		OHP 318	Den Haag	Retired, broke half shaft
130	AJ Tatham, I Davies					London	Retired
131	S Rostron, ON Pike, H Propp					London	111th o/a
132	E Elliott, D Wright	Mk IIA			MWK 17	London	36th o/a, 4th in class

Adriatic Rally, Yugoslavia, June 1954: Joe Lowrey of *The Motor* won his class in a borrowed works car, ODU 746.

Austrian Alpine Trial, June 1954: Sheila Van Damm and Anne Hall, class win and ladies' cup, in ODU 700, no. 46. Two US servicemen took part in an Alpine, result not known.

Alpine Rally, July 1954

No.	Entrant	Model	Notes	Reg.	Result
500	S Moss, J Cutts	Alpine	Works	MKV 21	9th o/a, 3rd in class, Alpine cup, gold cup
502	G Murray-Frame, J Pearman	Alpine	Works	MKV 22	4th in class
504	P Collins, L Garrad	Alpine	Works	MKV 23	Retired
506	G Hartwell, Dr Bill Deane	Alpine	Works	MKV 24	7th in class
508	Miss S Van Damm, Mrs A Hall	Alpine	Works	MKV 25	5th in class, ladies' cup
510	P Harper, P Miller	Alpine	Works	MKV 26	Retired, lost front wheel
512	Orr, Lewis	Alpine		OAD 333	6th in class

Viking Rally, Norway, September 1954: Sheila Van Damm and Anne Hall, third in class and ladies' cup, ODU 700.

Geneva Rally, October 1954: Sheila Van Damm and Anne Hall, second in class and ladies' cup, ODU 700, no.36.

MCC Redex National Rally to Hastings (fifth), November 1954
A total of 44 Sunbeam-Talbots took part but no works cars, the most important are listed below:

No.	Entrant	Model	Reg.	Start point	Result
36	AC Whatmough, BR Garlick			Manchester	3rd, closed touring car class to 2600cc
180	R Davis, GW Best	Mk III		Cardiff	2nd, closed touring car class to 2600cc
222	G Hartwell, Marshall	Mk III	PLJ 240	Plymouth	
286	J Nott, Corless	Ten dhc		London	Concours, open cars pre-1947
298	WG Edgerton, Lester			London	Concours, closed cars to £850

Second Great American Mountain Rally, November 1954: The team prize was won by three Alpines: Sheila Van Damm and Anne Hall, no.51; Stirling Moss and Ron Kessel, no.52; Kasimir Krag and William Giltzow, no.53. There were also two Mark IIAs and a further Alpine entered; F Guastini and V Massino won the Touring Car Class 1500-3000cc in a Sunbeam-Talbot.

1955

Monte Carlo Rally, January 1955

No.	Entrant	Model	Notes	Reg.	Start point	Result
20	J Canaroglou, P Milidonis	Mk III		Greek	Athens	267th o/a
52	RFD Seabrook, Mrs MV Seabrook	Mk IIA			Glasgow	Retired
70	GA Lewis, RW Ayres	Mk IIA			Glasgow	216th o/a
82	R Davis, Miss P Ozanne	Mk III		SYD 2	Glasgow	176th o/a
84	G Hartwell, ID Lewis	Mk III		PLJ 240	Glasgow	115th o/a
105	E Evans, E Colin (or C Edge?)	Mk III		KUX 2	Glasgow	111th o/a
109	RK Hooper, P Nelson	Mk IIA			Glasgow	259th o/a
119	W Humphries, S Charity	Mk III			Glasgow	Retired
126	J Trigg, K Best	Mk III		UPJ 291	Glasgow	191st o/a
131	HR Harrop, F Handforth	Mk IIA		TMB 185	Glasgow	Retired
198	Ingier, Schjolberg			C-234 (Norwegian)	Oslo	123rd o/a
201	P Malling, G Fadum	Mk III		A-68909 (Norwegian)	Oslo	1st o/a, *L'Equipe* team award
203	R Busch, H Mikkelsen			A-69162 (Norwegian)	Oslo	152nd o/a
209	N Garrad, J Cutts	Mk III	Works	PWK 603	Munich	122nd o/a
214	AB Fraser, RAJ Sinclair, WR Chipperton	Mk III		UKE 63	Munich	126th o/a

215

222	Miss S Van Damm, Mrs A Hall, Mrs F Clarke	Mk III	Works	PWK 604	Munich	11th o/a, *L'Equipe* team award, ladies' cup
223	JEG Fairman, L Smith	Mk III	Works	PWK 606	Munich	52nd o/a
239	LM Leader, BH Leader	Mk IIA		HAN 177	Munich	103rd o/a
251	P Harper, D Humphrey	Mk III	Works	PWK 605	Munich	9th o/a, *L'Equipe* team award

Canadian Winter Rally, February 1955: Two Alpines took part.

RAC Rally, March 1955
A total of 27 Sunbeam(-Talbots) took part, the most important are listed below:

No.	Entrant	Model	Notes	Reg.	Start point	Result
3	G Hartwell, EW Deane	Mk III		PLJ 240	Hastings	n/r
145	N Garrad, J Cutts	Mk III	Works	PWK 603	Blackpool	n/r
146	Miss S Van Damm, Mrs A Hall	Mk III	Works	PWK 604	Blackpool	1st Ladies
147	P Harper, D Humphrey	Mk III	Works	PWK 605	Blackpool	2nd touring car class over 2000cc
158	Elliott, Edmond	Mk IIA		MWK 17	Blackpool	4th in class (?)
178	PSR Smith, AW Rigling	Mk IIA		JJN 518	Blackpool	3rd in class
237	IA Maiden, D Healey	Mk III		KWM 616	Blackpool	2nd in class

Circuit of Ireland, April 1955: Four Sunbeam Mark IIIs competed in this rally, with first and second in class for Glover/Lynd (or Lund) (no.141) and Jones/Houston (no.142) respectively.

Tulip Rally (seventh), April-May 1955

No.	Entrant	Model	Notes	Reg.	Start point	Result
42	DM Hooft, R van der Werf	Alpine		PG-?0-?6 (Dutch)	Noordwijk	Retired
47	RLG Borgerhoff-Mulder, JL den Hollander	Alpine		Dutch	Noordwijk	145th o/a
54	NH Richards, T Clark	Alpine			Noordwijk	103rd o/a
74	JLFM Martin, BC Dresens, Mrs AMH Martin-Janssen	Mk IIA		Dutch	Noordwijk	Retired
76	HAA van der Laan, J Heeneman	Mk III		RK-91-42 (Dutch)	Noordwijk	129th o/a
77	RF Holland, JG Woodruff, WO Holding	Mk IIA		SBP 725	Noordwijk	94th o/a
78	Miss S Van Damm, Mrs A Hall	Mk III	Works	PWK 604	Noordwijk	15th o/a, 2nd ladies' cup
79	P Harper, J Cutts	Mk III	Works	PWK 605	Noordwijk	7th o/a, 2nd in class
81	JS Cohen, Miss J Nebig	Mk IIA		Dutch	Paris	79th o/a
82	KE Wits, J Pos	Mk IIA		Dutch	Noordwijk	Retired
85	A Syversen, G Fadum	Mk III	Works	PWK 603	Noordwijk	52nd o/a
87	P Malling, K Solberg	Mk III	(Works)	RDU 253	Noordwijk	68th o/a
90	G Hartwell, FN Scott, GS Sutcliff	Mk IIA		PLJ 240	Noordwijk	43rd o/a
91	AAJ Pennings, AJM van Stekelenburg, CAM Pennings	Mk IIA		Dutch	Noordwijk	100th o/a
96	JH Noble, FJ Kieran, Miss M Brown	Mk IIA			Paris	Retired
97	GWA Aitkenhead, D Handley	Mk IIA			Noordwijk	Retired

Alpine Rally, July 1955: This event was cancelled. Six Alpine works cars were prepared, registered RHP 700 to RHP 705.

Viking Rally, Norway, September 1955

No.	Entrant	Model	Notes	Reg.	Result
36	G Hartwell, WR Chipperton, EW Deane	Mk III	Works	PWK 605	
44	Miss S Van Damm, Mrs A Hall	Mk III	Works	PWK 604	3rd for Ladies' Cup
69	Malling, Jensen-Lund	Mk III	(Works)	RDU 253	
	Schjolberg, Stensrud			Norwegian	5th o/a, 3rd in class
	R Busch, H Mikkelsen			Norwegian	7th o/a, 4th in class

One of the two Norwegian cars was a Mk III registered D-27154. After this rally, Sheila Van Damm and Anne Hall were joint winners of European Ladies' Rally Championship for 1955.

MCC National Rally to Hastings (sixth), November 1955: There were at least six Sunbeams (probably more) in this rally. Not all results are known but AC Whatmough and BR Garlick (Mk III) were second overall. PH Brown and WJH Snelgrove were first in the 2600cc touring car class.

1956

Monte Carlo Rally, January 1956

No.	Entrant	Model	Notes	Reg.	Start point	Result
8	Canaroglou, Yanniscota	Mk III		Greek	Athens	Retired
146	L Potter, M Lawson	Mk III		NNY 872	Glasgow	Retired
154	R Davis, I Lewis	Mk III		VYB 2	Glasgow	90th equal o/a
168	R Hooper, P Nelson	Mk IIA		MYN 884	Glasgow	225th o/a
180	W Humphries, L Enion	Mk IIA			Glasgow	Retired
213	RE Evans, E Stephens	Mk III		KUX 2	Glasgow	152nd o/a
237	A Fraser, R Holmes	Mk III		UKE 63	Munich	58th o/a
283	P Harper, D Humphrey, P Elbra	Mk III	Works	PWK 605	Stockholm	3rd equal o/a, CF team award
284	Miss S Van Damm, Mrs A Hall, Mrs Y Jackson	Mk III	Works	PWK 604	Stockholm	122nd equal o/a, CF team award
292	I Eekrem, C Borch			Norwegian	Stockholm	193rd o/a
318	G Fadum, Solberg	Mk III	(Works)	RDU 253	Stockholm	Retired
323	Borgerhoff, J van der Laan	Mk III		Dutch	Stockholm	Retired
326	J Ray, J Cutts, J Waddington	Mk III	Works	PWK 603	Stockholm	10th o/a, CF team award
340	Christensen, Wang			Norwegian	Stockholm	Retired
346	Gordine			French	Stockholm	Retired

As this was the third time that the Sunbeam(-Talbot) team had won the Charles Faroux team award, they won it outright.

RAC Rally, March 1956

At least 15 Sunbeams took part, the most important are listed below:

No.	Entrant	Model	Notes	Reg.	Start point	Result
30	Mrs A Hall, Mrs Y Jackson	Mk III	Works	PWK 604	Blackpool	Team award
37	J Ray, Horrocks	Mk III	Works	PWK 603	Blackpool	
41	P Harper, D Humphrey	Mk III	Works	PWK 605	Blackpool	10th o/a, 2nd in touring car class over 2000cc
73	Whatmough, O'Hanlon	Mk III			Blackpool	Team award
97	HG Webster, C Varty	Mk III		ECB 888	Blackpool	Team award
105	E Elliott, D Wright	Mk IIA (?)		MWK 17 (?)	Blackpool	

Tulip Rally (eighth), May 1956

No.	Entrant	Model	Notes	Reg.	Start point	Result
62	MS Routley, DJ Tarratt	Mk III			Noordwijk	96th o/a, 14th in class
63	JH Suter, RC Boucher	Mk III			Noordwijk	139th o/a, 23rd in class
64	P Harper, D Humphrey	Mk III	Works	PWK 605	Noordwijk	138th o/a, 22nd in class
225	LJL Martin, A J Pennings, Mrs AMH Martin-Janssen			Dutch	Noordwijk	Retired

Rapiers were 11th, 19th, 39th and 49th overall.

Alpine Rally, July 1956

No.	Entrant	Model	Reg.	Result
504	G Hartwell, FW Scott (or Lewis?)	Mk III	SRU 502	21st o/a, 3rd (and first Group 1 car) in class 2000-2600cc

There were four works and two private Rapiers, the best placed was Peter Harper 23rd overall.

MCC National Rally to Hastings (seventh and last), November 1956: GV Howe, second in class for 2600cc production cars

1957

The Monte Carlo and RAC rallies were cancelled.

Tulip Rally (ninth), May 1957

No.	Entrant	Model	Start point	Result
27	H N Dixon, C Stanford	Alpine Special	Noordwijk	Retired
100	Miss M Handley Page, Mrs Wilton Clarke	Mk III	Noordwijk	134th o/a
102	J H Suter, M H Carreras	Mk III	Noordwijk	Retired

The highest-placed Rapier was 7th overall.

1958

Monte Carlo Rally, January 1958: At least one Mark III registered SLX 205 started from Glasgow but did not finish; this may have been R Hooper, no. 170.

RAC Rally, March 1958: There were three private entrants in Sunbeam Mark IIIs, R Hooper (no.54), RM Stead (no.152) and JT Shiel (no.55); results not known. This rally was won outright by Peter Harper and Bill Deane in a works Rapier Series II on its rally debut, the best result for a Rapier so far.

Appendix 4

Bibliography & Acknowledgements

Primary unpublished sources
In Leon Gibbs's collection: Sunbeam-Talbot sales ledgers 1948-56.
In the BMIHT archive, Gaydon: Nuffield Exports statistics 1947-54.
In the Coventry City Record Office: Coventry registration cancellation cards, ca.1945-50.
In the Coventry Transport Museum archive: Talbot and Sunbeam-Talbot Chassis Registers 1935-48; Coventry registration records, issue ledgers 1949-56; and other material.
In the Dorset History Centre, Dorchester: Bournemouth registration records.
In the Farnham Museum: Files relating to Abbott coachbuilders.
In the Warwickshire County Record Office: Motor vehicle registration records ref. CR 1827.

Primary printed sources – newspapers, journals and annuals
Automobil Revue (Katalognummer) (annual, Switzerland); *Autosport*; *Bilhistorisk Tidsskrift* (Dansk Veteranbil Klub, Denmark); *(Thoroughbred &) Classic Cars*; *Classic and Sportscar*; Earls Court Motor Show catalogues; *Glass's Car Check Book* (annual); *Modern Motoring (and Travel)*; *Motor Industry*; *Motor Sport*; *Motor Trader*; *Motor Trend* (USA); *Practical Motorist (and Motor Cyclist)*; *Precision*; *Proceedings of The Institution of Automobile Engineers*; *Road and Track* (USA); *Stardust* (Sunbeam Talbot Alpine Register); *The Autocar*; *The Automobile*; *The Daily Telegraph*; *The Independent*; *The Light Car*; *The Motor*; *The Motor Industry of Great Britain* (SMM&T annual handbook); *The Motor World*; *The Scotsman*; *The Spectator*; *The Times*; *The Times Survey of the British Motor Car Industry* (annual); *Time* magazine (USA); *Wheels* (Australia)

Rootes Talbot, Sunbeam-Talbot and Sunbeam literature: Various sales catalogues, handbooks and parts lists; Sunbeam workshop manual publication number WSM 110, 1956

Secondary sources – published articles and books
Adams, Ronnie *From Craigantlet to Monte Carlo* (Peninsula Print & Design, Newtownards, Co. Down, not dated)
Bailey, Tony and Skilleter, Paul *Mike Hawthorn Golden Boy* (PJ Publishing Ltd, Barton on Sea, Hampshire, 2008)
Balfour, Christopher *Roads to Oblivion* (Bay View Books, Bideford, Devon, 1996)
Baxter, Raymond, with Dron, Tony *Tales of my Time* (Grub Street, London, 2005, 2007)
Blight, Anthony *Georges Roesch and the Invincible Talbot* (Grenville Publishing, London, 1970)
Boddy, William *The History of Brooklands Motor Course 1906-1940* (Grenville Publishing, London, 1957)
Brägger, Bernhard *Die Geschichte der Rallye Monte-Carlo* (Edition Scriptum, Altdorf, Switzerland, 1989)
Bullock, John *The Rootes Brothers* (Patrick Stephens, Sparkford, Somerset, 1993)
Chambers, Marcus *Works Wonders* (Motor Racing Publications, Croydon, 1995)
Collins, Paul, and Stratton, Michael *British Car Factories from 1896* (Veloce, Dorchester, 1993)
Collis, Rose *The Life and Times of Nancy Spain* (Cassell, London, 1997)
Cook, Derek "Sunbeam Alpine at Jabbeke" in *The Automobile* July 2005
Couper, Mike *Rallying to Monte Carlo* (Ian Allan, London, 1956)
Cowbourne, Donald *British Rally Drivers Their Cars & Awards 1925-1939* (Settle Smith, Otley, West Yorkshire, 1996)
Cowbourne, Donald *British Trial Drivers Their Cars and Awards 1919-1928* (Settle Smith; Otley, West Yorkshire 2001)

BIBLIOGRAPHY & ACKNOWLEDGEMENTS

Cowbourne, Donald *British Trial Drivers Their Cars and Awards 1929-1939* (Settle Smith, Otley, West Yorkshire, 1998)
Culshaw, David *The Motor Guide to Makes and Models* (Temple Press, London, 1959)
Culshaw, David, and Horrobin, Peter *The Complete Catalogue of British Cars* (Macmillan, London, 1974)
Davis, SCH *Rallies and Trials* (Iliffe & Sons, London, 1951)
de Beus *Vijftig Jaar Tulpenrallye* (Europese Bibliotek, Zaltbommel, Holland, 1999)
Demaus, AB, and Tarring, JC *The Humber Story 1868-1932* (Alan Sutton, Gloucester, 1989)
Dowell, Bruce *Sunbeam "The Supreme Car" 1899-1935* (Landmark Publishing, Ashbourne, Derbyshire, 2004)
Dugdale, John with Cook, Michael *Jaguar in America* (second edition, Aztex Corporation, Tucson, Arizona, USA, 2001)
Frostick, Michael *A History of the Monte Carlo Rally* (Hamish Hamilton, London, 1963)
Frostick, Michael *The Cars That Got Away* (Cassell, London, 1968)
Frostick, Michael *Works Team: The Rootes Competition Department* (Cassell, London 1964, reprinted by Mercian, 1997)
Garnier, Peter, with Healey, Brian *Donald Healey – My World of Cars* (Patrick Stephens, Wellingborough, 1989)
Georgano, GN (ed) *The Beaulieu Encyclopaedia of the Automobile* (The Stationery Office, London, 2000)
Georgano, GN (ed) *The Beaulieu Encyclopaedia of the Automobile – Coachbuilding* (The Stationery Office, London, 2001)
Georgano, GN (ed) *The Encyclopaedia of Motor Sport* (Ebury Press and Michael Joseph, London, 1971)
Glass's Index of Registration Numbers 1929-1965 (Glass's Guide Service Ltd, Weybridge, 1965)
Harper, Peter *Destination Monte* (Motoraces Book Club edition, London, 1967)
Harrison, Zoë "1947 Sunbeam-Talbot 2-litre drophead coupé" in *The Automobile* September 1995
Hawthorn, Michael *Challenge Me the Race* (second edition, Aston Publications, Bourne End, Buckinghamshire, 1988)
Hawtin, David "Rootes Talbot The restoration of a 1938 3-litre" in *The Automobile* June 1991
Hudson, Bruce *British Light Cars 1930-1939* (GT Foulis, Sparkford, Somerset, 1975)
Hudson, Bruce *Post-war British Thoroughbreds* (GT Foulis, Henley-on-Thames, 1972)
Jodard, Paul *Raymond Loewy* (Trefoil Publications, London, 1992)
Langworth, Richard *Tiger, Alpine, Rapier* (Osprey; London 1982, reprinted by Mercian, 1999)
Laux, James M *In First Gear – The French Automobile Industry to 1914* (Liverpool University Press, Liverpool, 1976)
Lem, Ruud J *The Rootes Side-valve Motorcars 1936-1948 Talbot & Sunbeam-Talbot Register* (second edition, Sunbeam Talbot Alpine Register, 2007)
Louche, Maurice *Le Rallye Monte-Carlo au XXe siècle* (Editions Maurice Louche, Allein, France, 2001)
May, CAN *Wheelspin Abroad* (GT Foulis, London, 1949)
Montagu, Lord, with Sedgwick, Michael *Lost Causes of Motoring* (second edition, Cassell, London, 1966)
Montagu, Lord, with Sedgwick, Michael *Lost Causes of Motoring, Europe vol.1* (Cassell, London, 1969)
Motor Car Index 1928-1939 (Fletcher and Son, Norwich, reprinted by Autobooks, Brighton, 1964)
Newhall, LH, with Harrison, John *A History of Motor Vehicle Registration in the United Kingdom* (third edition, Newby Books, Scarborough, 2008)
Nickols, Ian, and Karslake, Kent *Motoring Entente* (Cassell, London, 1956)
Noble, Dudley *Milestones in a Motoring Life* (Queen Anne Press, London, 1969)
Plowden, William *The Motor Car and Politics in Britain* (Pelican edition, Penguin Books, Harmondsworth, Middlesex, 1973)
Pfundner, Martin *Alpine Trials & Rallies* (Veloce, Dorchester, 2005)
Pressnell, Jon "Fruits of the Rootes" in *Classic and Sportscar* Jul 1988
Pressnell, Jon "Norman Garrad – rallying's first professional" in *Classic and Sportscar* Apr 1992
Pressnell, Jon "The Mating Game" in *Classic and Sportscar* Sep 1996
Riden, Philip *How to Trace the History of Your Car* (second edition, Merton Priory Press, Cardiff, 1998)
Robson, Graham *A-Z British Cars 1945-1980* (Herridge & Sons, Shebbear, Devon, 2006)
Robson, Graham *A-Z of Works Rally Cars* (Bay View Books, Bideford, Devon, 1994)
Robson, Graham *Cars in the U.K. Volume One: 1945 to 1970* (Motor Racing Publications, Croydon 1996)
Robson, Graham *Cars of the Rootes Group* (Motor Racing Publications, Croydon 1990, reprinted by Mercian)
Robson, Graham "Going the Distance – MCC National Rallies 1950-1956" in *The Automobile* May 2003
Robson, Graham *Monte Carlo Rally – The Golden Age* (Herridge & Sons, Shebbear, Devon, 2007)
Robson, Graham *Rootes Maestros* (Mercian, Balsall Common, Warwickshire, 2008)
Robson, Graham *Sunbeam Alpine and Tiger* (Crowood, Marlborough, 1996, 2003)
Robson, Graham *The Monte Carlo Rally* (Batsford, London, 1989)
Sedgwick, Michael *Cars of the 1930s* (Batsford, London, 1970)
Sedgwick, Michael *The Motor Car 1946-56* (Batsford, London, 1979)
Sedgwick, Michael, and Gillies, Mark *A-Z of Cars 1945-1970* (Temple Press, Twickenham, Middlesex, 1986)
Sedgwick, Michael, and Gillies, Mark *A-Z of Cars of the 1930s* (Bay View Books, Bideford, Devon, 1989)

Staff, DJ "The Talbot & Sunbeam Talbot Notes for Newcomers" in *The Automobile* June 1983
Symons, Humfrey E *Monte Carlo Rally* (Methuen, London, 1936)
Van Damm, Sheila *No Excuses* (Putnam, London, 1957)
Walker, Nick *A-Z of British Coachbuilders 1919-1960* (Bay View Books, Bideford, Devon, 1997)
Walker, Nick *British Police Cars* (Veloce, Dorchester, 2001)
Whisler, Timothy R *At the End of the Road* (JAI Press, Greenwich, Connecticut, USA and Hampton Hill, Middlesex, 1995)
Who's Who in the Motor and Commercial Vehicle Industries (Temple Press, London, 1965)
Wood, Jonathan *British Postwar Classic Cars* (Osprey, London, 1980)
Wood, Jonathan "Supreme Sunbeam?" in *The Automobile* December 1999

In addition, a variety of one-make histories have been consulted.

Websites

thepeerage.com; wikipedia.org; http://forums.autosport.com; www.bilhistorie.no; www.bilnorge.no; www.kujawja.org/kolaczkowski.html; www.motorsportavisen.no; www.nacho.org.uk; www.npg.org.uk (National Portrait Gallery); www.sunbeam.org.au; www.sunbeamtalbot.info, Bob Hamilton, Canada; www.teamdan.com/archive/www2/; www.team.net/www/rootes.

Acknowledgements

First and foremost, I would like to thank the Sunbeam Talbot Alpine Register (web site: www.stardust.uk.com) for the tremendous reception they gave me when I told them that I, a stranger and complete outsider, was writing a book on their cars. In particular, my grateful thanks to John Badger, Chris Bryant, Peter Browning, Derek Cook, Chris Derbyshire, Ruud Lem, Roy Rogers, Paul Walby who wrote the chapter on ownership today, Peter Woodall and Guy Woodhams; and particularly to Leon Gibbs, owner of the ex-Stirling Moss Alpine Rally Sunbeam Alpine and of the 80/90 sales ledgers, which he gave me complete access to; as well as to the many members who shared photos of their cars.

In various museums and archives, at the JDHT I would like to thank my former director John Maries and our founder trustee Peter Mitchell who both looked upon this bit of moon-lighting with a benevolent eye, and also Karam Ram; at the Coventry Transport Museum, Steve Bagley and Lizzie Hazlehurst; at the Rootes Archive Trust, Tim Sutton; at the BMIHT, Gaydon, Gillian Bardsley and the archive team; at the Detroit Public Library, Mark A Patrick (now with Revs Institute for Automotive Research, Naples, Florida); at the Jaguar North America Archive, Mike Cook; as well as staff at the Coventry City Records Office, the Dorset History Centre and the Warwickshire County Record Office.

Of fellow historians and authors, Richard Langworth, Jon Pressnell, and Graham Robson have very graciously allowed me to share the results of their researches. Also Tony Bailey, Terry McGrath, Mark Morris (SAHB and Pook's Motor Books), Rinsey Mills, Bill Piggott, Professor Garel Rhys, Ole Emil Riisager (Danish Veteran Car Club), Michael Scott, Paul Skilleter, Nick Walker and the authors of all the works listed in the bibliography.

The following owners kindly allowed their cars to be photographed by Simon Clay: Richard Blackiston (Talbot Ten Airline saloon), Graham Jones (Sunbeam-Talbot 3-litre saloon), Roanne Langridge (80 saloon), Paul Rundell (90 Mark II convertible), Colin Moss (90 Mark IIA saloon), Chris Derbyshire (Sunbeam Mark III works rally car), and Leon Gibbs (Sunbeam Alpine works rally car, and chassis ditto).

Most archive photos are reproduced by kind permission of the Coventry Transport Museum (CTM) or are from the publisher's archive; other illustrations have been individually acknowledged. The author and publisher apologise if individual photos remain unattributed or incorrectly attributed. We thank all contributors for allowing images to be used.

This book is published with the support of the Michael Sedgwick Memorial Trust, with particular thanks to Michael Ware.

Finally, on a personal note, I would like to thank my publishers, Charles, Bridgid and Ed Herridge, and as always my partner David.